For Rachel,
with thanks for your
help in creating the
index.

Best wishes,
Jonathan Kolatch

China
MOSAIC

China
MOSAIC

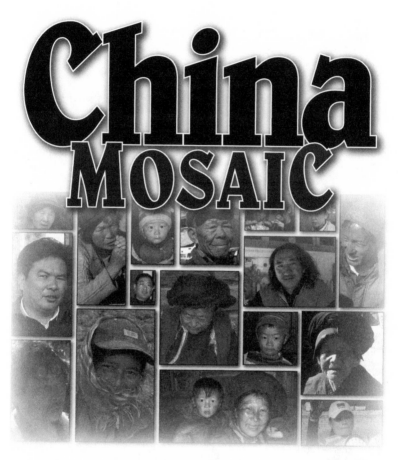

JONATHAN KOLATCH

JD | **JONATHAN DAVID PUBLISHERS, INC.**
MIDDLE VILLAGE, NEW YORK

CHINA MOSAIC

Jonathan David Publishers, Inc.
68-22 Eliot Avenue
Middle Village, New York 11379

www.jdbooks.com

2 4 6 8 10 9 7 5 3 1

Library of Congress Cataloging-in-Publication Data

Kolatch, Jonathan.
    China mosaic / Jonathan Kolatch.
      p. cm.
    Includes index.
    ISBN 978–0–8246–0470–7
    1. China—Social life and customs—1976–2002 2. China—Social life and
customs—2002– 3. China—Social conditions—1976–2000. 4. China Social
conditions—2000– I. Title.
    DS779.23.K65 2008
    951.05—dc22

                                                            2008026262

Maps created in part through data obtained from CHGIS, Version 4, Cam-
bridge: Harvard Yenching Institute, January 2007 (Lex Berman, editor), with
assistance from Scott Walker of the Harvard Map Collection.

Book design and composition by John Reinhardt Book Design

Printed in the United States of America

For Chongwu, the best of China
For "Sue," the best of mothers
For David, the best of brothers

Contents

Preface   ix

The Limits of Personal Loyalty   1

Hobnobbing with China's Rising Communist Stars...
and Penetrating the Veil of Secrecy of the
Communist Dynasty   33

Snubbed Again by Ningxia Royalty   71

Riding the Party Trail to the High Tibetan Plains   91

China's Mountain People   125

Beijing 2008's Dancing Logo   163

Back to the Coal Mines   171

Highway Dupe Foiled in Jinning County   181

The Chinese View of 9/11   189

Resurrected History: The Mysterious Jews of Kaifeng   195

A Mayo Clinic Prelude with a Double China Twist   209

Olympic Silver Medal Chronicle: U.S. vs. China   219

Recapturing Faded Olympic Glory: Training
    for Beijing 2008   225

China Goes to the Dogs   233

How Mousie Tongue Became Mao Zedong   239

They Wiggle and They Wriggle and They Squiggle
    and They Jiggle   243

Saving One Chinese Face   249

The Great Wall Scam   269

Riding Beijing's Buses   275

The Transparent Yellow Race   281

China's Quicksand   297

Index   339

Preface

□□□

AS BEFITTING a propaganda superpower—probably the most potent mind-molding super state in the history of civilization—the Chinese offer reams of processed information on almost any topic. Surprisingly often, for those unable to read Chinese, the information is available in English. And if you crave an up-close perspective, even in remote parts of China, the Chinese will organize a well-managed experience. But after more than twenty years of traveling to China, I have learned that, almost without exception, the most lasting Chinese memories and insights need to be scrapped for. Often the struggle teaches more than the success; unexpected windfalls emerge from a mistaken path.

For years I had yearned to understand how, at the beginning of the twenty-first century, when most of China had long since lost its interest in communism, a communist party then seventy-seven-million strong still functioned. I spent more than a week at the Sixteenth Chinese Communist Party Congress in 2002 buttonholing every delegate I could find, digging to see how deep I would have to probe until I hit living tissue. But it was during a visit to an ordinary village of seventeen hundred in northern Hebei Province after the Congress, where the local Party secretary showed me with pride how the local Party committee had satisfied Party guidelines, that I saw what fabulous psychologists the senior Party leaders in Beijing were.

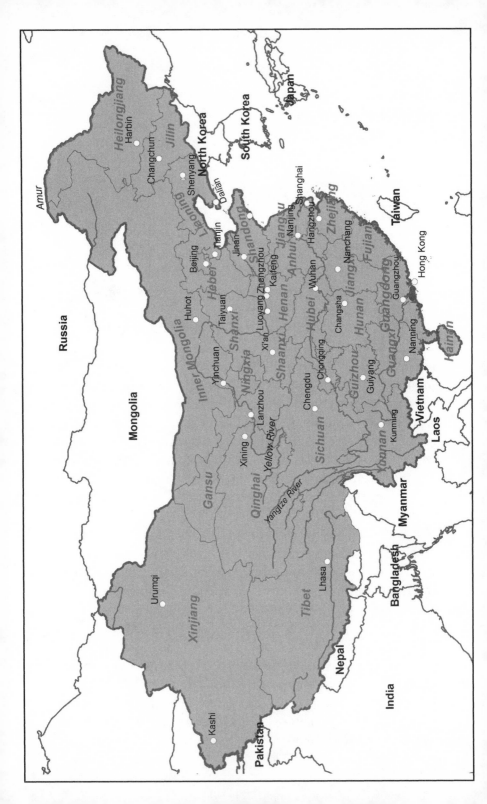

Walk into a Chinese restaurant or Chinese-run manufacturing business in any American city and you are almost sure to find illegal aliens, some of them smuggled in for five-figure sums, which their families in China scrimped for years to save. But it was only after I discovered that among the illegal Chinese population were people that I knew, smuggled in by a Chinese athlete I had brought to this country, that I began to understand the misconceptions and false hopes of America's illegal underclass and the deceptions that brought them here.

The efficient, successful Chinese sports machine is by now legendary, producing world champions in sports that a few decades ago were almost unknown in China. It is easy to see Chinese athletes as machines—robots who train for years under relentless coaches. But nothing provided as penetrating a light into the hearts of Chinese athletes as the ten days I spent with the Chinese National Softball Team at the Atlanta Olympics, as they fell a step short of beating the Americans for the gold medal. The bureaucrats who accompanied the Chinese team were as relentless as ever, isolating team members from any outside influence. But years of befriending the Chinese team and visiting their homes bred a stronger loyalty, and midnight telephone calls after almost every game clued me into the inferiority complex that is inbred into the Chinese psyche and has as much impact in sports as it does in the hardball international politics the Chinese play.

The Chinese government has been bucking corruption large and small as the scourge of Chinese society since the early 1990s. But it took a troupe of scammers working out of a bus heading for rural Kunyang in Yunnan Province to show me how far some Chinese were willing to go to squeeze the last cent out of their fellow countrymen.

The chapters that follow provide a vicarious Chinese experience for those unable to make the trip. And for those with a little film left in their cameras, there is a short stop in Japan on the way home.

The Limits
of Personal Loyalty

□□□

TWO MEMORIES LINGER from my fall 1991 visit to Sharon Chen's house in the Sichuan town of Ya'an. Like most Chinese flats, this somewhat dingy, four-story walk-up, attached to a kindergarten where her mother was the principal, was short on space. The Chens had come to own two refrigerators; one sat in the dining area and the other, diagonally across, in the living room. Sharon's father, a small-time movie producer and sometimes writer, was fleshy. The standing joke was that he got his exercise by running from one refrigerator to the other.

It is common when entertaining visitors in Chinese homes, just as conversation begins to lag, to trot out the family photo album. The Chens were very much of the photo persuasion, with imposing blowups of Sharon on several walls. Immediately striking about the Chen family album was that many of the pictures had been removed. Only the triangular photo ears remained. Ordinarily, this would have triggered a question. But I already knew the answer.

I first met Sharon Chen, whose Chinese name is Chen Jun, in 1988, while on a lengthy magazine assignment looking into sports in China. The Chinese run a tightly-structured, four-tiered sports system, sifting talent as young as four and five in some sports and moving it up the ladder to the national teams that compete at international events and in the Olympics. Relying on year-round, six-hour-a-day training, China, with fewer than two hundred adult softball players in the entire country, has managed to rank within a step of the U.S. (with hundreds of thousands of players) in world women's softball play, winning a silver medal at the Atlanta Olympics in 1996. Sharon Chen, then twenty-one (twenty-four according to others), 5 feet 9 inches tall, and an athlete-in-training since age eight, was one of China's ace softball pitchers; a befuddling change-up, which seemed to come out of her elbows, was her signature pitch.

In July 1988, I traveled to Oklahoma City to watch the Chinese softball team compete in the Tri-Nation against the U.S. and Japan. During the tournament, Coach Li Minkuan gave me a commemorative souvenir envelope signed by all of his players. As I counted the signatures, one was missing: Chen Jun's. Her room at the Days Inn wasn't far from mine, and I sought her out to sign my envelope. She gave me a coffee-stained Chinese drawing as a souvenir.

We again crossed paths briefly when the team overnighted at the Chinese Consulate in New York en route back to China. She quickly took the initiative: Could I please, please find her an American college that needed a softball player? Unable to refuse her imploring tone, I made a few inquiries, and, just as I was completing preparations to rejoin the National Softball Team at its winter base in Kunming, in China's Yunnan Province, I succeeded in obtaining a scholarship offer for Chen Jun from Oklahoma City University.

I wasn't at all sure that Coach Li would welcome the defection of one of his few prize pitchers. But how could I withhold information about an opportunity that could change Chen Jun's life? Our discreet conversations formed the undercurrent of my two-month stay in Kunming, during which time I lived the life of a Chinese athlete. Much of my time was spent trying to convey to Chen Jun—whose English vocabulary was little more extensive than "Let's go!"—such elusive American concepts as "athletic scholarship" and "eligibility." But she was also someone to fill in subtle points missed at team meetings because of language limitations, to introduce me to pine nuts, and to accompany me on my *de rigueur* pilgrimage to nearby West Mountain, where shills extracted 10 Chinese yuan from suckers with rope tricks, and hawkers peddled fried fish, local pineapples, and rice noodles. To ensure our outing, I handed her a note at breakfast the day before.

> Little Sister,
>
> Don't forget. Tomorrow we are going to West Mountain.
>
> Big Brother

Chen Jun was relentless in securing the ten or more approvals necessary for her to obtain a private Chinese passport* and government permission to study abroad. Final processing took place just as the Tian'anmen uprising was unfolding in May 1989. In one seven-day stretch, guiding and cajoling, I spoke to her seven times from New York, sometimes making the hundreds of dialing attempts then necessary to penetrate Sichuan's limited telephone circuits. It took extraordinary efforts to ensure her arrival in the U.S. at the end of August 1989. She spent her first days in the United States at our farm where we gave her an English name, Sharon, and taught her her first useful English phrase: "I don't drink water in the evening," a carryover from China's inconvenient bathrooms.

Chen Jun was determined to find her place here and, memorizing large chunks of the dictionary, saw her way through her courses at Oklahoma City University. In August 1991, two years after arriving, she married an OCU law student, James Frederick Strothman, the son of U.S. Federal Administrative Law Judge Frederick B. Strothman, sitting in Denver. Chen Jun assumed

---

* Her "public use" passport would have to remain with the team.

the married name of Sharon Strothman. Jim Strothman passed the bar, and, in 1993, set up private practice in Denver.

From her arrival in the U.S., Chen Jun exhibited questionable tendencies. It was difficult to get around spread-out Oklahoma City without a car. A lonely, retired oil worker, well into his seventies, by the name of Carl Huffaker, who used to hang around the OCU softball players, took a fatherly interest in Sharon, driving her where she needed to go. Sharon exploited his generosity by encouraging gifts worth thousands of dollars. She had this knack for always getting others to do things for her, giving a minimum in return. Just before her marriage to Jim, Sharon came to New York where our family threw her a bridal shower. She used the opportunity to purchase favors for her wedding guests. I remember watching her buy a leather change purse for $1.00 from a street vendor in New York's Chinatown, then, *using Carl Huffaker's calling card*, spending several dollars in phone charges to extol the virtues of each and every crevice of this $1.00 purse to Carl.

IN THE YEARS THAT FOLLOWED, our contact thinned, but I heard periodic rumors of Sharon's exploitation of Carl through a mutual Sichuan friend by the name of Christiane, who remained in touch with Sharon's family in China. Carl, she told, had paid for Sharon's plane ticket for a visit back to China. Serving as Sharon's advocate, and seeing that her scholarship promises were met, had been draining. Her marriage to Jim now absolved me of that responsibility, and I filed Christiane's rumors away. It was only in 1996, when Christiane arrived in Denver from China to take up residence with an American husband, that I began to hear rumors that were impossible to ignore: Sharon and Jim Strothman, now a member of the bar, had established a lucrative business smuggling Chinese into the U.S. Christiane and Sharon shared many of the same friends and acquaintances in Chengdu, Sichuan's capital (where the Sichuan softball team trained and Sharon had spent many years), and the illegal arrivals, or their parents back in China, would contact Christiane with complaints about Sharon.

Far removed from the situation, all of this likely would have remained in the realm of hearsay were it not for the original of a five-page letter, smuggled out from Yibin Correctional Facility in Sichuan, that Sharon had mailed to me five years earlier, in the fall of 1991, soon after her marriage to Jim. In the letter, Sharon's brother, Chen Wuchuan, serving five years for theft and assault, explicitly asked his sister for $800 to sweeten jail conditions and possibly buy an early release. Sharon sent me the letter, I surmised, in the hope that I would help with the sum. (At the time of their marriage, Jim Strothman did not even know that Sharon had a brother, let alone one who was a convicted felon.) Hence, the missing photos when I visited her parents in Sichuan later that fall.

Feeling deeply distressed for Sharon, I told no one of the 1991 letter—an expression of personal loyalty.

That loyalty began to erode rapidly in 1996 with word that Sharon's parents had arrived in the U.S., and with them her paroled brother, who had successfully concealed his prison past on his U.S. visa application. Further, according to Christiane, in order to prove to the U.S. Consulate in Chengdu that he had roots that would bring him back to China, Sharon's brother had gone out and married a local bar girl.

To send a message while maintaining my distance, in October 1996, I sent a letter to Jim Strothman's law office.

> Dear Mr. Strothman:
>
> As an officer of the court, and as the son of a retired federal judge, you need to be aware that your brother-in-law, Mr. Chen Wuchuan, is a convicted felon who has served five years in the penitentiary in Yibin, Sichuan, China. As such, he is in possible violation of U.S. immigration law, which requires full disclosure of such criminal past upon application for a non-immigrant U.S. visa...

Ethics is the core of the law. Murky pursuits, home
and abroad, trivialize its spirit.

Amicus Curiae
[Friend of the Court]

I enclosed a copy of Department of State Form 156 requiring disclosure of criminal past on visa applications.

The thought that my kindness in bringing Sharon to the
United States had led to the importation of a convicted felon
and the germination of a den of smugglers began to haunt me.
Every few months, Christiane would telephone me with an additional morsel about Sharon Strothman's activities. They always left me in sleepless turmoil.

The most disheartening case involved a nineteen-year-old
by the name of Li Jia, living in Denver with two other Chinese women in a house owned by Sharon. Li Jia, according to
Christiane, had been denied a visa to the U.S. nine times. In
the spring of 1997, Jim Strothman, impersonating a school official, had accompanied her to the U.S. Consulate in Chengdu
and finally secured her visa. Li Jia's parents had given Sharon
200,000 yuan (about $22,000)* in China. These details came
from Li Jia's father, Li Pingquan, who himself had given Sharon
$5,000 to get him a three-month visitor's visa to the U.S. Other
Strothman clients reported that Jim Strothman had masquerad-
ed as a college softball coach** and Li Jia as a softball player.

---

* Rather than personal wealth, these sums, fortunes to most Chinese, often
represented the pooled wealth of an extended family and money borrowed
from friends.

** In a letter that Jim's mother, Connie Strothman, wrote to U.S. District Court
Judge Richard P. Matsch in December 2003, she points to Sharon and her family as the possible catalysts for Jim's involvement in the smuggling scheme:

"After Jim's graduation from law school, he held his first job as a law clerk
for Judge Gaspar Perricone of the Colorado District Court. After this clerk-
ship ended he opened his own law office and practiced for a couple of years.
During this time the cultural differences became more apparent and, unfortunately, his practice did not develop as fast as his extended family thought it
should. By all accounts, Jim was a good attorney with a promising future, but
he elected to close his practice."

According to this version, $5,000 had gone to the Oklahoma City University softball coach, Phil McSpadden, for arranging a softball scholarship for Li Jia. McSpadden later confirmed receipt of the Strothman "gift" to the INS. Sharon had told Mc-Spadden that Li Jia was her cousin. As part of her softball masquerade, Sharon substituted Li Jia's name as the author of an essay on softball that Sharon had written and told Li to give it to the Chengdu Consulate when applying for her U.S. visa. Li Jia never attended Oklahoma City University.

In mid-September 2000, Christiane reported that a Chinese by the name of Song Chuan, whom she had met in an English class at Front Range Community College, had telephoned her, asking translation assistance in reporting a theft in the room he rented at 315 E. 112th Place in Northglenn, a suburb of Denver. In his statement, Song Chuan told the Northglenn police that four other unrelated illegal Chinese lived at this address, among them Sharon's brother, Chen Wuchuan, now known as Peter. Song Chuan accused Peter Chen of prying open his briefcase and taking $2,500 in cash. The examining police officer noted that both the basement bathroom and bedroom windows were open, but that the heavy dust around them was undisturbed. Song Chuan felt sure that Peter Chen, who was home alone all day in the house, and liked to play poker at an establishment known as Central City, had left the windows open as a diversion. Song Chuan, according to the police report, went on to explain that his absentee landlord was Sharon's husband, Jim Strothman, to whom he had paid $20,000 to obtain a U.S. visa. He estimated that Jim Strothman had arranged more than thirty such illegal entries from China.

My anguish turned to anger.

I followed up with the Northglenn police, learning that, the previous April, a prior complaint had been filed against Sharon's brother for harassment and domestic violence by one Luo Yang, a Chinese illegal to whom he had been married for a short period while living in Denver. Clearly, Peter Chen had brought his unsavory inclinations with him from China. Hoping to hasten his deportation, I faxed a copy of Peter's 1991 prison letter to Sharon to the Northglenn police, translating the most incriminating phrases.

Immediately, a cold reality surfaced: Because immigrants were involved, the Northglenn police contacted the Immigration and Naturalization Service (INS), then a branch of the Department of Justice, now a part of the Department of Homeland Security. Special Agent Eddie Melton, with whom I had been speaking for several weeks, instructed Detective Cindi Grein to lay off the case. He was after bigger fish. In fact, the local police had no effective way of dealing with non-English-speaking aliens. The 1991 prison letter remained in Grein's file.

Through the fall, Christiane, propelled by a genuine hatred for Sharon—whom she felt had bilked her out of $1,000 in conjunction with introducing Christiane to her American husband—widened her contact with the Strothman clients. Language limitations drove the aliens together and loneliness loosened their lips. One name quickly grew to nine, then to fifteen, then to more than twenty, virtually all from Sichuan. They ranged from factory worker to athlete to high school student to interior designer to real estate developer; their ages from seventeen to fifty.

The most common quasi-legal method used by non-student Chinese to enter the U.S. is to secure a six-month business (B-1) visa, then convert it into a student (F-1) visa under the name of any of hundreds of language schools which, through lawyers, will issue an official form I-20, certifying full-time-student status. The I-20 serves as the basis for the F-1 student visa. The applicant never sets foot near a school. Often these schools are hundreds or thousands of miles away from the "student's" place of residence. Student visas can be extended for several years, during which time the immigrant can marry an American, apply for a long-term residence visa on the basis of technical skills, apply for a permanent resident "green card," remain illegal, or return to his native country.

I had direct links to two of the Strothman illegals. The first, ZB,* an outfielder with the Chinese national baseball team, was the husband of a former softball teammate of Sharon. Sharon had sweet-talked him into coming with promises of a scholarship. ("If you come, I'll take care of you.") The B-1 business visa she would obtain for him, she said, was a necessary preliminary to a student visa. The $21,000 fee included a round-trip air ticket (to substantiate his business cover). During his first weeks here, ZB paid Sharon $200 per month to sleep under the stairs in the garage of the E. 112th Place house. The scholarship never materialized, and ZB became an embittered waiter in a Chinese restaurant.

The second illegal, LM, had been Sharon's teammate on the Chinese national softball team when I trained with them in Kunming in 1988. The teammate had spent much of the 1990s playing softball in Japan and had given Sharon $10,000 ("a discount," she said, because they were teammates) to prepare the immigration paperwork. To each of them, Sharon fed the same line: "My husband is a lawyer; my father-in-law is a judge." *Impressive words to foreign ears seeking a path to the "Golden Land."* This was the only truth she spoke.

These and other aliens produced documents directly implicating Sharon. Not only had she provided Song Chuan with a student I-20 from a school that he did not attend; shortcircuiting the process, she obtained the signature of the president of the Pacific Gateways English Academy, Keum M. Park, in Rowland Heights, California, on the I-20 and returned the signed form directly to Song Chuan without ever obtaining the approval of the INS or the F-1 visa. *A useless document for $1,200.* I had the form and the envelope it was mailed in. A few years earlier, in China, Christiane had taught me the Chi-

---

* Although full names eventually became available in open court documents, I retain the initials used in early court documents to fulfill a promise.

nese phrase *zhan pianyi* ("to look for the cheapest way out") in conjunction with Sharon. She always took the shortest route to personal advantage.

Song Chuan's original letter of invitation, in support of his business visa—from Marina Pool, Spa & Patio, in Lakewood, Colorado, to Hua Min Industrial Ltd. in Chengdu—tells as much about the weakness of the U.S. visa process as about the methodology of the Strothmans. The invitation is legitimate, but Song Chuan never worked for Hua Min Industrial, as a probing interview and a simple phone call by the U.S. Consulate in China would have revealed.

THIS MATERIAL AND OTHER LEADS went to Agent Melton at the INS. Since I was privy to much more data than he was, he readily exchanged information with me. On Li Jia, the "softball scholarship" student on whose behalf Jim Strothman was said to have intervened directly at the Chengdu Consulate, Melton readily pinpointed her May 28, 1997, date of entry and traced her original I-20 straight to the door of Oklahoma City University, where she never enrolled. Li Jia had married an American by the name of Wing Lam. Melton saw it as a bogus marriage. But in other aspects, the pace and manner in which Melton proceeded revealed basic flaws in the INS investigation process, and left grave doubts that the INS would ever complete the case.

I learned through Christiane, for example, that, on June 15, 1999, two of four Strothman clients en route to Denver were arrested at San Francisco Airport for possessing visas obtained fraudulently; both were summarily returned to China. Their documents could have served as indictable evidence against the Strothmans. Yet, when Melton contacted the INS at San Francisco, he found that the documents had been discarded. To contact the consulate in Chengdu, Melton said, he would have to go through the State Department, and that could take several months. In the end, it turned out that U.S. consulates retain nothing more than visa applications; discarding supporting documents.

I turned to contacts in China to retrieve as much as I could directly.

In October 2000, word came down through the illegal grapevine that two teenagers, one male, one female, had recently arrived in Boulder to attend college with the help of the Strothmans. To obtain their student visas, the Strothmans had arranged false TOEFL (Test of English as a Foreign Language) scores and, in collusion with the school (the Economics Institute, in Boulder), false scholarship documents. The juveniles had been seen at a karaoke hall, called DJ's, frequented by the illegals. This was significant because the two were the son and daughter of senior Public Security Bureau (China's multifaceted police force) officials in Chengdu. The deputy chief of public security in Chengdu, Zhang Longxue, whose son was also one of the Strothman illegals, was known to be an important referral cog in the Strothman smuggling operation. Further, there was information that the two juveniles would return to China during the Christmas holidays. This seemed just the time to apprehend them.

Yet Melton appeared almost reluctant to pursue them. First, he couldn't find them in INS entry records, a contributing problem being that, instead of recording border-crossing data automatically upon entry, the INS was still entering data manually, with a backlog of two to three months. Still, Melton could have gone directly to their school, a half hour from his office, and interrogated them. Finally, there was the problem of transcribing Chinese names. The boy's name was Shen Jun. "Shen" is an uncommon surname in Chinese. But in Sichuan dialect, "sh" becomes "s." To ease Melton's burden, I gave him all the possible romanized spellings and sound variations: Shen, Sen, Sheng, Seng. In mid-November, Melton came back with the misspelled answer: Shen "Jin." Still, since they were juveniles, Melton claimed he would have to go through the Chinese Embassy, something he expressed a distaste for. "Illegals are not a stable lot," I tried to tell Melton. They needed to be collared immediately.

DENVER

Fifteen days before Christmas 2000, shortly after 1:30 P.M., I heard a sharp rap on the door of my motel room, off of Interstate 25, in Northglenn, outside of Denver. It was one of those generic ground floor motel rooms with room-width windows facing directly onto the parking area. I peeked around the closed curtain and caught glimpse of a man's hand holding open a leather wallet to reveal a gold badge with the letters *U* and *S* on either side of an eagle-topped shield. No words were spoken. I redrew the curtain, nervously arranged the papers I had been perusing on the bed, and put them in their manila envelope. I returned to the window and asked who he was. He flashed his ID card: E. L. MELTON, Special Agent, U.S. Immigration & Naturalization Service.

Steeling myself, I opened the door to find a wide-shouldered, medium-height, pattern-bald, graying man who looked exactly fifty, no more, no less. He wore blue jeans, sneakers, and, though it was in the 20s outside, a short-sleeve, skin-clinging, knit shirt open at the collar. The shirt looked like it had either been slept in or worn many, many times. This was *not* how I had pictured Special Agent Melton. Looking outside the door, I could see a circa 1980 blue pickup. This was not a man to mess with. He looked like a Wild West cowboy, minus the hat.

Melton got right to the point in a Southwestern drawl as I struggled to gather my composure: "I hear you have some documents and a tape."

His out-of-the-blue, confrontational approach was totally disarming. In fact, just a half-hour earlier, I had left a message for Melton, hoping to come over to his office, as we had agreed by phone before I left New York two days earlier, so that I could give him copies of newly acquired documents from China and discuss the case. Apparently, Melton, with whom I had been working amiably over the phone for more than two months, a seasoned agent who had spent several years on the Mexican border, thought I was trying to escape with the evidence.

Even as the documents and tape were sitting right on the bed, I steadied my voice enough to tell him that I didn't have them. I had sent them back to New York, I implied. I asked him if he had a search warrant, which he did not, and that calmed the conversation.

No one in Denver knew where I was staying. What had happened, so said Melton, was that Christiane's husband, an investigator with the Department of Commerce who had initiated my contact with Melton, had given him the color of my white rent-a-car. Melton had spent part of Monday morning checking all of the motels, five or six, around I-25 in Northglenn. He figured that I would be staying there because many of the illegals lived nearby. Whatever credit due his diligence, in a matter of minutes, he had broken our mutual trust.

I HAD AGREED WITH CHRISTIANE to conceal the identity of any illegal who provided documents. That was a nagging moral dilemma, because if everyone were protected, there would be no case. On Sunday, at her home near Boulder, Christiane and I reviewed documents that had just arrived via Express Mail from China, and spent four hours talking with ZB, the outfielder, focusing on a twenty-minute telephone conversation he had recorded with Sharon Strothman during which she quotes prices for her smuggling service and discusses her plans for expanding it. ZB had made the tape in hopes of ransoming the money he had paid to Sharon. I had made it clear that I would take the tape back to New York and return a better quality dub than we could make on the spot. Nevertheless, whether out of anger that she was losing control of the case, or out of her all-consuming hatred for Sharon, the next morning Christiane, who had a nasty temper, directed her husband to call Melton, give him her file of documents, and betray the identities of all the illegals she had vowed to protect. Melton had spent part of that Monday morning interrogating ZB.

FOR THE NEXT FORTY-FIVE MINUTES, I lulled Melton into conversation. Tensions ebbed. He explained that, two weeks earlier, the Strothman case had been certified by the U.S. Attorney in Denver for prosecution and that had hamstrung him. The brusque investigative style of the INS didn't always find favor with the prim legalists at the Department of Justice. The U.S. Attorney now had to approve many of his moves. Whereas in the past there had been "give and take" between us, from now on, there could only be "take." That presented a problem for me, I told him. He was interested in convictions, notches in his belt. I was interested in seeing the Strothmans brought to justice and Sharon's brother deported. But I was also interested in understanding how a smuggling ring operated in China. "I am not an informant," I stressed to Melton.

Contrary to telephone impressions, Melton had worked hard and nurtured grand ambitions for what was dubbed "Operation Panda." He had already accumulated three thick folders, he said. His goal was to lay out a paper trail so clear that he didn't have to call any witnesses. To that end, he harbored the unrealistic hope of keeping the details of the case in as much of a vacuum as possible. The illegals, far from home and lonely, were a gossipy lot. The Strothmans, he surmised, could get two years in jail, more if tax evasion and money laundering were proven. But he wanted to close down the "schools" and collaborators that supported the Strothmans. Deep in his heart, he probably itched to link Judge Strothman, Jim's dad, to the case.

In recent years, the INS budget had been cut thirty percent. Melton's office was always having to scrounge funds from other agencies. Even getting $100 to trace phone calls was a problem. But equally as large a problem was that for Melton to penetrate the illegal Chinese immigrant culture was like moving to the moon. As he went out the door, mouthing the name of one of the illegals to see if he could coax recognition from me, Melton showed how far he had yet to travel. He asked me which part of a Chinese name was the last name and which part the first. I repeated for him the ditty I had learned back in high school: "Last name first; first name; middle name last." "Is it ABC or BCA?" he repeated, still trolling for confirmation on an alien I had sworn to protect.

"Last name first; first name; middle name last," I repeated.

I woke up at 4:30 the next morning with the heavy realization that a guy like Melton, who reported to work at 6:30 A.M., might just be crazy enough to get a warrant and come back to search my motel room. Without the tape and documents, my trip to Denver would be for naught. At what time would I be more vulnerable than dawn, I thought? So, in the dead of night, with the thermometer at 8 degrees, I placed the tape and documents in a plastic bag and buried the packet in the snow outside my room, under a spruce tree. Then, before 7:00, I retrieved them, and overnighted them back to New York from the post office a few blocks from the motel.

THERE REMAINED SEVERAL STROTHMAN THREADS in and around Denver to check into.

For five or more years, between Thanksgiving and Christmas, the Strothmans had been running a seasonal stand in the Westminster Mall known as Sharon's Gifts. The previous year, they had expanded, opening satellite stands at the Twin Peaks Mall in Longmont, near Boulder, and in Colorado Springs. The Strothman smuggling operation yielded a lot of cash in China. One of the things Melton was exploring was whether they were laundering some of this Chinese currency by purchasing goods in China later sold through their holiday outlets in the U.S.

A year earlier, in 1999, perhaps feeling that too much of their smuggling business was concentrated in Denver, Jim and Sharon, with their two daughters and Sharon's mother and father, had moved to Henderson, Nevada, near Las Vegas. During the holiday season, the six of them returned to Denver, living in the modest frame corner house on E. 112th Place, Northglenn, where brother Peter lived with three other illegals. Boxes reading "Made in China" were piled outside the garage. Sharon had purchased this house, in 1997, for $119,500, in the name of her parents, Zhu Huiqiang and Chen Weiming, the deed showed. The Strothmans owned a third house in Grand Junction, Colorado, not far from where Jim's father, Judge Strothman, had opened a winery after he retired. Sheltered Strothman assets were another Melton area of interest.

WITHOUT GOOD WITNESSES, the Northglenn Police had been unable to move on Song Chuan's theft charge against Sharon's brother, and the case had remained dormant since September. But Song Chuan had additional information about Peter Chen that might prove useful at a deportation hearing. To get it on the record, I arranged a follow-up interview for Song Chuan with Detective Grein at the Northglenn Police Station. I did the translation for Song.

Of particular interest was that, according to Song Chuan, Peter was involved in a scheme with a local driving school that, like other driving schools in Colorado, was authorized to administer written and road tests, and issue licenses. The client would give Peter $500. Peter would give the test administrator $250, and the applicant would pass the road test regardless of performance. Bribery in order to obtain a fraudulent driving license should have merited a vigorous investigation, further imperiling Peter Chen's murky immigration status. But it fell outside of Northglenn's purview, Colorado DMV was apathetic when Northglenn PD reported the case, and Melton of the INS didn't think it was a deportable offense.

SOON AFTER CHRISTIANE REVEALED the identities of the illegals to the INS, Melton confiscated the passports of as many of them as he could find to ensure that they would be available as material witnesses. Each was required to telephone Melton weekly. INS attention cost some their off-the-books jobs. Some hired immigration lawyers. One married an American to secure her status. Those aggressive enough to ask received employment authorization documents valid for as long as the case continued.

Previously a tightly knit group, several of the illegals changed their addresses and phone numbers to protect themselves from Strothman recrimination. (Melton had turned up a mob connection in one of Jim Strothman's front companies.) For a very few of the illegals able to offer compelling trial evidence, this turn in the case provided an opportunity to bargain information for legalized status. For most of them, it spelled the beginning of the end of their dreams for a stable life in this country.

THE SOUND TAPE I BROUGHT out of Denver was marginally audible. ZB had recorded it by placing a minirecorder next to one handset while speaking to Sharon on a second. Moreover, the conversation was spoken in Sichuan dialect. I had to search out a Sichuan native to catch a maximum of the nuances.

But the result rewarded the heavy leg work: an admission, in Sharon Strothman's own voice, that she was in the immigrant smuggling business.

CHINA

Spurred on by the realization that—due to blurry American laws, an inability to communicate with illegals in Chinese, inadequate record keeping and monitoring, meager budget, and poor resolve—the INS might underplay the Strothman case, in January 2001, I traveled to China determined to dismantle Sharon's smuggling operation. Beijing was my first stop.

When visiting China, Sharon often contacted her former softball coach, Li Minkuan; assistant coach Liu Yaming; and team leader Wang Mingchen. I informed each of them, as well as former teammates, that Sharon and Jim Strothman were currently under investigation by the INS and faced possible jail time. In full detail, I spelled out the sad, faceless lot of Sharon's clients, several of whom they knew. Removing the cover from the INS investigation, I hoped, would isolate Sharon in her native land.

The wide range of reactions by Chinese to Sharon's enterprise surprised me. The more sophisticated the individual, the greater the horror expressed; the more provincial, the more they saw Sharon's service as an expedient necessary to achieve a desirable end. Visas to the U.S. were hard to come by for Chinese, they reasoned; Sharon provided a useful service. Going through or around the back door was a time-honored way of getting things done in China. "Practical" and "illegal" were often only a hair apart.

A Chinese doctor friend now living in New York brought the Chinese attitude down to earth for me even before I had left for China. She was set to come to New York as part of a medical exchange program at a New York hospital. All of her papers were in order, but she had twice been denied a visa. A Beijing friend put her in contact with Sharon Strothman, who offered to facilitate her visa for $5,000—another "bargain" for another "friend." Both Sharon and the contact were dumbfounded when the M.D. refused the offer.

MY CHALLENGE IN CHENGDU, capital of Sichuan, 930 miles south of Beijing, was far more daunting: to locate anyone who had any knowledge about or involvement with the Strothmans. I was intent on disassembling the web of connections without which their smuggling scheme would be impossible. I arrived in Chengdu with no prearranged meetings; all contacts would have to be developed on the ground. Totally confounding, since so many members of the web knew each other, was ordering the interviews so that one party did not tip off another.

This was the percolating thought as I waited on the tarmac at Beijing Capital Airport for my plane to be de-iced. I budgeted eight days for the mission.

The approximately twenty Strothman customers from Chengdu fell broadly into two categories: those whom Sharon knew from her days as an athlete, and those recommended by or through associates of Deputy Police Chief Zhang Longxue.

My first contact was Hao Yue. Hao had provided the documents I had seen in Denver. She was the only one of Sharon's Chengdu customers with whom I had been in contact before arriving in Chengdu. I knew that Hao Yue wanted to help. But she has one of those voices that never bubbles. It was almost impossible to gauge how much she would open up. By the time she left my room at the Jin Jiang Hotel close to 11:00 in the evening, several more pieces in the puzzle had fallen into place, and my work schedule for the coming days had begun to take shape.

Hao, thirty-five, was a former provincial-level sprinter. In early 1997, Sharon proposed to arrange her visa to the U.S. for a sum of $18,500, $10,000 payable immediately. Hao, pregnant at the time, had dual motivations, she told me: (1) If her child were born in the U.S., Sharon had explained to her, the baby would automatically become an American citizen. (2) Hao worked as an interior designer, planning hotel lobbies and shops, and she was good at it. A period of study in the U.S., she thought, would help her career.

Hao's visa path went through several evolutions. In March 1997, in support of a business visa for Hao, Sharon prepared a false letter of invitation from Mountain States Chem-Oil, in Commerce City, Colorado, addressed to Tian Long Petroleum & Chemical, a bona fide business in Chengdu. Hao's cover would be as Tian Long Petroleum's financial officer. Tian Long's general manager was an associate of Deputy Police Chief Zhang. To facilitate Hao's application for a Chinese passport, Sharon's father, Chen Weiming, forged documents, complete with seals, addressed to the Border Document Division of the Chengdu

Public Security Bureau. For about $50, Miss Guo at the Bureau could expedite a passport.

Sharon did not return to Chengdu from Denver until February, 1999, and the Mountain States documents were never used. This time, Sharon brought with her a student I-20 document, issued by the National American University in Denver, granting Hao Yue a "Presidential Scholarship" for $18,480. The bogus scholarship was for visa purposes only. In preparation for her visa interview, Hao, with seven others, mostly teenagers, met two evenings per week for three weeks to practice basic English: "Why do you want to go to America?" "Why do you want to go to college in the U.S.?" "What will you do when you finish school?" The goal was to satisfy the consulate visa interviewer. Jim Strothman had written out the dialogue.

Claiming that her connections were not yet in place, Sharon aborted Plan B as well.

The scheme that eventually brought Hao Yue to these shores in June 2000 involved six people—three executives and three posing as their assistants: Peng Guoquan, president of the Jin Cheng Group, was paired with Hao Yue, his "assistant"; Deng Mei, vice president of the Jin Cheng Group, was paired with Sharon's former softball teammate, LM, who posed as her assistant; Li Shiyou, general manager of Tian Long Petroleum & Chemical, was paired with Guo Tongxi, an uneducated worker recruited from Sharon's hometown, Ya'an.

Crucial to Sharon's image were the contacts she claimed to have at the American consulate in Chengdu. "I'll invite the consul to dinner and the next week you'll have your visa," she would say. Sharon's former teammate, LM, reported that on occasion, when Sharon was talking with the consulate, she would shoo her out of the room. At the time the six were preparing to apply for their visas, the consulate in Chengdu was closed for several weeks while damage incurred in connection with protests of the NATO bombing of the Chinese Embassy in Belgrade was repaired. To keep on schedule, a Chinese national working at the Chengdu American Consulate by the name of Ou-Yang Dan, whom Sharon had cultivated, telephoned the consulate in Shanghai and made visa interview appointments for them. Thereafter, the six flew to Shanghai, where all of their visas were granted. American officials insist that there was no way that a Chinese national could have influenced the visa process. Ou-Yang continued to work at the Chengdu Consulate.

On June 15, 1999, four of the six flew from Hong Kong to San Francisco on United Airlines flight 806, arriving at around 2:00 P.M. Deng Mei and LM, whose U.S. letters of invitation had come from Judge Strothman's winery, the Rocky Mountain Meadery, near Grand Junction, Colorado, under Jim Strothman's signature, were admitted by Immigration. (Documents filed with the Colorado Secretary of State show that, although upon incorporation in October 1993 Jim Strothman was registered as Secretary of the winery—which has since assumed eight different names—by November 1995, his name had been deleted as an officer.) The letter of invitation carried by Hao Yue and Peng Guoquan, from Poly Steel, in New Mexico, was deemed fraudulent; the two were arrested, and sent back to China that evening. Deng, Peng's wife, returned to China with him voluntarily. Sharon's teammate, LM, continued on to Denver.

After Hao Yue returned to Chengdu, Sharon's father, Chen Weiming, returned $11,000 to her, leaving Hao Yue with a net loss of $7,000. Chen required her to sign a note stating that the matter was closed.

WHENEVER SHARON WAS IN CHENGDU, she would meet with her old Sichuan softball teammates. Going through their coach to break down their reluctance, I met three of them at Du Fu's Thatched Hut, which commemorates China's eighth-century, Tang Dynasty poet extraordinaire, and where one of the teammates, Li Mimi, worked as a tourist guide. In 1998, Li had given Sharon a fifty percent deposit of $6,000 for processing a visa to the U.S. When Li Mimi, whose husband did not know anything about this, bethought herself, Sharon returned the money, less a ten percent "service charge." "I have expenses," Sharon told her. Word that Hao Yue was caught by the INS in San Francisco spread like wildfire through China's sporting world, the teammates told me. Thereafter, Sharon avoided her old sporting friends. As far as they know, LM, ZB, Hao Yue, and Li Mimi were the only athletes to have contracted for Sharon's services.

VIRTUALLY EVERY APPOINTMENT WITH friends or associates of Sharon had to be carefully framed because I could not know that person's current relationship with her. One phone call to Sharon could have quickly alerted the others. Min Chunxiu, fifty-two, retired, an unpretentious woman to the extreme, was described by Hao Yue as "a good citizen" who had introduced many customers to the Strothmans. Min lived, with her husband, an executive with the prosperous Sichuan Power Company, and son, twenty-six, in a spacious apartment with twenty-four-hour domestic hot water, still a rarity in China. Whether this apartment was merely a job perk or reflected genuine wealth is impossible to say, but it would have been hard to ignore the three oversized TV sets I saw during a house tour.

I had introduced myself on the phone to Min as an American friend of Sharon who was interested in learning about "Chinese social customs." The Strothmans and their two children had been over to visit twice, I learned; so apparently they were on good terms. This, despite the fact that Min's son, a Sichuan University architecture graduate, had twice been refused a visa to the U.S. through Sharon's assistance. The son, without hint of bitterness, showed me his passport with the denials; the supporting documents, true to the Strothman pattern, had been whisked away by Sharon's father, he said.

During lunch, I worked the names of some of the illegals in Denver into the conversation with Min for hints of recognition. Most familiar was Li Jia, the softball player impersonator. Special

Agent Melton had surmised from her puffy photo that Li Jia was pregnant. "*Pang, pang,*" said Min. She was *fat.* The windfall at Min's house was word that a previously unconfirmed customer of Sharon was back from the U.S. for the midyear holidays. Min rang her up. This client wasn't "Petty," as I had heard in Beijing, but "Betty." She had completed a bachelor's degree in computers at Oklahoma City University, she said on the phone, and was now working on a master's degree.

When I returned to the U.S. in a few weeks, I would locate Betty, whose Chinese name was Huang Zhanghong. As she had done for Li Jia, in 1996 Sharon had arranged with OCU softball coach Phil McSpadden to issue an I-20 showing that Betty had received an athletic scholarship, though she was not an athlete. Sharon had told McSpadden that Betty was Sharon's niece. McSpadden later told the INS that he had written letters on OCU Athletic Department stationery to the U.S. Consulate in Chengdu, affirming that Betty had been awarded an athletic scholarship. Of the more than twenty Strothman clients with whom I was familiar, Betty was the only one who would turn out to be a bona fide student.

I walked in and out of Min Chunxiu's apartment several hours later with a sigh of relief and without having said a bad word about Sharon.

My next stop that evening was the Ba Bao Hotel. Sharon, together with a man in his forties by the name of Danny Wang, had invested in a disco there known as the Discovery Pub. The two were in dispute, the contact said: "He'll be talkative." I found Danny on the eighth floor in a white body suit, having his toes manipulated in the massage clinic.

Wang, an American raised in China by his grandparents, thought that Deputy Chief Zhang, who had brokered his partnership with Sharon, had sent me to adjudicate their disagreement. Wang proceeded to show me three generations of contracts in Chinese. The salient points: Wang was to have invested 510,000 yuan and Sharon 490,000 yuan, to create a 51-

49 split. But Sharon had paid in just 330,000 yuan ($40,000). Sharon had agreed to redraw the agreement to reflect her one-third ownership and had authorized her father's brother to manage the pub. But the brother had run off, leaving the Discovery Pub, once lucrative, closed for the last ten months.

There wasn't much I could do about any of this, but I had discovered where some of Sharon's smuggling windfall went.

THE TAPE ACQUIRED IN DENVER from ZB had described Strothman plans to establish official relationships with two of Chengdu's biggest universities: Sichuan University and the Southwestern University of Finance and Economics. Once a relationship was established, Sharon reasoned, she would be able to document her clients as university students and, under the exchange umbrella, simplify their visa processing considerably.

Starting out with no more information than the names of the two universities, working the phone, I was able to track down Jing Guang, deputy director of International Exchange Programs at Southwestern University. I detailed for Jing Sharon's situation and showed him her picture for confirmation. The previous spring, I learned from Jing, Sharon Strothman had been to see him to talk about establishing a TOEFL class and a continuing education program at Southwestern. Nothing had been finalized. Accompanying Sharon had been Larry Cross, president and CEO of the Economics Institute in Boulder, through which Sharon had smuggled the two juveniles, Li Wen and Shen Jun, the previous summer. According to the Denver tape, expanding her business through recognized Sichuan institutions was to be one of her prime missions when she came to Chengdu the following month. Jing Guang referred me to Ao Fan, a colleague at Sichuan University in international exchange, who I met the next morning. Unlike Jing, he didn't know of Sharon. But now he was forewarned.

Two more doors closed to the Strothmans.

THE JIN JIANG HOTEL HAD A ROOM SAFE, but that would be child's play for the Public Security Bureau. As I planned my final, potentially most dangerous meetings, I started to systematically discard copies of documents that were no longer needed and mailed home photocopies of my notes on a daily basis. I put pieces of scotch tape on the corners of the safe door so that I could tell if it had been opened.

Unlike Sharon Strothman's other clients, Deng Mei and her husband Peng Guoquan, principals of the Jin Cheng Group, were multifaceted, busy people. Their enterprises, which included real estate development, wines and liquors, foodstuffs, a restaurant, and communications interests in China and Britain, paid $1 million in taxes in 2000 on a gross of $35 million. Whatever their losses, they had no time and no incentive to revisit their misadventure with Sharon and Jim Strothman. In their possession were documents that might well tie Judge Strothman's winery to the smuggling scheme. Nevertheless, I deferred my original intentions of finessing documents and information about the Strothmans, instead telling Deng Mei, when I finally reached her cell phone in Guangzhou, that, on the recommendation of a friend at Win Honor Construction and Design Ltd. in Beijing, I was interested in doing a piece on their Jin Cheng Gardens housing development in Chengdu.

"No problem," she said.

When we met in their palatial executive suite on the nineteenth floor of the Jin Cheng Building two days later, Deng Mei, thirty-three, had a captivating, rags-to-riches story to tell. Her husband's family had been associated with the Kuomintang before the Communists came to power. As a result, her husband, Peng Guoquan, fifty-one, a junior high school graduate, was consigned to seven years of forced labor in the countryside during the Cultural Revolution. Returning to Chengdu in the late '70s, Peng found that he could buy oranges in Sichuan and sell them for seven times cost in Henan Province to the north, netting him $20,000 to $30,000 over a winter. From oranges, he branched into bulk liquor, yielding him tens of thousands of dollars per month. Peng would borrow money and repay in product, which could be resold at a large profit, providing him with easy credit. In 1991, Peng built Jin Cheng House, putting him in the building management business.

I spent almost four hours with Deng Mei, first in her top-floor office, then in her seafood restaurant, wondering all the while why a couple of such obvious wealth needed to turn to the Strothmans to arrange a visit the United States. Deng Mei, half a generation younger than Peng, and his second wife, were thoroughly straightforward. Without the airs of China's nouveau riche, she raised her own children, two and seven, rather than consigning them to grandparents, as do so many Chinese. She retained her old friends regardless of their social status. She liked to take simple vacations in the back country of Yunnan and Tibet. People of her means, Deng Mei said, stayed far away from politics, which they could not influence. Many had established a security residence outside the country in case policies in China changed.

Their intention, when Old Peng was arrested by immigration in San Francisco, was to establish themselves as investment immigrants. Chinese prefer to deal with Chinese, who share their language and customs. In this context, perhaps, Sharon Strothman, who spoke their Sichuan dialect, whose husband was a lawyer, whose father-in-law was a federal judge, provided an attractive option.

Any businessman in China who deals in real estate or liquor, no matter how pure his inclinations, cannot survive without a network of contacts—to secure permits, licenses, building materials, loans. Deputy Police Chief Zhang Longxue, who introduced Peng and Deng to Sharon Strothman, and whose portfolio at the Public Security Bureau was business affairs and the economy, would be a coveted contact. Even if they had reservations about the wisdom of the path to the U.S. Zhang offered, heightened by the knowledge that a portion of Stroth-man's fee would find its way back to Zhang, they might well have felt compelled to take it. And, if they expressed this hesitation to Zhang, he probably would have noted reassuringly that it was the Strothmans who had successfully brought his own son to the U.S.

As I surveyed the risks and prepared for my meeting with Deputy Police Chief Zhang Longxue, that son, Zhang Rui, provided my safety net as well.

I SKETCHED OUT A FLOW CHART OF THE thirty or so Strothman clients I had learned about. Fully sixty percent had some connection with Deputy Police Chief Zhang Longxue. But as he walked into the lobby at the Jin Jiang Hotel—out of uniform—at around 10:15 on a Friday morning—5 foot 2, thick black hair, unmatching rumpled pants and suit jacket—he looked as non-descript as any of millions of fifty-year-old, middle-level Chinese bureaucrats. I had started calling him the evening before, eventually reaching his Communist Party secretary (attesting to his importance). Earlier in the morning, I had finally spoken to him, asking to come to his office. He wanted to know what this was about. "*Danfo liu xuesheng.* The Denver students," I answered. He pressed me for greater detail. "We need to talk about this in person," I said. He was scheduled to attend a conference that morning, but would try to get someone to sit in for him, he said.

Immediately, as we sat down in the back lobby, a chess match unfolded. He asked for my card, I asked for his. He said he didn't have one. I said I didn't have one either. Finally, I told him I wanted to talk alone and he sent his burly, ominous-looking driver away. He asked for some identification to support my "researcher" cover. I showed him my Columbia University Alumni Library Card and wrote down a confirming e-mail address. That calmed him. I went on to tell him in great detail how I had studied about China in graduate school and gone on to do research on sports in China; about how I had met Sharon Strothman in 1988 during a research trip and about the current situation in Denver. I explained to him that the Strothmans had cheated many Chinese and were being investigated by the INS.

He interrupted to tell me—emotionless, convincingly—that he didn't know any Chen Jun [Sharon Strothman]. Perhaps someone else had used his name. I went down the list of illegals from Chengdu. Even when I mentioned his own son's name and looked deep into his eyes, he remained steel-faced. I took out a blowup photo of Sharon and Jim Strothman. He showed no reaction. "The students in Denver," he said, "have all been admitted to universities. If this Chen Jun has done something wrong, that is her responsibility."

"That isn't the way it works," I replied. He leaned away to make a cell phone call which lingered on for ten minutes. I used the interval to nervously return to my hotel room to see if the room safe had been tampered with.

In meeting with Zhang Longxue, I had two objectives. The first, to alert Zhang that the Strothmans were no longer reliable business partners, had already been achieved. Without Zhang aboard, the referrals and passport facilitation he could offer Sharon would dry up. The second was to encourage Zhang to obtain the jail record of Sharon's brother, Peter. Through Interpol, even for an American law officer, this would be virtually impossible. Zhang, through his connections, could get this document, *if it were to his advantage*. Since Zhang refused to acknowledge even knowing Sharon, this second objective had to be set aside.

When we resumed our conversation, Zhang agreed that I had performed a noble service by disclosing the Strothman situation but took the subject no further. We drifted into a discussion of the protocol of Chinese names. Both his sister and two brothers carried the word *long*, dragon, as a part of their names. His driver came back with a camera, and I told him not to take my picture. A photo circulated among law enforcement officers could impede my movement in China.

An acquaintance of Zhang in the cargo business from Taiwan came in. Zhang, it seemed, was holding court in the Jin Jiang Hotel. It was nearing noon and I told Zhang that I had a luncheon appointment with a friend. He suggested that I ask the friend to join us for lunch. I declined.

It had been a full morning.

AFTER MY MEETING WITH ZHANG, all my calls had to be made from public phones. The previous evening, I had finally obtained the name and telephone number of the ranking police officer in the Jin Niu district in north Chengdu. His son was one of the juveniles studying at the Economics Institute. I wanted to meet Shen Yong before word of my meeting with Deputy Zhang reached him. Calling from the Sheraton Hotel lobby, I reached him through his pager. He would be tied up in a conference through Sunday. It seemed imprudent to stay in Chengdu that long.

My mission in Chengdu was basically accomplished. Most of the documents I carried had been safely discarded. Content but jittery, I lulled myself to sleep reflecting on what a splendid liar Deputy Chief Zhang Longxue was. Until 3:00 A.M., when a phone ring wrestled me out of my sleep.

"Jonathan, *Wo shi* Sharon..." A lilting, pleading telephone tone I hadn't heard for four or five years.

Columbo would have seized the moment to tie together all the loose threads remaining after two weeks of field work. Sharon Strothman wasn't one to meter her mouth. But, heart thumping, head pounding, instinct prevailed. I hung up the receiver. The phone rang again. I told the hotel operator that I did not want to receive any more dead-of-the-night calls. Only Deputy Zhang knew I was staying at the Jin Jiang Hotel. He had notified Sharon.

The hotel message system had preserved Sharon's second

and third messages. I pressed my recorder flush against the handset to capture the faint voice:

"Jonathan, this is Sharon again...I don't know what's going on. Some people want to do something bad to you...My father would like to talk to you. It seems like he and you have something to talk about. I really don't like to give you problem. I need your help. So pl-e-a-s-e answer my phone.

"You help me come to U.S. And right now I'm in a difficult time. It feel like, you know, nothing go right with my life. So, Jonathan, help me out...But if you don't want to treat me as your friend, just forget about it..."

Vintage Sharon. Threatening. Begging. Anything to achieve her end.*

I LEFT CHINA IN JANUARY 2001 with a sense that, whatever the ultimate outcome of INS proceedings in the U.S., much of the Strothman smuggling network in China had been seriously compromised. It was now up to the law to mete out punishment.

ON DECEMBER 4, 2002, a federal grand jury in Denver indicted Jim and Sharon Strothman, together with two officials of the National American University who had assisted them. The charges against the Strothmans were: conspiracy, inducing illegal entry, and harboring illegal aliens, with a maximum pen-

---

* Even as she was trying to reach me in Chengdu, Sharon was calling my mother and brother in New York, monologuing about her two children and how hard she had worked in the U.S. As Sharon became more desperate, the tone changed. An anonymous phone call in Chinese put me on notice: "If anything concerning immigration happens to Chen Jun [Sharon] or to anyone else in her family, you will bear responsibility. I warn you."

In the months ahead, according to grand jury testimony, Sharon aggressively tried to gag her customers. Client Yan Xiaoyu testified that Sharon told her not to talk to investigators and that Sharon's husband, Jim, could represent her. ZB was threatened by Sharon's brother. Sharon promised to refund Song Chuan's money if he went back to China. Deputy Police Chief Zhang's son, Zhang Rui, testified that Sharon told him not to give any information to the INS.

alty of five years in jail, a $250,000 fine, restitution, and a $100 special assessment.*

In an affidavit dated July 23, 2003, ZB informed government prosecutors that he would return to China within two or three weeks to attend to his mother, who, he said, was dying from lung cancer. ZB's true motive for leaving the U.S. was fear for the safety of his family in China, which had received threatening phone calls. U.S. Prosecutor David Bybee concedes that the loss of the chief government witness, ZB, who had taped Sharon's smuggling plans, could have softened U.S. conditions for a plea agreement.**

On August 5, ZB returned to China without giving a deposition and without any government effort to keep him here by offering him permanent residence and protection.

On August 8, 2003, Jim and Sharon Strothman pled guilty to a reduced charge of one count of conspiracy.

On February 27, 2004, breaking federal sentencing guidelines, which, after discounts for cooperation, required a prison term of six to twelve months for Sharon (branded the "organizer or leader" by the court), Judge Richard P. Matsch sentenced her to three years probation, home detention for six months (during which time she would be required to wear an electronic monitoring device), and a $100 assessment. Jim Strothman

* The indictment was weakened by the government's failure to call three pivotal witnesses known to the INS at the time that the grand jury was sitting. They were Phil McSpadden, Sharon's softball coach at Oklahoma City University, and the two Strothman clients that McSpadden assisted to come to the U.S. under softball player guise—Betty Huang and Li Jia. Bringing these three before the grand jury would inevitably have broadened the indictment. Instead, the involvement of the three Oklahoma City witnesses was buried in a post-indictment motion. While the Strothmans were known to have smuggled in more than twenty aliens, just seven were called to testify before the grand jury.

** In response to a government motion to permit ZB to be deposed before he left for Chengdu so that his tape could be introduced as evidence at the trial, the Strothmans arranged for a Chinese lawyer in Chengdu to interview ZB's father and have the father sign and affix his fingerprint to a document stating that ZB's mother's cancer was in remission and that she was able to lead a normal life. The document was clearly not in the father's handwriting.

was sentenced to three years probation and a $100 assessment. He also pledged to relinquish his law license. There was no fine and no restitution.

In his sentencing colloquy, Judge Matsch drops clues to his leniency toward Sharon. He finds more fault with the government bureaucracies, both here and in China, and their laws and procedures than with the lawbreakers. He spares no effort to comfort Sharon. Her probation, he tells her, "...doesn't mean you're bad, or that you're evil, or that your intentions here were simply mercenary....I understand that you could justify what you did." He offers no sympathy to the victims, most of whom wasted the prime years of their lives because of Jim and Sharon's deception, and returned to China with broken lives.*

---

* A further clue arises in a letter Jim's mother, Connie Strothman, wrote to the judge on December 9, 2003, in advance of sentencing: "...his father [Judge Fred Strothman]," Connie Strothman tells Judge Matsch, "believes it would be inappropriate to write to you due to his professional association with you many years ago." Should Judge Matsch have recused himself?

Hobnobbing with China's Rising Communist Stars... and Penetrating the Veil of Secrecy of the Communist Dynasty

□ □ □

IT WAS FAST APPROACHING MIDNIGHT, two days after the Sixteenth Chinese Communist Party Congress ended in November 2002, when I was awakened by an extraordinary phone call. It was from one of the delegates from Ningxia, in the western part of China.

What made Ma Fu's call exceptional was that a week earlier, during the Congress in Beijing, our interview almost broke up over the issue of whether China was really a socialist country. When I first visited China in 1984, I told Ma, all of the shops along Chang'an Avenue, the major east-west boulevard cutting through Beijing, were state owned; now they were almost all privately owned. Further, the overwhelming majority of China's farmers, representing some seventy percent of the population, were outside of the state system. This carried no weight with Ma, who had a canned response to everything. "Don't the farmers all live on state-owned land?" he quibbled. That the government was now considering allowing them to *sell* this land (or more precisely, the rights to this land), he dismissed with a huff.

"If that's what you think," he said, "then we have nothing in common." Despite my best efforts, the rest of our seventy-five-minute discussion limped along to a dispirited conclusion.

Apparently, however, I had made a lasting impression on Ma Fu. "There were some sticking points," he said on the phone, "but we had a very good conversation." Now he was inviting me to come to Ningxia to see the local situation with my own eyes. And not only that, he would pay my expenses.

This was surely a gift from heaven. Ma Fu, forty-three, was not yet a top-echelon politician. But he was very young for a delegate to the Party Congress. And his current position, as Party secretary of the Ningxia branch of the Communist Youth League, was a well-worn path to higher office. Hu Jintao, the heir to Jiang Zemin, had served a stint at the Youth League on his way to the top Communist Party position. Being able to call Ma directly, at home, without having to go through a secretary, made coordinating a visit so much the easier.

MORE SO EVEN THAN ITS WEIGHTY historical significance—the changing of the guard, the inauguration of the first post-revolutionary generation to lead the world's largest country—the Sixteenth Communist Party Congress presented an opportunity to meet a large number of upper-echelon Chinese leaders. I would learn what I could from them in Beijing, and then perhaps forge enough of a relationship with a few to visit them in their hometowns after the meeting. The Chinese have a saying: "The central government has its policy, and local governments have their own counterpolicies." I wanted to meet local leaders and see if I could penetrate the mask of unanimity they all appeared to wear. I wanted to see flesh and blood in place of the mannequins and parrots they appeared to be in public. I needed to understand how, at the beginning of the twenty-first century, when most of China had long since lost its interest in communism, a communist party still functioned. And how that party was adapting to the everyday needs of a modern society.

The Chinese made nothing easy.

Any delegate could be interviewed. But to request an interview, an application had to be filed at the press center. To apply, a name was needed. But though the delegates were chosen five months before the Party Congress opened, no published list of the 2,114 delegates was to be found.

But there were opportunities. Before the opening ceremony began in the Great Hall of the People, the delegates and the press were free to mingle in the vast reception area outside of the assembly hall. In thirty minutes, I managed eleven potluck interviews, whose sole purpose was to copy the name of the delegate from his badge, learn his delegation and telephone number, and possibly grab a business card. I avoided anyone old or fuddy-duddy. I was after rising stars—China's new generation of leaders.

The thirty-eight delegations met, morning and afternoon, for seven days, to "deliberate." Three half-day sessions were partially open to the press. I exploited them by running from end to end of the Great Hall of the People—a structure on the scale of the Pentagon—to gather further interview targets. *As much an athletic feat as a crash course in political science.* In this way I was able to file forty-five interview applications. By the end of the Congress, I had managed to meet a wide range of upwardly mobile delegates from all over China.

Many of the delegates were one-timers, inserted to add diversity to the delegation. Among them were athletes, actors, college presidents, simple workers. For decades, China, the defining standard when it comes to propaganda, has paraded out model citizens, people so pure and goodwilled that they hold angels to shame. Officer Li Tiejun—thirty-two, strapping,

Wheaties-box handsome, a policeman from the 911 unit of a district in a small city in Fujian Province, along China's east coast—was all goodness. He held a junior college degree in criminology and saw his role in life as helping people, as a bridge between the people and the law. He was as excited to be interviewed as I was happy to meet a local icon. After I finished asking my own questions, I spent fifteen minutes answering his: about the American justice system, about ethnic diversity, about overlapping constituencies, about the role of the FBI.

The Party Congress provided only bones and a road map; it was just a prelude. As soon as it ended, I prepared to travel around the country hoping to find some meat. Four of the Party delegates I had interviewed were subsequently elected to senior Party positions. I would visit some of them. Two weeks of hobnobbing with top Party officials had made several things very clear: viewed from the top, the grip of the Communist Party remained very strong. The Party controlled the government—most senior government officials held parallel Party posts. The Party controlled the army—enough to marshal seventy thousand policemen and troops in Beijing during the Congress. The Party controlled the media—the day the new Politburo was elected, the entire national TV newscast was suspended, replaced by a word-for-word reading of the official biographies of each new member that ran one hour and fifty-four minutes.

What made this possible? *The absence of any audible dissenting voice.* Intimidation or apathy? *The people simply didn't care.*

The entire Chinese Communist Party endeavor is an exercise in discipline—mental and physical. To retain just enough control to stay in power, but not to the point where it constrains China's march forward. For, if the Party were to smother the people materially, it would fall from power. This parallels the dynastic principle that has governed China for 2,100 years, from the first emperor, in 221 B.C., to the last, in 1911. After five decades in power, the Communist Party had finally succeeded in reinstating the dynastic cycle.

That is why the Party gives careful identity to each communist "reign." **Mao Zedong**, the revolutionary, the founding father of the Communist Dynasty, who took China out of the mires of thirty-eight years of civil war and foreign occupation, as had the First Emperor of Qin (*Qin Shi Huangdi*) 2,100 years earlier. **Deng Xiaoping**, the second Communist "emperor," who turned China toward the West, toward material well-being. **Jiang Zemin**, the third generation, who continued on Deng's path by instituting a market economy—"a special breed of socialism with Chinese characteristics," he called it. **Hu Jintao**, the new leader, the fourth generation, who is empowered with seeing China's integration into the world economy, punctuated by China's entry into the World Trade Organization (WTO) and Beijing's hosting of the 2008 Olympics—all without compromising Party authority.

Communist authority has two arms: (1) physical control through the army and the state police, whose domain stretches, without a gap, from Beijing to the most remote village; and (2) thought control. In an era where the common Chinese people, the *laobaixing*, have more physical and economic freedom than ever before, mental discipline is essential if the Party is to retain control. One of the points of emphasis in Jiang's Sixteenth Party Congress address was "party building." The Communist Party needed to make party membership attractive enough to recruit a critical core (set at about five percent of the population). Such loyalty is built by making Party membership a criterion for jobs that would seem to have no connection with communism, such as being the president of a hospital or the coach of a team in China's powerhouse sports system.

I was finally beginning to understand the end purpose of all the slogans and unfathomable catch phrases—the "two" thises, the "three" thats, the "four" other things—that have been the hallmark of Communist China all these years. Propaganda disciplines the Party; the Party disciplines the people. The physical act of forcing all Party members to talk the same way, in time, makes them think the same way. The Chinese call it "thought unification."

Unifying thinking, brainwashing, deciding everything in closed forum, then presenting consensus to the people—while providing the people with an ever more comfortable life. That remains the secret of Party power.

Even avowed non-communists such as my friend Hua Weili, a businessman who has prospered under the communist system, sees advantage in the discipline cast by Communist Party control. "Mao Zedong, Deng, Jiang Zemin, I don't see where they made any basic mistakes. China is too big; if there were multiple parties, they would just tear each other to pieces and the common person would suffer."

EVERY MAJOR TRANSITION REQUIRES A rallying call, something for the entire Party membership—all sixty-seven million*—to latch on to. That was the function of the "Three Represents," the clarion call of the Sixteenth Party Congress and the bridge between the third emperor in the Communist Dynasty, Jiang Zemin, and the fourth emperor, Hu Jintao.

The "Three Represents" was Jiang Zemin's bid for immortality; his attempt to enter the Communist Chinese pantheon alongside Mao Zedong and Deng Xiaoping. Introduced two years before the Sixteenth Congress, the "Three Represents" got off to a difficult start, befuddling millions of Party members. The Party, it said, (1) **represents** the needs of progressive production forces, (2) **represents** progressive cultural trends, (3) **represents** the basic needs of the overwhelming majority of the Chinese people. It seemed to be speaking in tongues.

The "Three Represents" was subtly redressed several times,

---

* As of 2002. By 2007, the number had grown to 73,363,000. Although to many people in China the Communist Party is an anachronism, since 1997 the Party has added thirteen million members to its rolls.

and by the time the Party Congress began in November, it was finally upgraded to read, "Three Represents *Important Thought*"—intoned in one breath. One can only imagine how many hours Jiang and the other core leaders spent debating the two words "important thought."

What "Three Represents Important Thought" was preaching, it finally became clear, was inclusion. The Party was trying to be everything to everyone. Even a capitalist, it was saying, could be a communist.

Still, there were questions...which, once consensus was reached, no Party member dared to ask.

First, the semantic question: If the "Three Represents" was the ideological breakthrough claimed, why did it have to be termed "important"? "Mao Zedong Thought" sought no qualifying adjective. "Deng Xiaoping's Great Theory" at least merited a superlative. It was a little awkward listening to Jiang Zemin repeat "Three Represents Important Thought" nineteen times during his hour-long report at the Sixteenth Congress opening session. But with repetition, it had to be acknowledged, one got used to it. Worthy of note: although Jiang abbreviated the printed text considerably in his oral presentation, he didn't cut any of the references to "Three Represents Important Thought."

The "Three Represents" is (1) the Party's main rationale for existence, (2) the cornerstone of its authority, (3) the source of its strength.

ONE OF THE PARTY'S KEY points in accommodating capitalism was the idea that China's 900 million farmers (who, in contrast to city dwellers, own the rights to the land they live and work on) might soon be able to sell those rights—either to get out of farming entirely, or to consolidate small plots into larger operations. Rural Zhuolu County, in Hebei Province, several hours north of Beijing—moderately prosperous, somewhat progressive, about as average as you can get—was a good place to check out the ramifications of land reform. I used the limited express train time to Zhuolu County to complete my own mini-survey on the "Three Represents." Things did not look good for the Party public relations effort. The "Three Represents" recognition factor on the train stood at less than 1 "Represent" per interviewee, and that excluded the rural villages where attention to politics is nil to none.

Zhang, forty, a junior high school graduate who long-hauled coal in his own truck for a pretty good living, pulled me over to his seat on the train and hit the point home harder than most: "Those Party Congress delegates, they are all a bunch of fakers. Politics doesn't have *anything* to do with our lives. What we care about is *money*. If you want to understand China, talk to the common people." He gave me his phone number.

The Chinese Communist Party (1) represents the needs of progressive production forces, (2) represents progressive cultural trends, (3) represents the basic needs of the overwhelming majority of the Chinese people.

WHAT BROUGHT ME TO ZHUOLU County was a chance to get into the farm villages where most of China still lives. Mao's revolution began in the villages and, if the villagers don't get their share, it could one day resume there. The villages are falling further and further behind.

China is organized as a series of circles within circles within circles. Provinces* usually contain anywhere from five to ten cities, each made up of a city center surrounded by rural counties. The counties in turn are composed of a county town or seat surrounded by rural villages, themselves grouped

---

* Confusing. Administratively, they number thirty-one, exclusive of Taiwan (considered a province by the mainland), and Hong Kong and Macao (both considered special administrative regions). Twenty-two of the thirty-one are designated provinces. Five are designated autonomous regions instead of provinces because of a heavy minority presence. The Ningxia Hui Autonomous Region, for example, contains a heavy Hui Muslim population. Four of the thirty-one—Beijing, Tianjin, Shanghai, and Chongqing are cities under the administration of the central government. Administratively, the thirty-one are all of equal rank.

into smaller administrative units. The land whose rights they own aside, what distinguishes the peasants in the villages from townspeople is that they pretty much fend for themselves. City dwellers, if they work for a government business or organization, benefit from a measure of social security.

Since the 1990s, Chinese villages have developed unevenly. I had stayed in villages in rural Yunnan Province near Vietnam and Gansu Province in Western China and had seen how basic they could be. I would see prosperous villages outside Tianjin. Zhuolu's villages sat in the middle. In Zhuolu County, I hoped to understand to what extent Chinese communism was alive and well in the back country, the quality of life in the villages, and how land reform might alter the balance of rural life.

My original thought had been to ease my way into the villages with the support of Yang Deqing, the Party secretary from Zhangjiakou, the city that governs Zhuolu County. But one brief discussion with Yang at the Party Congress in Beijing told me that I had made the wrong choice. Instead, my entrée to Barefoot Temple* Village came from a Beijing friend with a slew of cousins in Zhuolu Town. The friend, through her cousins, had hired Little Fang, then twenty, as a nanny to care for her son. This gave Little Fang the opportunity to accumulate some cash in Beijing before returning to Barefoot Temple Village to marry. Now, eight years later, Little Fang was in the village, tending the family's corn plots with her father and caring for her own five-year-old son. Her husband was in Beijing working with a building demolition crew, one of one to two hundred million Chinese farmers in China's cities hoping to build a nest egg; his at the rate of $125 to $175 per month. Little Fang's entire corn crop would earn no more than $400. Particularly in late November, there weren't many men to be found in Barefoot Temple Village.

AT 7:00 A.M., THE DAY AFTER I ARRIVED in the village, a voice blared over the loudspeaker: "Cover your corn, it's snowing."

* *Chijiaosi* in Chinese.

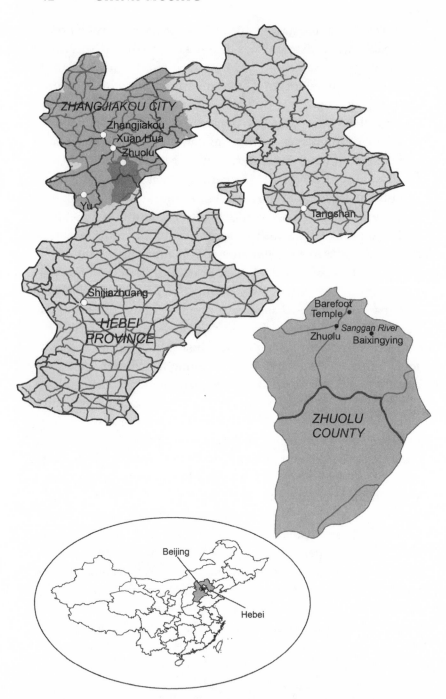

Sure enough, there was a half-inch of large flakes on the ground. But Little Fang, aided by a fifteen-year-old helper, had been well ahead of things. Neatly folded plastic sheeting covered three twenty-foot rows of dried, husked corn piled waste-high, like a New England wood stack. You could learn a lot about Little Fang, Barefoot Temple Village, Zhuolu County, and land reform in general from this corn, which represented most of the agricultural cash income her family, and the other families in Barefoot Temple Village, would reap this year.

Barefoot Temple was a quaint enough place. Its name came from a legend about a well dug long ago in the village, whose excavation yielded a bronze Buddha with bare feet. As in much of rural China, poplar-lined, earthen lanes flanked the courtyard compounds that are standard in China's countryside. Little Fang kept a neat five-room homestead with a color television, a telephone, and outbuildings. The brick-enclosed latrine in the courtyard was tidy if inconvenient, but the night bucket Little Fang handed me took care of most post-bedtime emergencies. Bathing was generally suspended in winter, replaced by a thorough basin-washing of face and feet. Sleeping was on a *kang*, a brick-framed, earth-filled bed that is covered by a mat or blanket and heated by burning wood, corn stalks, or coal in oven-like openings near the bottom of the *kang*. It could get into the single digits in winter in Zhuolu County, and on such occasions, inch-thick cotton quilts did the trick. The key to village life was getting into the rhythm.

The problem with Barefoot Temple Village was its corn. Though land-wise the one thousand farmers in the village were better off than most in the county, with one-third of an acre per person, corn simply didn't fetch a high enough price to generate prosperity. Elsewhere in the county, farmers had moved to fruit crops, especially grapes, which generated four times as much cash. Whose fault was this? Partly the farmers themselves. Little Fang appeared particularly conservative, not one to plunge into new waters. Part of the blame lay with the heavy clay soil in the village, which the villagers flooded before the soil froze in winter so that expansion and contraction induced by the freeze and thaw would break up the clumps. Party Secretary Zhang, the most powerful person in the village, was innovative enough to engineer a basic central heating system in his own spacious home. As village Party secretary, as farmer, and as head of the village credit union, he had three incomes. But maybe he didn't provide enough of the push that more progressive villages enjoyed.

Not that Barefoot Temple was backward. In the village elementary school there were eight shiny computers for the one hundred students. And each home had cable television provided free of charge. But little by little, Barefoot Temple Village was losing ground.

Baixingying Village on the other side of the Sanggan River—more adaptable—was converting to grapes now that the price for pears had fallen through the floor. In Baixingying Village, there were two cold storage facilities to house those grapes—destined for faraway markets in Manchuria and Inner Mongolia. Barefoot Temple, in contrast, barely managed a simple machine shop where three men hand-turned stainless steel arms for bulldozers.

The 1,705 residents of Baixingying Village had half the acreage of Barefoot Temple Village, but they enjoyed as much as twice the income. That was why the village lanes in Barefoot Temple turned to mud when it rained while those in Baixingying were paved. The day was quickly dawning when a village such as Barefoot Temple, always short of cash, could not survive.

I walked the lanes and fields of Barefoot Temple and Baixingying with Party Secretaries Zhang and Liu. One thing both could agree to was that land reform in either village was highly problematic. The plots the peasants worked, measuring about forty by sixty feet, with a family's holdings often scattered throughout the village, made mechanized farming impossible.

But consolidating the fields and selling them off to enable scale agriculture, the idea Jiang Zemin had raised, would destroy the fabric of the village. Before this could be allowed to happen, there had to be a fundamental change in employment opportunities in Zhuolu Town, the county seat. Zhuolu County's peasants couldn't *all* work in Beijing. The urbanization of China's two thousand counties went part and parcel with land reform.

If the villagers were to leave farming on a permanent basis, they had to have something to do. To have a job, they needed skills. To obtain skills, they needed education. To obtain such education, they needed money and good schools. For the county to provide such opportunity, it had to prosper. For the county to secure investment, it needed skilled labor. To provide skilled labor, it needed to provide better education. I could see the day, five or ten years down the road, when villages like Barefoot Temple—airy, spacious, just fifteen minutes by car from Zhuolu Town—would become leafy suburbs of a small city. Many farmers would fall through the cracks during the transition.

Before the transition could begin, a swept-under-the-rug aspect of the work situation in Zhuolu and towns and cities throughout China had to be addressed: premature retirement. The web of connections that provided me entrée to Barefoot Temple and Baixingying involved five classmates, all fifty-three or fifty-four. Barefoot Temple Party Secretary Zhang was one. The other four all lived in Zhuolu Town. Two of the four (a department head at the local post office and a hardware company manager) had been eased into early retirement to provide advancement opportunities for the next generation. A third was still employed in the Zhuolu Cultural Affairs Office, where there wasn't much to do. *Three idlers at fifty-four.** Only the

---

* The official retirement age for ordinary male workers in China is sixty; for women fifty-five—though for senior officials it can be extended to sixty-five or seventy. In non-productive government-owned businesses, workers might be forced to retire at fifty or below.

fourth, who, using his earnings as a bulldozer contractor, had recently opened a haberdashery, displayed any real initiative. Zhuolu Town, now forty thousand strong, was growing, and the new highway and its proximity to Beijing were pluses for the county. But it would take a long time for the town to generate enough growth to provide work for any significant portion of the 320,000 farmers and townsmen who lived in Zhuolu Town and the dozens of surrounding villages.

What was the Chinese Communist Party's primary interest in this? Order. For two thousand years, the hallmark of Chinese society has been the ability of the government to keep tabs on and control populations in even the most remote areas. That is the function of the Party secretary present in each and every village. The Party is everywhere. Promptly at 9:00 A.M., on my second day in Zhuolu, no less than three hundred Communist Party members from throughout the county flocked into the meeting room just a few feet from my door. The day-long meeting's theme: "Studying, Publicizing and Implementing the Sixteenth Party Congress Spirit." *Discipline.*

In Barefoot Temple Village proper, there were forty-seven Party members; in Baixingying, there were seventy-nine: about the same proportion as elsewhere in China. But the energy with which the two villages executed their Party study responsibilities differed significantly. In Barefoot Temple, it mostly took the form of watching TV reports. In Baixingying, Party Secretary Liu—more vibrant, more interested in the outside world than Secretary Zhang in Barefoot Temple—went out of his way to take me to the Party meeting room, which was filled with placards detailing just how much study time was expected from each Party member. Slogans hailing Jiang Zemin's "Three Represents" plastered the walls. In Baixingying, they had turned the "Three Represents" from an abstraction into a reality. That would strengthen the village's standing with the Party chief in Zhuolu Town.

It was "market day" in Baixingying, with villagers from

throughout the area coming to peddle their wares as has been the custom in China for centuries. As we strolled down the village lanes, munching on sticks of candied crab apples, Secretary Liu pointed to a towering cell-phone antenna. "Progressive production force," I whispered to Liu in Chinese. He howled. Party activism and recompense—was that part of the difference between Barefoot Temple and Baixingying?

The Chinese Communist Party (1) represents the needs of progressive production forces, (2) represents progressive cultural trends, (3) represents the basic needs of the overwhelming majority of the Chinese people.

THE INTERVIEW SCHEDULED WITH THE Tianjin delegation during the Congress was supposed to have been with the top Party man in charge of rural affairs. But the executive vice mayor, Xia Baolong, whom I had met at the opening reception, came along instead, my name card in hand, and pretty much took control. He handed me a book filled with glossies of Tianjin—a city of ten million, and one of the most heavily invested in by foreign companies in China—and let me know that he wanted to see these pictures in print in the U.S. He had ambitious plans for Tianjin, foremost of which was raising its per capita gross domestic product (GDP) from $2,500 to $6,000 by 2010.

Xia was a bit miffed that I hadn't paid sufficient attention to his talk at the open Tianjin delegation group discussion and was making him retrace covered ground. He was a strong orator, but I had been preoccupied with writing down names in preparation for future interviews during his speech. Xia walked me through Marx, Mao, Deng, and Jiang Zemin, explaining how each of the three paramount Chinese leaders had adapted Marx's basic theory to the needs of his time. The contribution of each was precisely equal, he insisted like a cleric; nothing could budge him. Mao freed the common people from generations of exploitation by the moneyed class. Deng turned backward China toward the path of modernization. Jiang expanded on Deng and solidified China's opening to the outside world. Xia was as unswerving and unflappable as he was affable. He was on the fast track and didn't hide it.

Xia Baolong mentioned that thirty percent of Tianjin's industries were privately owned, and that triggered a semantic debate on the nature of China's socialism. "What if that proportion were reversed and became the national trend throughout China?" I probed. China, he insisted, would remain socialist no matter the percentage of private businesses because "the companies would need to be stock-based in order to expand, meaning that they would be owned by the people." It was hard to imagine how the president of IBM would react if he were called a socialist because he headed a publicly owned company.

Of course, defining China as "socialist" was crucial to the entire Chinese Communist enterprise. If China were to cease carrying a socialist tag, the legitimacy of the Communist Party would evaporate.

Vice mayor Xia had studied philosophy and liked to argue. He promised me a hearty debate when I came to Tianjin.

BY THE TIME WE MET IN TIANJIN FOR DINNER several weeks later, the career of Xia Baolong, fifty, feisty, a natty dresser, had taken a further step forward. He had been re-elected as an alternate member of the Party Central Committee. As such, he would attend all Central Committee meetings, and could participate in Central Committee discussions, though he could not vote. The benefits were enormous, both in enhanced status in Tianjin and as an opportunity to mingle with and be scrutinized by China's upper crust.

By custom, Chinese leaders remain enigmas, even to their own people. A biography of Hu Jintao appeared in Chinese several years ago without even mentioning his wife's name. Xia was of the same cloth. I fished a little into his background between toasts, and his response was tepid. I tried to cajole him, saying that he was a "likeable" fellow and that his personality might some day be a strong asset when China turned to a direct electoral system. When that didn't work, I pointed out how ridiculous it would appear if one day, say as the Chinese ambassador to the U.S., he would be interviewed on CBS and, in response to a question about his hobbies, were to answer, "No comment."

In fact, Xia was playing the system like a virtuoso, giving the impression of one poised to implement rapid change, but at the same time plugged solidly into the present. Revealing himself to the foreign public by telling me a little bit about his family would score no points with China's elite leadership.

Despite his reluctance, over a truly plush dinner, I succeeded in extracting a few bare details.

Xia Baolong had grown up in Tianjin, where he had spent his entire career. He had graduated from elite Beijing University, majoring in economics and also studying philosophy. He had worked as a high school teacher, school principal, and local Communist Youth League secretary, and had stepped through all of the Party and government positions from the county level on up. Almost all senior Party officials serve a stint, sometimes decades, away from their hometowns. Hu Jintao, for example, who grew up in the eastern part of China and began his work career in Beijing, spent seventeen years in three remote provincial posts, including four years in Tibet. "Cadre rotation," as they call it, is intended to ensure a dispassionate, incorruptible view of the local situation at a price of insensitivity and sometimes ignorance. At fifty, Xia Baolong—focused, ambitious—might yet have to pack his bags as he continued his climb.*

Chinese as a people are a gossipy lot. But pulling personal information out of Chinese officials is like trying to pull a hat out

---

* True to the system, one year later, lifelong Tianjin resident Xia Baolong was appointed deputy Party secretary of Zhejiang Province by the Chinese Communist Party Central Committee.

of a rabbit. I went to great lengths to point out to Xia Baolong that, until ten or fifteen years ago, Chinese officials used to conduct all of their official socializing with foreigners without their spouses. But when China began to court the West aggressively, Chinese officials discovered that bringing one's spouse along was *de rigueur*. So, for the first time the public learned the names of the wives of China's leaders. When he became an ambassador, Xia said, he would consider amending his style. He opened up only a bit. When he is truly bushed, he allowed, he plays the piano for half an hour and comes back as good as new. We digressed into a discussion about aping the West and discarding Chinese values, and he told me that his son, twenty-two, could play not only the violin, but also the traditional Chinese string instrument, the *erhu*. "And, I can tell you, I have a wife."

The big scoop.

IN CONTRAST TO MOST OF CHINA, which is overwhelmingly rural, the balance in Tianjin, seventy miles southeast of Beijing, is fifty-fifty. Heavy industry dots Tianjin's outlying areas, and in some Tianjin villages land reform has already begun. The day might not be far off when almost all of Tianjin's ten million people will be urbanites. Tianjin is one of the best places in China to view the process of urbanization unfolding. I was anxious to see, up close, from the farmer's point of view, how feasible land reform was in rural Tianjin. Xia Baolong arranged with the Party secretary in charge of rural affairs to put his deputy at my disposal.

To anyone familiar with Chinese villages, Shijiazhuang Village, in southwestern Tianjin, would appear to be a fairy tale. In 1985, under the guidance of a returning son of the village, Shijiazhuang, a hamlet with about 500 people and 330 acres, began to industrialize. It sent villagers outside the village to study, brought in instructors, and developed a group of enterprises, the most prominent of which is an electric wire and cable factory with a yearly turnover of some $50 million. At the same time that it was industrializing, it underwent land reform, which saw all the villagers transfer their privately owned plots to the village in return for shares in the resulting cooperative. This let the village consolidate land not used for industry into

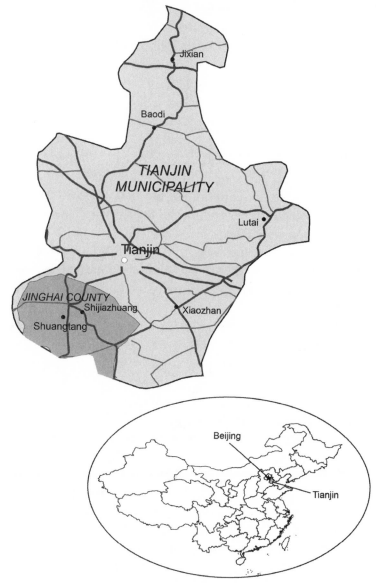

fields suitable for mechanized farming. They now grow corn, cabbage, wheat, sorghum, and apples. What Shijiazhuang Village established in effect was an Israeli kibbutz.

Its success has enabled the Shijiazhuang cooperative to build a cottage for every family in the village and to provide each with a private car, computer, and telephone. I visited several of the two-story cottages and they are bright, airy, and thoroughly appealing. In addition, the village provides health insurance; tuition; retirement benefits; an allotment of fruits, grains, and vegetables (which can be sold); and about $1,700 in cash per person per year. The only palpable blot on this perfection was the carton of still-green apples they gave along when we left.

It occurred to me that everything I had seen in the village was staged; that the Tianjin government, hoping to encourage investment and transition in other villages, had underwritten the cost of the comfortable life that made Shijiazhuang a place most Westerners would be happy to call home. And, if the government of Tianjin had indeed done so, it might well have made a wise decision. The Sixteenth Party Congress set as a core goal to provide everyone in China with a "well-off" standard of living within twenty years. Shijiazhuang is the perfect model.

West Shuangtang, about thirty minutes from Shijiazhuang, was more believable because it was less perfect. West Shuangtang has twice the population and five times as much land (about two square miles) as Shijiazhuang, but little more than half the income per villager. The moving force here was a handicapped man by the name of Chen Lixin, fifty-two. Chen is a dwarf who left the village for thirteen years, during which time he became wealthy trading in commodities—vegetables, hardware, lumber.

In West Shuangtang, the villagers opted for much the same type of cooperative arrangement as in the first village, with half the annual cash allowance. There were no free cars or computers, but it was possible to borrow a communally owned car. The factories here were more modest, including a leather processing factory that turned imported Australian sheepskins into sofas, rugs, and futons sold in Japan; and a tableware factory that made forks, knives, and spoons.

As interesting as the overnight stay in the home of Zhao Chunmei (where, encouragingly, the plumbing leaked) was the chance to talk about politics and communism with communists: Zhao Chunmei, the hostess and a Party member, worked as a bookkeeper in the cooperative's import-export department; her husband, Guo, who handled Party affairs and the eighty-nine Party members in the village; Rural Affairs Party Deputy Secretary Zheng; and his driver. Chinese have always been stingy with their lighting, continuing to favor—even with prosperity—25-watt bulbs. Inevitably, darkness induces candor faster than sleep. *You reach some unexpected conclusions in the dark.*

Communism, we all agreed, was about power, discipline, and control; ideologically, it had long since lost its meaning. When he first introduced his radical reforms in the 1980s, Deng Xiaoping defused sometimes raucous internal conservative opposition with a simple saying: "On the question of whether to call it [the Chinese system] 'socialism,' or to call it 'capitalism,' we won't debate that at present." *Then as now.* To defer an identity crisis and the potential loss of Communist Party power, "Capitalist" China was postponing this debate indefinitely.

Tianjin bucked the national trend. Half of Tianjin's 3,870 villages (having the Deputy Party Secretary for Rural Affairs at hand for statistics has its conveniences) were collectively owned. But nationally, the picture was just as I had seen in Little Fang's village: more than ninety percent of the farmland in China was privately owned and the villagers liked it that way. "Where conditions allow," the Sixteenth Party Congress Report suggested, land rights could be sold to make way for mechanized agriculture. In most of rural China, the time was not yet ripe. Ironically, in going against the popular tide, the two collective Tianjin villages I had visited were moving closer to communism. That was something for Party theorists to mull over.

The real rural China, as it happened, lie just over the bridge, one hundred yards from West Shuangtang Village. I told Deputy Secretary Zheng that I would be setting my alarm for 6:00 A.M. in order to fit a look at East Shuangtang Village into our crowded schedule. He wasn't used to jogging in pre-dawn light.

The only thing East and West shared was a common elementary school. East Shuangtang Village was devoid of any rural charm. The rutted earthen lanes were strewn with corn stalks and litter. None of the white poplars that grace almost every village in China were on the horizon. Most of the villagers were sleeping when Deputy Zheng gave a hearty call through the door, but you could glean well the state of interior affairs by a look at the disheveled courtyards, none of which had even an outhouse. But if this large village of three thousand was poorly managed, it was well monitored. For sanitation reasons, the county health authorities had mandated collective outhouses. That spelled and smelled compliance and inconvenience.

We finally found a household that was awake. Jin, sixty-two, and his wife, Yang, fifty-seven, were remarkably cheerful and hospitable for 7:00 A.M.

"But wouldn't you say life is much better than it used to be?" Deputy Party Secretary Zheng tried to coax. They were in a complaining mood. The streets were crumbling and there wasn't enough land. The big beef though, was that, over and above the permanent population, two thousand migrants from Manchuria who worked in the local dairy had crowded into the village. Their footprints were everywhere. The contradiction was that Jin and Yang, like many of their neighbors, had rented out their son's house to the migrants to exploit the earning opportunity.

When you ponder a while, you realize that prosperous farm

villages like Shijiazhuang and West Shuangtang in Tianjin are not miracles. Rather, they are the result of organization and funding—not very far in concept from the tens of thousands of factories established in coastal China over the past fifteen years. Previously independent farmers agree to pool their labor and land in return for a package of salary and benefits. The $75 to $150 per month cash benefit in the Tianjin villages is roughly what rural migrant labor in export factories all along China's coast receives. Villagers receive perks that migrant labor would never merit. But in return they contribute their land and provide the cooperative a particularly reliable source of labor. Since the cooperative is non-profit, perks many Chinese would view as luxuries are available for the shareholders. Worth remembering is that many village industries are low-tech, cashing in on the locomotive that has pulled China so far so quickly: cheap labor. The key in these villages is a willingness on the part of the farmers to give up their source of independence—their land—and progressive, far-sighted leadership. Neither is in plentiful supply.

WHAT DREW ME TO DELEGATE ZHU WEIQUN was his straight talk. He suggested that we meet after the Congress when things would be less hectic. And we did—in his office just across the street from Zhong Nan Hai, the government complex facing Tian'anmen Square. Unlike most of the delegates, who represented a geographical area, Zhu was a part of the delegation representing departments directly under the Party Central Committee. Zhu's bureau was somewhat unique. His United Front Work Department—the term "United Front" refers to cooperative efforts between the Chinese Communist Party and the Nationalist Party (Kuomintang) during the war against Japan beginning in 1937—coordinates between the Communist Party and the eight non-communist "democratic" parties through which China pays lip service to political diversity. It also serves as the Party's link to religious groups, intellectuals, and other non-affiliated groups in China. An anachronism in most respects.

By the time we met, some weeks later, Zhu had been elected to the Party Committee on Discipline Inspection, the body that oversees the personal conduct of Party members and manages the Party's ongoing war against corruption. On the corruption issue, which had seen the expulsion of several top Party leaders including the former mayor of Beijing, Zhu felt that the system was partly to blame because there wasn't enough scrutiny. On other issues, he proved to be generally conservative.

Exploiting this rare opportunity to chat with a Party disciplinarian, I probed the cult of secrecy that surrounds China's top leaders, asking whether it was against Party rules to talk about one's career, family, and personal interests. In response, he proceeded to outline his own background: born in Jiangsu Province, grew up in Beijing, attended college in Beijing, majoring in Chinese language and literature. He worked as a teacher from 1970 to 1972, and then in the propaganda office of various government and Party departments until 1980, before working as a regular beat reporter for the *People's Daily* from 1980 to 1998. In 1998, he became deputy department head in the United Front Work Department. His hobby was reading. Forthcoming by Chinese standards.

As we prepared to end the interview, Zhu made a request. Given language and other potential misunderstandings, could I run my copy by him before publication? Later that day, after reviewing my notes, I gave his secretary a call to clarify his early work history, his attendance at the Central Committee Communist Party School, and the name of the North Carolina university where his daughter had studied economics.

One point remained out of whack. The transition from eighteen years at the *People's Daily* to senior Communist Party bureaucrat was too steep. There are positions at the *People's Daily*, the Party paper, that carry high rank, but Zhu's wasn't one of them. I asked a reporter friend with long tenure at the paper to look into this and her comeback was that Zhu hadn't worked at the paper that long, maybe only eight or nine years. Had my discussion on transparency with a member of the Party Committee on Discipline Inspection yielded a liar? Or was Zhu—assuming that I had no way to cross-check—just trying to fudge over a period of his life he couldn't talk about publicly?

I went back to Zhu's secretary for a third round. Another revision. He had, in fact, worked for the Party paper from 1979 to 1992. From 1992 to 1998 he had worked for a "Party Central Committee branch organization," without elaboration. I told the secretary that that was like George Bush saying that "he worked for the government."*

AS I WAS TRAVELING AROUND CHINA, seeing how the Party was functioning at the grassroots, I was trying to understand why, in a country with four times the population of the United States, almost every politician, no matter the issue, came out sounding like a recorded announcement.

For many years I had nurtured a yearning to attend the Central Committee Communist Party School,** the institution in Beijing where senior Party and government officials from all over China learn to be good communists. Insights to be gleaned aside, sitting in on a class full of communists in the twenty-first century just seemed very quaint. Not a simple wish. But now it seemed within grasp. I had faxed a letter with my request from New York to a friend who had a friend who taught Communist Party history at the Central Committee Party School

---

* At the Seventeenth Party Congress, in October 2007, Zhu Weiqun was selected to be a member of the Central Committee.

Much like a mid-term U.S. presidential race, in which the incumbent stands without challenge, the Seventeenth Party Congress was a tame affair. The top four Party officials retained their ranking and there were no ideological "breakthroughs" comparable to Jiang Zemin's "Three Represents." With five years ahead in which to leave his legacy, Hu Jintao's dominant theme was a non-specific: "Building a Harmonious Society through a Scientific Outlook."

** Official name: Party School of the Central Committee of the Communist Party of China (*Zhong Gong Zhong Yang Dang Xiao* in Chinese).

and whose parents had also taught there. Within an hour, I had a call from Beijing saying that he would be happy to have me attend his class and would introduce me to the head of the department. There wouldn't be any need to go through the customary energy-sapping, formal application procedure.

It proved to be a tortuous effort.

When I arrived in Beijing, I immediately linked up with the Party School contact and we headed right over to the home of his friend. Well on our way, my contact unveiled some unhappy news. The Party School teacher who was so welcoming from afar had had a change of heart. The entire staff of the Central Committee Communist Party School had been warned not to talk to reporters during the Party Congress. No amount of cajoling could get me inside. There was genuine fear on the part of the Party School teacher.

I decided to pursue a second Party School path. The Central Committee Party School sits at the head of a national network that radiates down to the provincial level and below. If not the Central Communist Party School, then the Beijing City Communist Party School certainly was an acceptable substitute. The approval of the Beijing City Foreign Affairs Office would first be required, but the sister-in-law of a friend's father's colleague would walk my request through the system. I cranked out my letter of application with supporting documents.

A week later came the approval of the Beijing Foreign Affairs Office. But that wasn't enough for the Beijing Party School. It said it needed more specific information. Postponing the approval until I would no longer be in China seemed to be their strategy. I rephrased and refaxed. Six days later came a second reply: my "status" precluded attending classes, *but* they would arrange *one* interview for me with the Party School vice president. *However*, that could not take place until the following week because the Party School president would not be in until then to give his approval. In any case, the vice president needed time to "prepare."

Seeking to expedite, we (the friend's father and I) headed proactively to the Beijing Communist Party School, an impressive enough, six-story, brick building in the old communist style, to finally locate a Mr. Qin. In sequence, Qin told me first that I could not attend classes; then, that there were no classes of the type I wanted; finally, that there were only night classes. ("Seek the Truth" is the Party School system motto.) The approval, which would only be available the following week, had in fact already been received. He showed me the approval. He could now arrange the interview.

But something far more interesting was beginning to reveal itself that says a lot about the state of communism in China. I had noticed that there was no restricted entry at the main gate, as could be found at any sensitive institution in China. Anyone could walk right in. Further, a second organization shared this campus: Beijing Administrative College, a junior college for tax collectors, middle level bureaucrats, and the like. Mr. Qin, in fact, allowed that the Party School didn't have any regular students. There were occasional short courses lasting two or three days, such as one that had been held the week before focusing on the Sixteenth Party Congress spirit, and there were a limited number of night courses that would contribute to a largely fictional junior college diploma. In fact, the Beijing City Communist Party School existed virtually in name only.

When I finally met Professor Luo Zhongmin at the Beijing Communist Party School ten days later, his business card confirmed that reality. He was introduced as the chairman of the Department of Party History at the Beijing Communist Party School; his business card read: Professor, Department of History Science, Beijing Administrative College. He confirmed that they were one. He had not taught any Party School courses during the past term. Once a vibrant institution, the Beijing Party School was now little more than a nameplate.

Just as enlightening was the spring list published in the

Beijing Daily of all the courses offered by the branch Party Schools under the Beijing City Communist Party School: business management, accounting, computer studies. All practical courses that would generate tuition income. No offerings in communism. Nevertheless, it remained crucial to maintain the Party School façade in order to give teeth to the illusion of a national Party School system.

THE CHINESE HAVE A SAYING: "At home rely on your parents; on the outside rely on your friends." That hadn't worked. But the urge to see the Central Committee Communist Party School from the inside remained strong. At the same time I was making arrangements to attend classes at the Central Committee Party School through contacts in the Communist Party History Department, I was also faxing the same request to the school vice president, Comrade Yu Yunyao. I wrote what I thought was a compelling letter, addressing him as Respected Comrade Yunyao. It hadn't worked. He had read the fax and ignored it, I learned from his secretary after arriving in Beijing.

As I got on public bus 801 headed for the Central Committee Party School, located near the Summer Palace, I couldn't help but contrast this uninvited visit with my visit to Tianjin the week before, when the executive vice mayor had sent a car to Beijing to pick me up and reserved a room for me at the Hyatt so that I would have a place to rest between activities.

I walked briskly past the soldiers to the reception center outside the main gate and, showing them a copy of the unanswered correspondence, gave them the name and telephone number of a Mr. Chen, a ranking official in the Foreign Affairs Office of the Party School. I implied that I had spoken to Chen just that morning. Fifteen minutes later, I was escorted into a lavishly carpeted reception room with doilied, stuffed chairs—the kind of which can be seen only in China.

Unlike many of the directors of foreign affairs who pass their days twiddling their thumbs, Mr. Chen Guoji, in his early fifties, with neatly plastered-back hair and a moderate Hunan accent, was clearly a man of stature and a first-rate propagandist. Chen was somewhat intrigued by my Chinese, which seemed to get better under the pressure of the challenge he presented. He ran through the basics as I peppered him with questions: at any one time sixteen hundred students, mostly in their thirties and forties, are in residence, supported by three to four hundred instructors and professors, giving mainly three-, six- and twelve-month courses to top- and middle-echelon government and Party officials. All of the courses center on "The Three Basics" (Chinese Communist theory) and "The Five Contemporaries" (contemporary world issues). The students test either *good* or *excellent*. There are no failures.

Because all of the students are decision makers, the school is able to attract world-class lecturers such as Michael Dell of Dell Computer; Chris Patten, the last British governor of Hong Kong; the president of General Electric; and the prime minister of Australia. It was Chen's job to arrange these lectures—supplemented by talks by leading Chinese academics, bureaucrats, and businessmen. A trip to the bookstore for Central Committee Party School Vice President Yu's text, *On the Vital Problems of the Contemporary World,* explained how far the Party had evolved. IT, WTO, DNA. Marxism-Leninism wasn't nearly enough any more. Advanced knowledge with a Chinese twist.

Chen arranged for a tour of the campus: two hundred manicured acres with a lake, numerous quadrangles, a modern instruction hall, dormitories—a self-contained city, the antithesis of much of China. It would take a staunch individualist and a master stoic not to conclude, from the surroundings alone, that a very important mission was taking place here and that he was indeed fortunate to have been selected to attend this course. That was an integral part of the brainwashing.

Virtually every top-level politician I interviewed had passed through the Central Committee Communist Party School.

That was one of the reasons they all sounded like parrots. Attendance was a prerequisite for political power.

A HEAVY FOG SHROUDED BEIJING the day I left for Yinchuan to spend a few days in the capital of the Ningxia Autonomous Region with Ma Fu, the delegate who had gone out of his way to invite me home.* Ma Fu forgot to give my rearranged flight schedule to his assistant, leaving me stranded for three hours at Yinchuan Airport without a city destination. No hard feelings. When I finally reached him on his cell phone, he told me that he was about to give a talk and couldn't meet me personally at the airport.

"A talk about what?" I asked.

"The Sixteenth Party Congress spirit," he said.

The assistant's instructions were to take me to a guest house to rest, but I was intent on hearing Ma Fu's speech, a rare opportunity for an outsider. That it was being given at the Yinchuan City Communist Party School made it all the more alluring.

I arrived at the Party School just in time to hear Ma deliver his fourth of five points to about one hundred Communist Youth League workers. As the form required, Ma's talk would parrot and localize Jiang Zemin's Party Congress Report. Ma Fu was an animated but low-key orator with the habit of twirling his arms as he lectured. He spoke with passion and without notes. He had delivered the same speech all over the region about a dozen times since returning from Beijing two weeks earlier. In every nook and cranny in China, as muted cell phones testified, Party Congress delegates were going through the same exercise.

Ma was hitting on one of the key points of the Party Congress: "completely" achieving a "well-off society" within twenty years. The Party had already declared that a "well-off society"—a Party goal for five years—had been achieved. That was characteristic

_____

* See page 72 for a map of Ningxia.

of the Chinese propaganda machine—achievement by declaration. But, the Party admitted, it was a low-level "well-off society," achieved unevenly. Ningxia was one of the laggards.

"They define a 'well-off society' as having a GDP of $800 per person," Ma began. GDP, recited in English, had become an everyday part of the Chinese lexicon and was one of Ma's favorite subjects. "In Shanghai," he continued, "the GDP is more than $3,000. Ours is $680. We have a lot of work to do…" (Part of the problem, Ma Fu had explained in Beijing, was that, unlike coastal China, the western provinces had no Overseas Chinese constituency, no landsmen to invest in their "hometown." Another was that doing business in the West, hundreds or thousands of miles from seaports, was simply inconvenient.)

Ma's fifth point was a call to continue Party-building—strengthening the appeal and control of the Party—by implementing the "Three Represents."

"Progress brought many problems to China," Ma had said rather eloquently in Beijing, and the "Three Represents" provided the guidance to resolve them. Under the banner of "progressive production forces," the concept of labor was changing: "sweat equity" was moving over to accommodate mental labor. In the past, peasants worked the land and nothing more. Now there were eighty million farmers working in Chinese cities. Urbanization was the Chinese trend. Cultivating talent and encouraging creativity under the banner of "progressive culture" were two more applications of the "Three Represents." All of this was to serve "the basic needs of the overwhelming majority of the people." Ma flipped through Jiang Zemin's speech with the dexterity of a preacher surfing Scripture.

"Three Represents Important Thought," "Three Represents Important Thought," "Three Represents Important Thought…."

"We live in very turbulent times," was his parting remark to the Youth League audience, citing the World Trade Center and attacks on Israelis in Kenya. He gave two deep bows—a touch of genuine humility—in acknowledgement of his applause.

OVER DINNER, MA BEGAN TO OPEN UP. He liked to spend at least two hours each night on the Internet—his connection to the world. That was the reason that he was often unreachable in the evening. Except when playing bridge, that was the only time he shut off his cell phone. It turned out that Ma Fu had spent ten years as an instructor at the Ningxia Communist Party School. He could fill in a lot of gaps. Part of his work as the top man at the Ningxia Communist Youth League was to recruit new Party members. Ningxia (technically an "autonomous region" in deference to its one-third Hui Muslim population, but practically equivalent to a province) was exceptionally small with just 5.7 million people. But each region, no matter how backward or far removed, was expected to maintain its quota. "Party building" was crucial to the Party's future, which made Ma one of the PR point men for the Communist Party in Ningxia. That spelled pressure. Public relations aside, Party recruitment also included a certain amount of social service work, such as bringing agricultural experts to the villages—to improve yields and to show that "the Party is looking after you."

In Beijing, Ma Fu had mentioned vaguely that he had a bone to pick over American treatment of Muslims. Now, he gave the details. It seems that every year six or seven Communist Youth League leaders from across China were chosen to visit the United States as part of an exchange program. It is an exceptionally competitive program, and Ma Fu had been selected to join the group. His wife had already spent a year in the U.S. and he himself had traveled widely in Europe. He was especially keen on visiting the U.S. But his visa application had been rejected by the U.S. Embassy on the grounds that he was "too old." Ma was certain that, in the context of the World Trade Center attack, it was his Muslim background, which appeared clearly on his ID card, that was the culprit.

But that story paled in the face of the big news. It turned out that I had had the extraordinary good fortune of arriving in Yinchuan the very day Ma Fu had been informed that he would be the next mayor of Ningxia's most populous city, Guyuan. As soon as next week, Ma would be leaving for his new assignment. That was why he had forgotten me at the airport.

MA FU SAW ME BACK to my room. At about nine, he said, he, his wife, and his daughter would be coming over and we would go for some karaoke. Within the hour, that was cancelled. Something had come up, but we would meet the following afternoon. I took a walk in the dark and bought some local apples.

I could feel the days Ma Fu had allotted to chat leisurely and show a new friend around Ningxia evaporate before my eyes, replaced with a picture window view of the evolution of a rising political star.

The schedule continued to change like the winds on a spring day. Ma Fu would clear away a few morning matters, and we would spend some time together. At his suggestion, I spent the first part of the morning at the local museum studying Ningxia's past. By the time I finished with the museum, the late morning meeting was pushed back to the afternoon.

Ma Fu surprised me for lunch, joined by his wife, an economist and powerhouse in her own right, just appointed the director of the Ningxia Academy of Social Sciences. Talk centered around his new job. Guyuan was poor and backward, but Ma felt an affinity for the place because it was his "hometown." Not that he had ever lived there, but his ancestors had. His work with the Communist Youth League had taken him all over Ningxia. He felt he knew the place.

His new job as mayor of Guyuan represented not only a change of location, but a change of direction. At the Communist Youth League, his primary focus was public relations, politics—strengthening the Party. As mayor, his responsibility was economic—bringing the two million people of Guyuan closer to a "well-off" life. His education wasn't the best (college in neighboring Gansu Province at an institute for minority studies and graduate studies at the Party School in Xi'an), but it centered on economics. Ma Fu was a self-made man. He was primed for this challenge, he said.

For Ma Fu, who didn't read Arabic and wasn't well steeped in his religion, being a Hui Muslim was both an advantage and a limitation. He would have ample opportunity to rise high up in the Ningxia government and Party structure, but would likely find it difficult to rotate into senior positions in other provinces. China's minority policy was a complex mix of affirmative action and discrimination. Minorities were proportionally represented in the provincial government and Party apparatus, but vigorous advocacy was short-circuited. The four mayors of Ningxia's cities were all Hui Muslim, but the top man in each, the Party secretary, came from outside. In any event, the higher a minority official rose, the more he sounded like a majority Han Chinese.

Our 3 o'clock activities were pushed to 4:00, then 5:00. Ma Fu's assistant took me for a walk around Yinchuan, a city of about four hundred thousand. Yinchuan is—literally and figuratively—an oasis in the desert. The approaches to the city recall China's more progressive cities ten and fifteen years ago—building roads, altering landscapes, but with backward equipment and a lot of handwork. Yinchuan City itself, especially at night when the lights went on, was an okay, agreeable place—well-stocked department stores, a pedestrian mall, a KFC. Outside Yinchuan, it was another story.

When we returned to the guesthouse near 7:00, after unspectacular bowls of noodles with side dishes of pickled turnip, Ma hinted to his assistant via cell phone that maybe we could postpone that day's appointment. Getting the drift, I shook my head in his face. Tomorrow would be even worse. The assistant told Ma Fu that I *had to* have two hours with him. I used the waiting time to quiz Ma's assistant on basic information so that I could use my shrinking time with Ma Fu fully.

Ma was being pulled in every direction from early morning to late at night: he needed to review the candidates for the job he was leaving, to appoint a new staff, to ground himself in the situation in Guyuan City. He needed to show his gratitude and listen to the wisdom of the provincial leaders who had nominated him; and he had to ingratiate himself with the local leaders in the city he was now about to govern. (If they weren't happy, his nomination could be rejected by the local People's Congress in Guyuan, a measure of democracy.) One thing he did not have to concern himself with was relocation. His wife and daughter would remain where they were and he would return home—five hours by rutty road in each direction—on the weekend.

Finally, at 9 o'clock that night, there was a knock at my door. Ma Fu stood there with a blank stare on his face, the look of a lush who had just emerged from a stupor, minus the alcohol. He was exhausted. After we finished talking, he still had two appointments to keep.

I sat Ma Fu in a chair, set my own rump on the edge of the bed, and turned into an inquisitor. This would be our last meeting. I wanted to understand to the core how a political career in China evolved and pressed him for every detail.

Right after graduating from college in 1982 at twenty-three, he was assigned to the Ningxia Communist Party School where he spent most of the next two years working in the library. "I was too young" is the way he described his first job.

After two years in graduate school in Xi'an, he returned to the Ningxia Party School, where he taught for six years until 1992. I wanted to compare what I knew about the Beijing Party School with what Ma had experienced. I zeroed in.

"What were the classes like? Were they at night or during the day? How many hours did you teach each week? Give me an idea what a typical week was like at the Party School."

"Daytime. Eight to twelve hours. Ten to twenty students." Only phrases, no sentences.

"Eight to twelve hours isn't much work for an entire week. Were you busy? Did you do anything else at the same time?"

"Nothing else. There was 'a lot of time' to study."

"What did you teach?"

"Economics."

"What kind of economics? Communist economics?"

"We call it *political* economics."

"What happened after you left the Party School in 1992?"

"You don't have to go into such detail."

"People want details. I'm trying to draw a picture. What happened?"

"I worked for a company."

"What kind of company?"

"An international company."

"Was it a foreign company?"

"A government company."

"What kind of work did you do? Was it Party work? Did you work in the Party cell inside the company?

"It was economic work."

At this stage in his career, Ma had not yet faced the need or developed the skill to boilerplate himself. I was probably teaching him as much as he was teaching me. We digressed a bit to talk about his day and the transition ahead. I commiserated with the pressure he was under, then headed back on course.

Two years earlier, in 2000-2001, Ma Fu had spent a full year studying at the Central Committee Communist Party School in Beijing. I plumbed him for the details. Business, economics, I learned, not politics, was the thrust of the course, which turned out to be more flexible than I had been told in Beijing. Self-study and communist style "discussion"—a Talmudic, Socratic mix—were the main tools.

It occurred to me that a major function of the Central Committee Party School for the students was network building. Ma said that about six of his classmates had been delegates at the Party Congress, but downplayed the idea of networking as a function of attending the course.

"The major purpose of the Party School is to train cadre [Party and government officials]," he said.

"And to make everyone think the same way?" I pushed.

"To *train cadre*," he reiterated, slumping back in his chair.

I was homing in on a Party contradiction that intrigued me: the contradiction between the Party's call to "unify thought" and its call to "liberate thought" so as to encourage creative solutions to new problems and "keep up with the times"—one of the Party's newest slogans. (The Central Committee Communist Party School Press had even published a book entitled *Unifying Thought While Liberating Thought*.) But it was already 10 o'clock and Ma Fu just sat there pumped out.

"These are things you don't have to think about," was all he could muster.

My final request from Ma Fu was to let me see the Party School in Yinchuan where he had taught. I asked him to write a note so they would let me in; or at least to take me there for a visual impression. He balked. Out of my own frustration and fatigue, I began to lecture him mercilessly.

"Your responsibility is to bring economic progress to your people. You have to think the way the larger world thinks. If you tell them that they can't look at a building, or what they can and can't think about, they will think that you have lost it. It might be that in five or ten years this entire communist system will collapse. Then, you will have to rely on your economics. It will be to your benefit to get used to the ways of the world."

Ma Fu just fiddled with his ears.

"There will be other times to talk," he said, after a picture and a parting handshake. For the entire hour, he had not raised his voice once.

"In another week," I said, "your cell phone number will be replaced by a secretary."

"But my e-mail address won't change."

Just to be sure, when I sent New Year's e-mail greetings to Ma Fu, I sent a copy to his wife.

The next day I received return wishes for a fruitful year.

It was signed: "Ma Fu's Wife."

Snubbed Again
by Ningxia Royalty

□ □ □

I T WAS NOW A YEAR since I had traveled to Ningxia at Ma Fu's invitation following the Sixteenth Party Congress. In the interim, I had made a conscious effort to keep in touch with him, apologizing for the intensity of my interview, sending him pictures from the visit, wishing him well during the SARS scare as he took on his new challenge as mayor of Guyuan City. Acknowledgement always came from his wife, Wu Haiying, director of the Ningxia Academy of Social Sciences and by now herself a local celebrity.

In one of her responses, Wu Haiying mentioned explicitly that I was welcome to visit Ningxia again. I took her up on that and, months before my trip, wrote to her about my plans, giving a six-week window for the visit, so that there could be no chance of a schedule conflict. She said she would pass along my letter to Ma Fu. Thereafter, her responses became non-committal. Ma Fu had reason to be wary. I had been rough on him.

I wasn't overly hopeful when I rang him up soon after arriving in Beijing.

Sunday was a good time to call Ma Fu at home in Yinchuan, I knew, because on the weekends he would return home from his post in Guyuan. He got right on the phone and asked me to

71

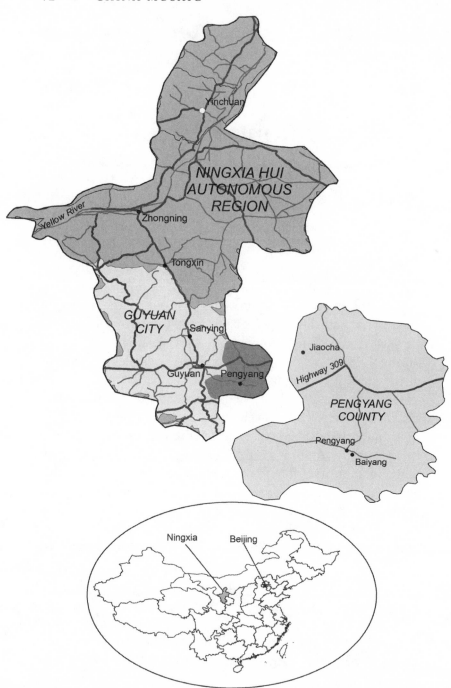

e-mail what I wanted out of my visit. He would open the e-mail in the afternoon and call me back in Beijing in the evening.

These political letters are always tricky. When a Chinese official wants to help you, they aren't necessary; when he leans toward giving you the brushoff, no letter can satisfy him. Tianjin vice mayor Xia Baolong hadn't needed any letter to arrange a two-day program around his city for me after the Party Congress.

With Ma Fu, I decided to take a personal tack wrapped around a little psychology. I reminded him how incomplete my visit had been the year before, that the day I had arrived, at his invitation, had been the day he was selected to be the new mayor of Guyuan, and how our plans had been waylaid. I recalled how excited he was that day because Guyuan was his ancestral home, and how meaningful it would be for me to hear from him how it felt to be returning home as mayor. Guyuan City, I tried to preempt, was a poor, underdeveloped place. I knew that. What interested me was not the end result, but the process of revitalizing Guyuan. The Chinese language word processor I had recently installed had paid its way.

'IT'S THE WRONG TONE,' HE IMPLIED, when he phoned me that evening.

He was now in government. He needed a more formal, more specific letter spelling out just what I proposed to see before he could issue me an invitation. That didn't make much sense; he was the mayor. He didn't need specifics. But I had to go along with him. He would return to Guyuan the next day. He gave me his personal e-mail address and home phone number in Guyuan. He wasn't building any wall around himself as most Chinese politicians did. He would open the revised letter the following evening when he got to Guyuan and give me a call.

I took his phone call and the access he was providing as a positive indication for the visit.

I headed my revision: "American Writer Jonathan Kolatch's

Trip to Ningxia: Goals and Wishes." I stripped it of anything personal, skipping over my previous meetings with Ma in Yinchuan and Beijing, not even mentioning his name once. In its place, I outlined my nineteen years of reporting experience in China for publications famous even in China. On this trip, I said, using Ningxia and Guyuan City as examples, I wanted to home in on one of the focal points of the Sixteenth Party Congress: growth and development in China's perennially backward West. I took care to include all of the right catch phrases, laboring sentence by sentence to the last line: "Most important is an opportunity to understand what kind of a place Guyuan is and what kind of dreams its people harbor for their future."

Ma Fu didn't buy it.

"*Bu hao* [no good], I can't give you an invitation," he said.

"I don't need an invitation," I countered. "Just give me the name of a hotel in Guyuan. All I want is an opportunity to talk to you and a little direction."

"If I give you the name of a hotel, it's like inviting you."

I went fishing, pointing out to him how officials at much higher levels had no trouble encouraging me to visit. "It's a small place here," was his rejoinder. I recalled for him how anxious he was to invite me last year. "Last year I was Youth League secretary, now I am a mayor," he said.

"It's the same system," I countered.

Ma could only sigh to no productive end.

"You are interested in Ma Fu the mayor."

"I am also interested in Ma Fu the individual. Can't you distinguish between public and private?"

"I have no private life."

"Is it because you're new?" I baited.

Ma Fu didn't answer.

He left one sliver of light. If I found my way to Guyuan, there was a chance I would get to see him. There were many hotels in Guyuan and many taxis and buses from Yinchuan, the capital, to Guyuan, five rickety hours to the south.

FOR A WEEK, I TRIED HARDER THAN EVER to plug into Ma Fu's thinking. From his perspective, to allow me to carry out my mission, I
needed to have been dispatched by an official entity: a newspaper,
a magazine, a think tank. Application had to be made in the name
of that organization, which then had to be accepted by an official
Chinese organization such as the Chinese Writers' Association.
"Independent" didn't cut it in official China. What allowed him to
talk with me a year earlier, Ma said, was that I had been accredited
to attend the Sixteenth Party Congress by the Foreign Ministry.

Ma was tripping all over himself. In inviting me to visit him
in Ningxia, he had gone out of his way to make the point that, to
avoid a lot of trouble, he was inviting me as "a private individual."
As mayor, he certainly had that capability.

Ma Fu was taking me back almost twenty years to my first visit
to China. I had an assignment from TV Guide to write an article
on Chinese television. The Chinese Consulate in New York had
set up an invitation from China Central Television, the national
network. Just before setting off for China, I had landed another
assignment from The New York Times Magazine to write a piece
on sports in China. When I arrived in China, I started to work
on both tracks only to find that, without CCTV's approval, the
Chinese Sports Commission would not open its doors to me. In
a jealousy common to those times, CCTV refused, and the Sports
Commission refused to help me. To break the bureaucratic logjam,
I would have had to, literally, reenter China with a different invitation.

The contradiction was that much of China had long since moved
away from such rigidity. Ma Fu had lured me to visit Ningxia a
year earlier with an expression of flexibility that he was now finding he did not have.

I WAS DETERMINED TO GO to Ningxia and find Ma Fu. But it
would be a lot easier if I would be able to earn his welcome in
advance. I appealed deferentially to his sense of honor:

Dear Old Ma

Chinese have a saying: "At home, rely on your parents; away from home rely on your friends."

I hope that it's still that way over there when I arrive
in Guyuan.

Little Ke*

Ma still wouldn't buy in.

THREE WEEKS HAD PASSED SINCE our last contact. I timed my
arrival in Ningxia to be on a Sunday when Ma Fu would likely
be at home for the weekend. My perfect scenario was to be
invited to ride south with him to Guyuan the next day. I was
now not in far-off Beijing, but a mere bus ride away. I thought
that might move Ma Fu.

As soon as I reached Yinchuan, I rang him up. He was at a
meeting, his wife said; he would open his cell phone at about
5:30. She gave me the number.

Ma Fu was no more yielding when I reached him in the
evening than he had been a few weeks earlier from Beijing. He
had no time; he would be traveling to Shandong for two days.
"I made myself perfectly clear," he said.

Wouldn't he at least provide me with a contact in Guyuan?
By reflex, he suggested the Foreign Affairs Office. With a phone
call or two, Ma Fu could have opened up the entire town to me
as had Executive Vice Mayor Xia Baolong in Tianjin. Guyuan
was small enough. He chose not to. His sole concession was to
give me the name of two hotels in Guyuan.

Apparently, Ma Fu had come to the conclusion that he had
revealed too much of himself to me and was now trying to
reestablish distance. The whole thrust of communism is the
"collective self." Allowing individuality to show through was
taboo. Maybe Ma Fu was just being a good communist. Maybe
he just didn't want me to see the real Guyuan.

* My family name in Chinese.

I decided to go to Guyuan and see what he might be hiding. Traveling there was no problem; there were many buses. But without a focus, all I could do was walk the streets and maybe visit a few of the outlying farm towns. Guyuan, in the southern part of Ningxia, I knew, was the poorest of the four cities that made up China's smallest province. I had been told many times how poor remote parts of China were, but had never actually seen such extreme poverty. Here was the opportunity.

The road down to Guyuan, 205 miles south of Yinchuan, showed the contrast between modernizing China and the dirt-poor China of the past. Ma Fu made this trip twice weekly and would have found it hard to ignore. All along the Yellow River north of Zhongning, and down past Tongxin, at homestead after homestead, there were well-tended apple plantings. Corn stalks, already dried, were bunched in sheaths, ready to be sold. In front of virtually every house was a carpet of yellow—corn ears in their final stages of drying, soon to be stripped of their kernels. At a few farms, the bagging process had already begun.

All of this meant reliable cash for the farmers. Irrigation water piped from the Yellow River was what made this bounty possible. A modern four-lane highway paralleled this corridor of yellow. The greenbelt effort—thousands of white poplar trees astride the toll road—was equally impressive. Ecology was on the national agenda and, to answer it, nurseries raising white poplar saplings had sprung up, a new source of peasant income.

The irrigation system had been extended into Guyuan's northernmost county and removed it from the poverty rolls. But it could not be extended much further south. The resources of the Yellow River, brackish to begin with, were limited. Most of Guyuan, six thousand feet above sea level, was hill country, making pumping impractical to impossible. When completed in a year or two, the new highway would inject life into Guyuan City and establish it as a vital crossroads between Gansu and Shaanxi Provinces. But the perpetual shortage of water that hamstrung rural Guyuan defied solution.

AS THE BUS ROLLED INTO downtown Guyuan, with just a little imagination, you could see its past and future. Just a few miles to the north, in the rural hub town of Sanying we had just passed through, it was market day, one of two designated days per week when peasants from the outlying villages came to town to buy and sell every conceivable commodity—from chickens to bed frames to candied crab apples to bicycle seats. A mile-long corridor of vendors lined either side of the dusty, pockmarked road as customers, clutching the day's purchases, came and went—by foot, by donkey cart, by motorbike, by tractor. At the entrance to Guyuan City, gleaming shells of new apartment buildings provided the ultimate contrast. Ten years earlier, the market scene at Sanying would have sprawled out exactly where Guyuan's future was now growing.

Chinese are extra sensitive about showing China's warts. Even poor areas had pockets of relative prosperity. My priority was to ensure that the poverty that I would be seeing was the extreme. Ma Fu had thrown down a challenge. No maneuver was out of bounds.

As soon as I got to Guyuan, I inquired about the best hospital in town. Though greater Guyuan, Ma Fu's bailiwick, had a population of 1,800,000 and covered an area of 6,000 square miles, Downtown Guyuan, an agreeable, far from decrepit place at first view, had just 100,000 residents. It could be walked through. I had no trouble finding the Second People's Hospital, where I asked for the office of the hospital president. The guard pointed to an adjacent building. The fourth floor, he said. I was shown to the president's office, an exceptionally large open space with two desks. Sofas and easy chairs lined the wall. Half a dozen people milled around. A meeting had just broken up or was about to begin.

Once introduced, I motioned the hospital president to the side and spoke to him in hushed tones. I told him that my family had a small charitable fund and that we were interested in considering making grants, in the form of medical equipment worth about $30,000, to the poorest areas in Guyuan. I emphasized the word *poorest*.

Continuing quietly, while the others in the room strained to listen, I told Dr. Zhu that I had already visited backward areas in Sichuan and Hebei Provinces. I could promise nothing, but had heard that the outlying areas of Guyuan were very poor and wanted to visit them to see if we could be of help.

Within ten minutes, Dr. Zhang, from the Guyuan Department of Health and Hygiene, was at the hospital. At the outset, I stressed to him the importance of confidentiality.

He asked what type of equipment I had in mind, and I told him that it would be emergency room equipment to stabilize patients and might include portable generators and blood-testing equipment. He understood. Specifics lent credibility.

We took the elevator down together and, with a detour through the market to buy a sweet potato, Dr. Zhang walked me a few blocks in the direction of the Post Office Hotel. He would meet me in my room at 6:00.

By the time he arrived with two colleagues, including the head of his department, he had already contacted the health department in Pengyang County, about thirty-five miles away. I had inquired on the bus down from Yinchuan, and from a taxi driver in town, about the poorest places in Guyuan, and had circled four county towns on my map. Pengyang was truly dirt poor, just the type of place I was interested in seeing. The health department in Pengyang would send a car at 8:30 the following morning to take me to some of the poorest parts of this very poor county. Because of the remoteness of the villages, I might need to stay overnight. I prepared a small bag and paid for an additional night's lodging at the Post Office Hotel.

I made one request of the three as we walked to the adjacent building for dinner: that the matter be kept totally within the department. I certainly didn't want it to appear in the papers, I told them. Ma Fu was out of town, so there was no danger of being introduced to the mayor to soften me up. But I needed to be sure that no other government department knew the details, I said, until something definite was decided. Guyuan was a small enough place. If Ma Fu were to catch a whiff of this, it would be curtains for me.

OUR DESTINATION THE FOLLOWING MORNING was Jiaocha Township,* a cluster of seven villages, about fifty miles from Guyuan Town, along the northwest spine of the county. *Jiaocha* means "crossroads" or "junction," about as nondescript as you can get. The name was well chosen.

As we rode out of Guyuan, I tried to put my finger on the source of the abject poverty that I was about to witness. Was it a simple lack of water revealed by the parched layers of eroded yellow loess soil that punctuated the landscape everywhere? Or was it the roads themselves? Even before we crossed the municipal boundary of Guyuan City, National Highway 309 rode like it had just been plowed. Mr. He, a ten-year veteran behind the wheel, drove the four-wheel-drive Jeep like he was barebacking a bull in Cheyenne during Rodeo Days. Then, we turned off the main road, and things got even worse. We were swerving around mountain trails in fog so heavy that we could not see the valleys that plummeted below. Mr. He was overly generous with the gas and very sparing with the brakes.

Jiaocha Town itself, when we reached it an hour and forty-five minutes later, was a string of low-slung, one-story, gray brick buildings astride an earth-packed road that offered basic

---

* The term "township" (*xiang* or *zhen* in Chinese) generally refers to an administrative center that controls a group of villages. The township offers basic government services such as schools, health, and police, as well as basic commercial services. The larger the township, the more sophisticated the services and the greater the number of people living in the township town. In some cases, the township town might contain factories employing sizeable numbers of people. In the remotest areas, however, the number of people actually living in the township town is minimal, and the town may be little more than a walled compound with Party and government offices.

services: a general store, vehicle repair, a restaurant, a truck for hire. The flavor was dust; the aroma: burning coal. Up the slope was the township compound that housed the government and Party offices. Over to the side was a junior high school.

The Jiaocha Clinic, the only medical facility available to the seven thousand in the surrounding villages, was right out of *National Geographic*: six or seven unheated, stone-floored rooms, with soiled plaster walls. The Ob-Gyn examining room contained a battered wooden chair, a writing table, and a bare examining table with rusty legs. Outside temperatures were in the low 30s; inside temperatures not much warmer.

All of the eight "doctors" working at the clinic had been assigned to Jiaocha Township from outside the area by the county health office. Most were in their twenties or thirties. Dr. Yang Zhihui, baby-faced, was the dentist. Like all but one of the other doctors, he was a junior high school graduate with three additional years of "junior specialist" training. He uncovered the white enameled pans that contained his implements: a few syringes, a pair of pliers, several forceps, vials of anesthesia. There were no drills and none of the probes and explorers normally found in a dental office.

I asked him if he could do root canals, he being the only dentist for at least thirty miles.

"*Banbuliao,* I can't do them."

"Fill cavities?"

"*Banbuliao.*"

The only dental services that Dr. Yang could offer were to prescribe pain killers or, when that failed, pull teeth. Cost of an extraction: 60 cents. That explained in an instant the toothless smiles that were the norm in rural China. A plastic false tooth could later be purchased in Pengyang, the county town, for $1.25. I repeated the amount to be sure that I hadn't misheard.

A couple came into the clinic carrying a toddler wearing a white ski cap with a pompom. He had a cold. Chinese are very particular about treating colds. The caseload for the eight doctors at the clinic was a mere five or six patients per day. Yet none of the doctors rushed to minister to the toddler.

I next spoke to Dr. Hai. Unlike the seven other doctors, he was older, in his late forties or early fifties, and had a "senior specialist" certificate, representing three years of training past senior high school. The years had jaded Dr. Hai and he showed none of the humility of Dentist Yang. He was responsible for clinical diagnosis, and took care of the only surgical procedure performed there: tubal ligation, what the Chinese call "family planning operations." These were all but compulsory after a third child was born to the villagers. Because the population in Jiaocha was entirely Hui Muslim, one of fifty-five official minorities, couples were permitted three children instead of the normal two permitted rural Chinese couples.* (Though they live in the most rural of settings, the doctors in Jiaocha are considered "urbanites" and are subject to urban child limitations.)

Dr. Hai performed about fifty tubal ligations each year. The charge was $12.50 per procedure, with Dr. Hai keeping ten percent. That added another $60 to his base salary of $110 per month—a respectable sum in the context of local incomes.

The only room in the Jiaocha Clinic that was fully stocked was the caged pharmacy, larger than any of the examination rooms and under lock and key. "Western medicine," the sign read, but there were Chinese herbal remedies as well. If norms held, the doctors at the clinic profited handsomely from selling medicines, a heavy inducement to overprescribe to a very vulnerable clientele.

The problem in rural Chinese medicine wasn't a lack of equipment as I had assumed. It started with a lack of trained personnel. Without training, any amount of equipment would be superfluous. As if a high school education weren't insufficient enough, only two of the eight staff "doctors" at the clinic had passed the qualifying national Ministry of Health exami-

---

* In urban areas, Han Chinese couples are permitted one child and minorities two.

nations. Even if they never passed the exams, these doctors would be allowed to continue working, though at lower rank and pay. For anyone living in Jiaocha who faced a life-or-death emergency that required immediate medical attention, virtually nothing could be done. That was the reality in much of rural China.

THE STORY OF GUYUAN'S POVERTY was up in the hills. The point-to-point distance between Jiaocha Town, where the clinic was located, and Jiaocha Village was probably little more than a mile. But it took us fifteen minutes, driving into and out of valleys on sometimes barely discernible, grassy mountain roads until we parked high on a treeless hill looking down into a clearing where Mrs. Jin Denglian was busying herself with late autumn tasks. We had doubled back more than once to find the best access because you could never see more than one valley ahead. A hefty, tan-coated sheep dog, chained to a like-colored doghouse, howled his disapproval as we climbed down the steep slope after parking our four-wheel-drive higher up on the mountain.

Back in the 1930s and '40s, in their pre-power, renegade days, Mao Zedong and the fledgling Communist Party holed up in the caves of Yen'an in nearby Shaanxi. Sixty years later, according to Driver He, who had been to almost every one of the 150 villages that make up Pengyang County (total population: 240,000), eighty percent of the rural population of 200,000 still lived in caves.

These weren't quite the jagged-mouthed caves with rough stone interiors that I had envisioned. Instead, they were carefully excavated, Quonset-shaped structures dug into the bone-dry, yellow loess hills, conjuring images of the Scottish Highlands. A wood-framed doorway with a window covered by a curtain provided a formal entrance to Mrs. Jin's cave, whose height was more than ample to stand in comfortably. The interior walls were sandpaper smooth, reflecting a building technique refined over many years. That the soil in this part of Ningxia contained a minimum of rocks simplified construction.

It was difficult not to compare Mrs. Jin's bare, drab walls with the fine sense of beauty of the Tibetan homes I had visited. Simple utility, not artistry, was the dominant theme here. The caves were cheap to build, requiring almost no materials, cool in summer, and warm in winter. An electric cord strung from a utility pole powered a single light bulb. The front section of the cave contained a *kang,* the brick-framed, earth-filled bed that is traditional in cold climates in China.

To the rear of the cave, partitioned by a curtain, was a storage area filled with potatoes. Wheat, potatoes, and corn, some of which would be sold, were the traditional crops in this part of China. Chickens, a cow, and sheep provided food and sometimes a paltry additional income.

MRS. JIN'S HUSBAND, MA ZHENGGAO, was said to be a medic of sorts. This was one of the reasons that brought us here. But exactly how he fit into the health system wasn't very clear. And since he was out on call, there was no way to find out. What I found when I initially opened his first-aid bag—a shoulder-strapped brief case with a Red Cross insignia and the Chinese characters for "Serve the people"—wasn't encouraging. Inside was an empty box with the wording "Hepatitis B" and three other small containers. Only later on, after I translated the wording on the containers, did I resolve something that had long perplexed me: The average lifespan in China is remarkably long for an underdeveloped country—in excess of seventy years. With the current level of health care in rural China, how was that possible?

The answer lies in the preventive care China gives its children. Although the ongoing health care provided adults in rural China is meager, the immunization of young children is remarkably efficient. The vast majority of Chinese children, urban and rural, receive a complete complement of vaccines. In the countryside, this is achieved, not through the local clinic, but by dispatching a practical nurse, trained in administering vaccines to children, directly to each village on a regular basis.

In addition to the hepatitis B vaccine, Ma Zhenggao's bag contained TB vaccine; a comprehensive vaccine against whooping cough, diphtheria, and tetanus; and a measles vaccine. Mrs. Jin's husband was the area circuit vaccination specialist.

NEITHER MRS. JIN, ILLITERATE, nor her seventeen-year-old daughter, could provide any details about the family's yearly income. They simply didn't know. But in the adjacent homestead, I found another Mr. Ma, a man in his sixties, who was busy threshing wheat with a wooden roller pulled by two donkeys who seemed to be eating as much as they were threshing. This Mr. Ma told us that his household of five had a total yearly income of $287: $57 per person. That was all the cash they had to buy supplementary food, clothing, implements, and anything else they required. Buying a simple light bulb was a serious purchase. This was far, far distant from the $680 average in Ningxia as a whole, and even further from the $800 that the Communist Party used to define a "well-off" lifestyle.

In most rural Chinese villages, the houses are situated in clusters, surrounded by fields, creating a pastoral sense of community. But as in the high Tibetan plains of Western Sichuan, the houses in rural Jiaocha Township are scattered. It took us another ten to fifteen minutes to reach the homestead of the village head, yet a third Mr. Ma (a common name among Muslims), who gave us the village vitals: 190 families, 800 people. That was lower by about ten percent than the figures I had gleaned from the township government offices. A slow but steady population outflow was in progress, encouraged by the hardscrabble life in Jiaocha, and Mayor Ma's figures were more up-to-date.

Village head Ma's own situation showed what a difference a little cash could make. Though he took special pride in showing off his animals, and in particular his cute-as-a-button little white lambs, his farm income wasn't much better than the others in the village, a bit over $60 per person per year. But his job as village head brought him an additional salary of $35 per month. And that allowed him to live in a four-walled house in place of a cave. Thirty percent of the village men, he said, were working outside of the village for extra cash. They could add as much as $500 to $600 per year to their incomes. Their extended absences did little for family life, but were much the norm in rural China.

ALTHOUGH THE RAINFALL WATER SITUATION was pretty much uniform throughout Guyuan's five rural counties, about twenty inches per year, the fertility and topography were not. At Guankou Village, where the fields were longer and flatter, with more uniform sunlight, Hai Xiuke and his wife, both in their early thirties, managed a better yield and an income of $250 per year to support themselves and their one child. The gleaming yellow corn drying in the courtyard would soon be ready to be marketed.

For domestic water, Hai, like the other villagers in Jiaocha Township, deployed a concave configuration of cement tiles that pitched toward a cement cistern buried in the ground. It could hold several hundred gallons of rainwater, enough, in most years, for family needs and to water the animals. Like all the local farmers, Hai relied on the heavens to irrigate his fields.

To compensate for the grudging soil they had to work, farmers in Pengyang County were allotted ten *mu*, almost two acres per family member, compared to the one or two *mu* per person common in most of rural China. Because Hai's family numbered only three, they had appreciably less land than larger families in the village. But they also had more modest needs.

In any event, five acres pressed the limit of the amount of land that Hai and his wife could work physically.

Like most of the peasants in the area, Hai took the winter off. He said he was bored. After the corn was sold, his only activities until spring would be watching television and playing with his baby. Hai seemed more in step with the modern world than other villagers. He had recognized a long time ago, he said, that the health facilities in Jiaocha Township weren't worth the energy to make the trip. When absolutely necessary, he bundled his toddler in the cart attached to his two-wheel tractor and chugged twenty-five miles to the adjacent township where he perceived the treatment as a tad better.

What spelled luxury for this couple was that they had a second cave: the first for sleeping and lounging; the second, right next door, for cooking and storage. Without proper ventilation to relieve cooking odors, a separate cave for cooking was a significant improvement.

THE EXTENT TO WHICH PHYSICAL LOCATION could have a drastic impact on farm income was provided by a brief stop at Baiyang, a village just outside of Pengyang Town. Because Farmer Han Zhiren had access to town water, he could irrigate his corn and wheat crops. By dint of fate, his soil was also superior. As a payback for these advantages, his five-member family was alloted just over one acre to work. But, with far less labor, he achieved yields comparable to what Hai could manage on his five acres, providing spare time for other labor that, together with the farm income, gave the family $750 per year.

AS I WALKED AROUND DOWNTOWN GUYUAN after returning from the villages, I itched to be able to gauge just what kind of a job Mayor Ma Fu was doing. Urban Guyuan, I said to myself, was a decent place, even if it lagged ten years or more behind China's more dynamic cities. Under better circumstances, I could have walked the few blocks to his office and talked to him about his challenges. The few people I questioned seemed to say that he was more progressive than the previous administration, more aware of the need for change.

The dismal scene I had observed in the countryside was certainly not Ma Fu's creation. But it was easy to see how he might have felt that opening up his modest city to me offered him only negatives. Or maybe in the short space of a year he had so thoroughly steeped himself in the Chinese political cult of personal anonymity that he didn't want to take any chances with his budding career.

Dr. Zhang at the Guyuan Department of Health was eager to have my impressions. Personal mission accomplished, I couldn't ignore the person who had made it possible.

What I said could not have made him happy. It wasn't a new building or new equipment that would make a difference at the township clinics in Guyuan, I said. It was the quality of the staff members who used them. That was a very complicated problem that dollars alone would not solve. I promised to be in touch.

Maybe Ma Fu had reached the same conclusion.

A week after I left Guyuan, Mayor Ma Fu announced a plan to provide nine years of free education to every child in Guyuan, urban and rural, by 2007. The program would cost $66 million. The immediate obstacle was that Guyuan was currently short 4,173 junior high school teachers. At present, just eighteen percent of the elementary and junior high school teachers in Guyuan met the educational requirements for their jobs. The shortage ran across the board: language arts, math, foreign language, music, physical education, technical education. Taking English teachers as an example, Ma Fu said, in urban Guyuan City, there were no more than six teachers who had graduated with a major in English.

It was not only in the health field that Guyuan was short of human resources.

Cherchez la femme.

Ma Fu's wife, Wu Haiying, director of the Ningxia Academy of Social Sciences and a delegate to the National People's Congress, is a powerhouse herself. An economist, she spent a period at the University of Chicago as an exchange fellow. She had joined us for lunch in Yinchuan the year before.

Ever cordial if always elusive, after several phone conversations, she finally invited me to visit the Academy of Social Sciences after I returned to Yinchuan from Guyuan. What I was really after was more detailed information about how their family life had changed since Ma Fu had been appointed mayor.

When I reached the academy, a modest building in the western part of Yinchuan, the guard said that Wu had not come to work that morning. I had him ring her cell phone, but there was no answer. No one knew where she was. The Ningxia Academy of Social Sciences, whose ninety staffers do research in six areas, including economics, local history, and ethnology, offers no classes and awards no degrees. Its informal work style suited Wu Haiying's multifaceted lifestyle perfectly.

Snubbed again by Ningxia royalty.

IN OUR PHONE CONVERSATIONS, WU Haiying had mentioned a vice president at the academy by the name of Lei. I had the guard ring him up. I had prepared my interview questions for him in advance to accommodate this contingency.

Professor Lei Xingkuei gave a very informative hour lecture on the root of poverty in Guyuan that tied loose threads together nicely. The source of the problem, he said, was not the lack of rainfall, but the dearth of groundwater. Guyuan, with about twenty inches annually, had the most abundant rainfall in Ningxia. But its groundwater shortage was the most acute in Ningxia. In some places in Guyuan, it was necessary to dig down six to eight hundred feet to reach water. It was the absence of groundwater that had sponged the moisture out of the soil, making possible construction of the earthen caves where the bulk of the population still lived. This groundwater situation prevailed not only in Guyuan but in adjoining Gansu and Shaanxi provinces—where people also still lived in caves.

There was no solution to the groundwater problem, Professor Lei summarized. Water available from the Yellow River was limited and in any case was not of the highest quality. "Why do they call it the *Yellow* River?" he asked rhetorically. "Because its water is yellow." In any event, pumping river water one thousand feet higher than its source was impractical if not impossible. The only solution was to relocate a portion of the population from the most severely affected areas to decrease the population pressure on the available supply of water.

Lei said that some 140,000 people from Guyuan had already been relocated successfully. He circled for me on the map the area where they now lived. Relocating populations in China, most recently to accommodate people displaced by the great new dam under construction on the Yangtze River, has a very low constituent satisfaction rate in China. For Ma Fu to propose to move large numbers of people from their homes with the aim of achieving economic prosperity would be a prescription for political suicide. Proposing free education was certainly more prudent.

As a self-made man, whose formal higher education had been more political than academic, Ma Fu appreciated more so than most the necessity of solid schooling. In trying to assure that his own shortcoming became his constituents' blessing, he was heading in the right direction.

Riding the Party Trail
to the High Tibetan Plains

□□□

MY ATTACHMENTS TO TIBET were sketchy. In high school we read James Hilton's *Lost Horizon*, set in Shangri-La; that was a long time ago. In more recent years, there were images of the heavy Chinese hand that had subjugated a restive Tibetan population. Over the last fifteen years, always under imported Chinese leadership, efforts had been made to mend fences with the local Tibetan population. Still, in 1995, the Communist government had insisted on installing its hand-picked *ban chan*, the Panchen Lama, ranking second in reverence to the Dalai Lama in Tibetan Buddhism. Before coming to Beijing in 1992, Hu Jintao, the Chinese President, seemingly more progressive, had spent four years in Tibet as the Party secretary, the leading political position there. He knew the area well. That was somewhat encouraging for the future.

DURING A CHANCE VISIT to the Sichuan delegation at the Sixteenth Chinese Communist Party Congress a year earlier, I had buttonholed delegate Yang Suping and taken down her cell phone number and portfolio: Party secretary from Kangding County in the Ganzi Tibetan Autonomous Prefecture. As

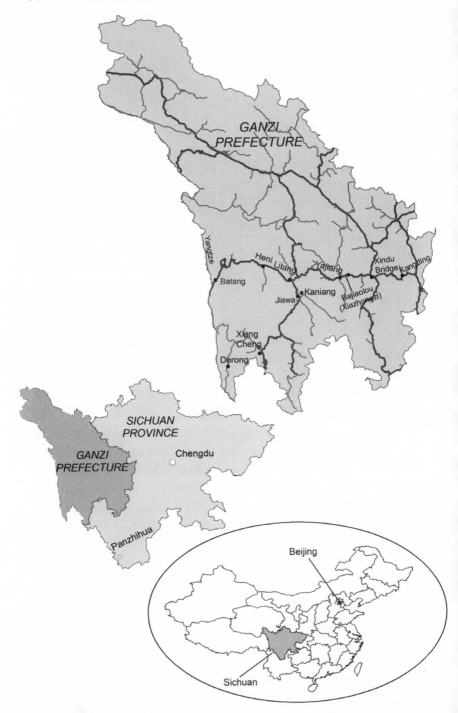

did many of the delegates from minority areas, Yang Suping, who uses her Chinese name in daily life instead of her Tibetan name, wore moderately traditional Tibetan dress. We met later during the Congress on a blustery November Beijing day outside of her heavily policed hotel, where the Sichuan delegation was housed. (Arranging an indoor meeting, while possible, involved too many bureaucratic footsteps.)

Her speech before the Sichuan delegation was delivered in a strong, authoritative tone, reinforcing yet again the brilliance of the Party line as interpreted by Jiang Zemin's "Three Represents." At our private meeting, shivering in the cold, she was much softer, less doctrinaire. The dichotomy was appealing. Forty-four, slender, average height, with wire-rimmed glasses, she cut a pert figure. The discussion was very basic: place of birth, education, general thoughts on the Party Congress. Yang took a moment before we parted to note that outside criticism of China's Tibet policy was unfounded. We didn't go any further. Back in New York, I sent her some Congress pictures that I had taken of her to maintain the contact.

TIBET ITSELF, THREE TIMES THE SIZE of California, was impenetrable to an outsider. With poor roads and a single railway line, a visit of any depth would take months. In heavily Chinese Lhasa, standard Mandarin could get you by. But outside of Lhasa, in traditional Tibet, it would be almost useless.

Yang Suping's Ganzi Prefecture, the western backbone of Sichuan, and occupying about twenty percent of its territory, was much more accessible. Almost seventy-five percent Tibetan (close to one hundred percent in the villages), it was an authentic continuation of Tibet as implied by the Chinese term for Tibet, *Xi Zang* (Western Tibet). Travel far enough west in Ganzi Prefecture and you are in Tibet. More Tibetans live in Sichuan (2.5 million of a total Tibetan population of 4.8 million in China) than in all of Tibet (2 million).

Yang Suping's initial response about a visit, when I reached her ten months later from New York, was positive. But the fax I sent a few weeks after that, outlining what I wanted to see, didn't go through; and a phone call revealed that she had been transferred to Chengdu, the provincial capital. We agreed that we would meet in Chengdu, which in any event had to be passed through on the way to the Tibetan areas, and she would circle places on the map that were worth a visit. I expected that she would provide some contacts as well and, riding her own status as the senior Party official in Kanding, gates would fly open.

As it turned out when I rang her up from Beijing, she had returned to Kangding from Chengdu for a few days for a Communist Party meeting. If I arrived before she returned to Chengdu, she could give me on-the-ground help.

Immediately, complexities surfaced. The road from Chengdu to Kangding, she alerted me, was being rebuilt. Buses traveling in the Kangding direction only plied the eight-hour route on even days.

The Chinese designation for Monday, Tuesday, Wednesday...is Weekday 1, Weekday 2, Weekday 3...The day I planned to travel from Chengdu to Kangding was Weekday 3, the 24th of November. Was Weekday 3, the 24th, an even day (24) or an odd day (Weekday 3)? Another call to Yang Suping. She was washing clothes. The *calendar date* was decisive, I learned.

Many long-haul bus routes in China leave only in the early morning to avoid reaching their destination in the dead of night. If I arrived in Chengdu from Beijing just before noon, would there still be an afternoon bus to Kangding? If not, I could only arrive in Kangding two days later, the next even day. By then Yang Suping might be returning to Chengdu. She was losing patience. She didn't take public buses; she didn't know about such details. To be sure, she said, better fly to Chengdu immediately.

To establish just who I was, and thus make my work easier,

Yang Suping said emphatically, I needed a letter of introduction from the media company I was representing. She had never mentioned this before. How was I going to get a letter of introduction when my flight to Chengdu left in two hours?

I opened my computer, fashioned a letterhead from a book publisher I work with, wrote the letter of introduction, and faxed it to myself through the hotel business center.

"YOU MIGHT NOT KNOW MUCH ABOUT KANGDING," Yang Suping sometimes remarked during her speeches and interviews away from home, "but you probably know the 'Kangding Love Song.'" An oldies but goodies Chinese staple.

> At the top of a cloud-shrouded mountain,
> Where the horses paced and pranced.
> Sat a town by the name of Kangding.
> A-A-A-h, A-a-a-h.

> In Kangding town, there was an eldest sister from the house of Li.
> Who had a very fine disposition.
> And there was an eldest brother from the house of Zhang.
> Who noticed her and her disposition.
> Who noticed her and her disposition.
> A-A-A-h, A-a-a-h.

> The first time he saw her, he noticed her disposition.
> The second time he saw her, he noticed her family's possessions.
> He noticed her family's possessions.
> A-A-A-h, A-a-a-h.

> Women of the world, it's up to you to seek love.
> Men of the world, it's up to you to love.
> A-A-A-h, A-a-a-h
> A-A-A-h, A-a-a-h.

BY THE TIME WE MET AT the Kangding Hotel just past noon two days later, I had already paid an uninvited morning visit to the Hui Min Elementary School, where the principal had outlined for me the highlights of Tibetan culture. (Yang Suping, who was tied up in meetings throughout the morning, had suggested the visit.) Schools and teachers, who can be counted on to speak good Mandarin, are always reliable sources of information in remote parts of China. I had no idea where I would be headed or what I would see; the overview would help me retain perspective. The lesson began right outside the school door.

Clothing and jewelry. Particularly the distinctive hats (with summer and winter variations) worn by the men, and the earrings and jewelry by the women (even when working in the fields). Even in Kangding, where Chinese were the majority, the variety in dress was eye-catching.

Eating and drinking. The highland barley firewater drunk every day. The men in China are big drinkers, the women are usually let off the hook. But among the Tibetans, both men and women drink. Principal Yuan, not Tibetan herself, ranked them among the top three in liquor capacity in China.

And the yak-butter tea, which non-Tibetan stomachs often could not hold down. (Recipe: Add *zan ba* flour, made from highland barley, to fermented milk. Add yak butter. Add sugar. Add to Chinese tea.)

Song and dance. The Tibetans have a saying, Principal Yuan said: "If you can talk, then you can sing. If you can walk, then you can dance." "Mountain High Blush" was the perennial vocal favorite. The song title referred to the pink cheeks of mountain girls.

Death and Burial. Aerial burial is most common. The corpse is left in open air and devoured by birds of prey, usually within a day. Once the flesh is stripped, the bones are crushed and the birds eat them as well. Water burial is another method. The corpse is fed to fish, revered by Tibetans. Because of this reverence, Tibetans do not eat fish. (Tibetan Buddhists, including monks, are, however, permitted to eat meat.)

Sports. Principal Yuan couldn't show me the horse races held during festivals in the summer, but she did arrange for me to see a Tibetan-style tug-of-war performed in the playground by her students: opponents (singles and pairs) loop ropes over their necks and, at the signal, try to pull the opposite member across the center line.

Still left to cover was the influence of Tibetan Buddhism; far too complex for a morning briefing.

Principal Yuan also gave me the ethnic breakdown in her school, which, its Muslim name notwithstanding, was open to any ethnic group. This breakdown was important because although Ganzi Prefecture (population 900,000; Tibetan population 675,000) was overwhelmingly Tibetan, there was a strong, deliberately managed ethnic Chinese presence in each of the eighteen counties, and particularly in Kangding Town (two-thirds Chinese), the administrative center for the prefecture. This was the way the Chinese keep their fifty-five minorities, over one hundred million people, in check.

ON THE PHONE, BEFORE WE MET in the afternoon, Yang Suping continued to stress that I needed to register with the prefectural foreign affairs office. In all the years that I had been traveling to China, I had managed to avoid such offices, which inevitably cause trouble. In anticipation, I set out to neutralize her request. I prepared as many documents for her as I had with me, including the business cards of senior government and Party officials who had opened themselves and their avenues up to me without my registering at the local foreign affairs office (which can be found at every administrative level in China, even where there are no foreign affairs to conduct).

I began to sense a change in attitude when we met. At my persuasion, Yang Suping finally agreed that going through the foreign affairs office would only complicate things. She

sketched out a six-day itinerary, restructured it after some discussion to give me a broader picture, and phoned the Party
secretaries in Yajiang and Litang Counties from her cell phone.
Each Party secretary gave her a contact and a phone number.
The entire process took ten minutes.

All doors but one flew open.

Yang Suping was adamant about not talking about herself.
She had already told me the year before in Beijing that she
was a member of the first post-Cultural Revolution class to
attend National Minorities University in Beijing beginning in
1977. Her major was Chinese language. Minorities University
is known to be a brainwashing institution, part of the Chinese effort to neutralize dissent in minority areas by training
able students who then move back to their home areas with a
stronger loyalty to the government. Since the establishment of
the People's Republic in 1949, the Chinese have systematically
pumped ethnic Chinese into minority areas to serve in key administrative posts. But it was equally important to have a core
of local residents loyal to the government. Yang Suping was
part of that strategy.

The ring on her finger told that Yang Suping was probably
married. She had attended elementary school in Batang, at the
extreme western edge of Ganzi Prefecture, almost on the border with Tibet, and junior high school in the Sichuan capital,
Chengdu, when her parents, "cadres," were transferred there.
When pressed about what specifically her parents did, she narrowed the description to "administrative officials."

Yang Suping had spent most of her career in Kangding, first in
the county government, rising to county executive (mayor) and
Party secretary (the top position). Following the Sixteenth Party
Congress, she had been promoted to the Standing Committee of
the Ganzi Prefecture Party Committee that oversees Kangding
and the other counties that make up Ganzi. She was a rising star.
Her present appointment, several months at the Sichuan Provincial Party School, was a part of the grooming process.

ENTRÉE TO THE GANZI INTERIOR ASSURED by the Communist Party, I booked a 7:00 A.M. bus ticket for the next morning to Yajiang County, ninety miles due west of Kangding. Its final destination, Xiang Cheng, was two days away. The four-and-a-half hours anticipated for the trip to Yajiang presaged the terrain ahead. The story of Ganzi is its mountains and elevation. Aside from Xindu Bridge, a dusty market hamlet with petrol stations, repair shops, and feed depots, the stretch from Kangding to Yajiang was for the most part uninhabited, far too steep to support agriculture in any form. In much of China, farmers, desperate for fuel wood, have denuded the forestland. But here a vigorous campaign to preserve the forestland was under way, and lush vegetation—larch, birch, fir—carpeted the steep slopes up to the timberline at about 14,000 feet. One of the portfolios Party Secretary Yang Suping carried was tourism. There was a lot to work with here, if only the access could be improved. Route 318, snaking around mountain after mountain, was the main artery between Chengdu and Lhasa, but it rode like a county lane that had been chopped up by a column of tanks. About the norm for Ganzi roads.

For the two women next to me on the bus out of Kangding, altitude sickness was the topic of constant discussion. Headaches, nausea, and dizziness were the symptoms. Kangding, at about 6,500 feet, didn't trigger any reaction. But as we headed west toward Yajiang, where I was going, we started to climb, passing a peak that topped out at over 15,400 feet. This was a momentary tease of what was ahead. The older of the two women gave me a vial of Chinese medicine intended to enable the body to use oxygen more efficiently. I would put it to good use the following week.

As the topography west of Kangding changed, fresh vistas opened up. The younger Tibetan woman across the aisle was fluent in Chinese, and I peppered her with questions about the unfolding landscape. We reached a modest-sized range of pasture dotted with houses—sturdy, attractive two-story buildings—and I wanted to know if we had reached the fabled "high plains." *No, said Liu Yan, this was just a modest river valley.* From time to time, triangular batteries of flags could be seen on the mountain slopes. *They commemorated the dead, but not the burial place. There is no interment in Tibetan tradition.* The herds of shaggy bovines? *They were yaks, the mountain cattle raised by Tibetans for their milk, meat, wool, and hides; and to plough their fields.* The orderly piles of stones with rounded tops standing about chest high? *Drying yak dung to be used as fuel.*

Liu Yan, in her early twenties, was returning to Derong, in the southwest corner of Ganzi, after a conference in Kangding—a two-day bus trip. Like many of the passengers headed that way, she would overnight in Litang, where altitudes soared above 15,000 feet, at one of the rudimentary inns renting sleeping space at $2.50 per night. Hers was a familiar story of unrequited parental dreams. Like many in Ganzi Prefecture, her parents, at great sacrifice, had sent her to junior high school in Chengdu. But she had not passed the high school qualifying exams and instead had settled for a three-year course in accounting in Kangding. She was a veteran of the trek from Kangding to Derong. From Liu Yan, I learned that there was indeed a Shangri-La. It was on the map. You could get there in about three hours from her place.

THE BUS PULLED INTO YAJIANG and, on her cell phone, Liu Yan rang up the number of the Communist Party contact Yang Suping had given me. There was no answer.

Liu Yan couldn't wait; the bus was ready to roll.

Yajiang Town was not a large place—just a few terraced streets following the contours of a narrow mountain valley. I headed for the local Party offices. We were now at about 10,000 feet, and the altitude weighed on me slightly as I pigeon-toed up the slope to steep concrete stairs leading to the street above. A thoughtful soul took my bag and led me to the Communist Party building.

It was lunchtime and there wasn't a person to be seen in the dark, cement-floored corridors. I camped on the stairwell between the second and third floors, pondering what to do. A woman walking up the stairs caught sight of me.

"*Ni shi na li*? Who are you?"

I was looking for Zhou Zhi, I told her.

She went to find the assistant administrative director.

Things move along briskly when you are on the Party trail. Faster than I could assimilate, Zhou appeared on the stairway landing. He got on his cell phone and summoned an associate. Before I knew it, we were walking through the streets of Yajiang and found ourselves in a modest hotel. I stopped them in their tracks. Five thousand people lived in Yajiang Town; forty-five thousand farmers surrounded them. Rural was what I wanted. I repeated for my hosts a lesson that I had learned many times in China: "The closer you are to the county town, the more prosperous the villagers and the less typical the experience." Their instructions had come from Yang Suping, a powerful Party official. They needed to please me.

Within minutes, an SUV arrived and we were on our way thirty minutes out of town to Xiazhongzi, one of a cluster of villages with a population of about a thousand.

Xiazhongzi, like the other villages in the area, was designated "agricultural," meaning that its primary land use was to raise crops. The few animals the villagers kept (cows, mules, pigs) were supplementary. In fact, raising any more than a few animals was impractical in much of Yajiang County because most of the villages were woven through narrow valleys without sufficient open space for large herds. Other villages in Ganzi Prefecture, situated in more open areas, were termed "herding" villages. Their principal land use was grazing; they did not break the soil. As such, they received government subsidies per household member to compensate them for the fact that they did not possess workable land. The distinction between agriculture and herding or ranching, which popped up again and again, was difficult to latch on to because in the U.S. ranches and farms that raise animals often cultivate vast cropland to feed them.

The homes of those who work the soil in rural Tibetan villages, unlike villages in most of China—where homes are clustered, with cropland surrounding the cluster—are widely spaced, sometimes hundreds of feet apart, with cropland adjacent to the house. There is less of a sense of community in Tibetan villages than elsewhere in China, and much more privacy.

Chinese see Tibetans as dirty—unwashed and uncultured. I carried that prejudice into the villages as well. But one step into Zhaxi's house put that to lie. Chinese village homes are typically made of drab brick (clay or mud), with little or no attention to architecture, and interior decoration a seeming afterthought. For Tibetans, artistic detail is an integral part of the construction process. On the bus ride in from Kangding, I had already glimpsed from a distance how much Tibetans value artistry. The hand-decorated exterior window frames, carefully chiseled in a delicate checkerboard pattern at the top of the window and at the eave line, with a distinctive white flare painted at the bottom of each window frame, recalled quaint village homes in southern Bavaria.

Like most Tibetan homes, Zhaxi's had three floors. The first floor, of packed earth, was for storage, farm implements, and animals—a brooding pig, a calf. In the center of the first floor were stout wooden pillars, resting on large rocks, that support the living quarters above. The second floor, reached by a steep set of wooden stairs, consisted of a vast open space—forty to fifty feet long and almost as wide—with wooden-plank flooring, far larger than most Chinese houses. The cooking area was located along one wall. Sleeping is traditionally on mats placed on the floor, providing open living space during the day. In some homes, there are additional rooms for sleeping or lounging. With three generations often living together, they provide a modicum of privacy.

The support pillars on the second floor of Zhaxi's house were decorated in bright, multicolor, oriental patterns, which extended to the beams that stretched across the high ceiling. The walls were graced with pictures and tapestries. Plastic flowers in bright colors sat atop the television set and on cabinets. The windows were adorned with lace curtains. On one sofa sat embroidered bedding; on another, elaborate ornaments worn at weddings and festivals. And on the southern wall there was a small Buddhist pantheon. As she prepared dinner, Zhaxi's mother intoned a brief prayer.

The third floor, made of cement, was for drying corn and other crops, and for storage. A portion of the third floor is sometimes left open to the sky, lending a distinctive hacienda look to the Tibetan landscape.

THE SYMBOL OF TIBETAN CULTURE is its yak-butter tea, served at every meal, and offered to guests as a greeting of hospitality. Definitely an acquired taste.

I had my first sip in Zhaxi's house. One was my limit.

Tibetan names can get confusing. Although Tibetans have a clan (family) name—Zhaxi's was Niu Wu Fu—officially, they use only first names. Since they are Chinese citizens, for school records, ID cards, and other official documents, Tibetan names are transliterated into Chinese characters, which inevitably leads to mispronunciation. For convenience, Tibetans who have frequent dealings with Chinese often use Chinese names. Virtually no one called Party Secretary Yang Suping by her Tibetan name, Gesang Yangjing.

There was something uninviting about Zhaxi's house. Maybe it was the absence of smiles. Maybe it was the large areas of empty white wall space that gave the room a cavernous feeling. Maybe it was the small inn right next to the house that Zhaxi ran, serving food and providing beds for the truckers, officials, businessmen, and tourists traveling between Lhasa and Chengdu. I didn't want to risk being coaxed into sleeping at an inn.

The reception across the road was far warmer and more patient.

There was something about Wang Dongshou and his wife, Pu Yulian, that said, "Welcome." (Both used Chinese names, though their children carried Tibetan names.) They took me into every corner of their home, and into their ledger book as well. Because Wang was a second son, his widowed mother, following Tibetan tradition, lived with his older brother. Wang and Pu, both thirty-eight, were mild mannered people. But they acknowledged that living in a household with just two generations simplified matters, because there was no mother-in-law to offer opinions (which had to be heeded).

Wang didn't work the two-thirds of an acre that the family owned. That was left to his wife, who tended a sloping plot about a hundred feet from the house, where she grew mostly corn and potatoes. Instead, from April to September, he worked repairing walls and gathering *chong cao*, a traditional plant pharmaceutical found high up in the mountains, said to benefit the lungs and liver. It took about ten days to gather a pound of *chong cao*, which brought in from $250 to $650. According to Tibetan lore, in winter, when dormant, *chong cao* resembles a worm, and in summer, when actively growing, a blade of grass; hence its name: "worm grass." The mountains of Ganzi were loaded with *chong cao*, and many of the Tibetans relied on it for cash income. Herb gathering and wall repair brought Wang, his wife, and their two children over $2,000 cash per year. That gave them a comfortable life.

Whereas Zhaxi's house was dominated by empty white walls, the interior of Wang and Pu's house was graced with paneled wood. The dark, textured wall lent a more intimate feeling than did Zhaxi's house. On one of the walls was a certificate of merit earned by their sixteen-year-old daughter, a junior high school student in Yajiang Town. I asked her mother, Pu Yulian, whether she would rather her children pursue traditional Tibetan lives or study, with its implied measure of assimilation. She came down without qualification on the side of education.

Because it was impractical for Wang and Pu's daughter to commute to school from the village, she boarded at the school during the week and returned home on Saturday. Her place was taken seamlessly during the week by her cousin, a sixth grader whose home was up in the mountains. Because commuting to school from the mountains was impractical for the cousin, she stayed with Wang and Pu during the week, attending elementary school a mile or so down the road with their fourteen-year-old son. Surrogate parents, surrogate siblings. It seemed to be working.

Winter, when the men are at home, is house-building time among Tibetans, and the house going up adjacent to Wang's was typical. The outside walls were made of plentiful stone packed with mud. Two craftsmen were hard at work planing window frames. The endless mountains in this part of Ganzi Prefecture carried abundant timber, and locals were permitted to harvest it for their own use, provided they planted a new tree for every one cut. The new owners, husband and wife, were hard at work as well. Sweat equity is a vital component of Tibetan house building. It cost almost $4,000 to construct a new home.

Evenings come early at the end of November and, after an appetizer of homemade noodles, mixed with potatoes and flavored with ginger, the TV went on and with it the news. Satellite dishes are common in the mountains, even among poorer families. Later, a plate of cow intestines, a Tibetan favorite, was brought out. But TV chatter provided mere backdrop to the main evening activity: gossip punctuated with popping sunflower seeds. As people streamed in and out of the house, it was hard to keep track of them. Any subject was fair game, including, this evening, what I would eat. To suit my palate, Pu Yulian had roasted some potatoes in the hearth, and made potato dumplings spiced with onion, garlic, and ginger. She added a cake made from corn meal, ground from her own harvest.

From time to time, as we sat around on the wooden floor or on squat wooden stools, Pu would move glowing chunks of charred wood from the cooking stove into a three-legged iron canister. A wide opening cut into the ceiling above the cooking area vented any smoke that might have filled the room, but also ensured that the room would never feel warm. The canister could be moved around the room, providing an opportunity to warm your hands. At almost 10,000 feet, temperatures fell rapidly into the 20s after dark. Sips of tea and extra layers of clothing provided supplementary warmth.

Understanding their heavily accented Sichuan dialect would have taken weeks of exposure. Most Tibetans have at least a passive knowledge of Mandarin from watching television. Being able to speak Mandarin is an entirely different issue. Living as they do in Sichuan Province, many Tibetans in Ganzi Prefecture understand and speak Sichuan dialect quite fluently. But the deeper you travel into Ganzi, the more Tibetan is relied upon. Pu alternated between Tibetan and Sichuan dialect without seeming effort.

Within the ethnically concentrated Tibetan areas of Sichuan, traditional life remains vibrant. But the dominant Han Chinese culture is forever lurking in the shadows—in schools, in dealings with bureaucrats, on television. In the villages, some Tibetan might be taught in elementary school. But in county towns, Tibetan children are likely to study English before Tibetan. By the time they reach high school, Tibetan disappears from the curriculum. Except for those who study Tibetan as part of post-secondary courses, many Tibetans turn out illiterate in their mother tongue. Part of this is the end result of the unified Chinese curriculum, which aims to fashion a unified Chinese people. Many Tibetan parents feel they have no choice but to encourage their children to learn Chinese at the expense of Tibetan, because only full fluency in Chinese will buy them a solid future.

Here the difference between Tibetan life outside of Tibet

(where most Tibetans live) and inside Tibet is fundamental. Tibetans inside Tibet have two cultural influences: the official Mandarin Chinese culture imposed by television, schooling, and dealings with Chinese officials and businessmen on the one hand; and the native Tibetan language and culture on the other. Tibetans living in Tibet constitute a majority in their immediate cultural sphere. Tibetans living in Sichuan on the other hand, face a third challenge: Sichuan language and culture. Two-and-a-half million Sichuan Tibetans; eighty-six million people in Sichuan; one billion three hundred million people in China. The forces of assimilation are everywhere. The same situation applies to Qinghai, Gansu, and Yunnan, the other principle Tibetan diaspora communities in China.

At about 10:00, after a peripheral washing of hands, face, and feet in a shallow basin, we headed off for bed. Wang and Pu had a gravity-fed water tap in their house, but heating enough water for bathing was impossible. It took more than an hour for my body heat to warm the ice-cold, inch-thick cotton quilt—resting on foam padding placed on the cold wood floor—so that I could fall off to sleep. Though the house sat just feet from the main road to Lhasa, not a car or truck passed by the night through.

With little work to do and the sun coming up well past eight in this part of China,* Tibetans sleep late on winter mornings. I was up before everyone to perform the morning's first vital task without pressure. On the way to the outhouse, I met a cow. "*Ni hao* [good day] brown cow," I said.

As outhouses go, Wang and Pu's rated near the top. Its shortcoming was its location: the need to descend a steep flight of wooden stairs and then leave the small courtyard to reach it. The structure itself was very solid: stone walls packed with mud, a roof made of planks, covered with a layer of cement. The floor

---

* Though just a bit larger than the United States, most areas of China are in the same time zone. Thus, the further west you travel, the later daylight arrives in the morning.

was made of planks with ample space between them. Better empty your money pockets before attending to business.

Before returning to the house, I took a stroll up the road in the direction of the elementary school, marveling at the detail that went into every house, noticing how cozily each nested in the steep slopes that rose up on either side of the road, nodding 'Good Morning' to a pig, admiring an apple orchard, testing a rope bridge that spanned the modest river that ran through the valley.

Turning my head back toward the house for a moment, I caught sight of an agitated Pu running in my direction. Seeing my bedding empty when she woke up, she was afraid that I had wandered off and lost my way. As we walked back, she begged me to stay on another day, and to promise, really promise, that next year, in July or August, when everything was green, I would return for another visit. For the moment, though, yet higher pastures beckoned.

MY TRANSFER FROM YAJIANG COUNTY, where Wang and Pu lived, to Litang County had its moments of uncertainty. According to the plan arranged by Party Secretary Yang, I was to call a Mr. Huang when I reached Litang. But this was the weekend and these were rough-edged places. I asked my Yajiang contact, Zhaxi Ciren, to call ahead before I left Yajiang.

It turned out not to be a working number.

Probably, she had written down the wrong number, Yang Suping said when Zhaxi reached her; someone would be waiting at the bus station in Litang when I arrived.

The trouble was, how would they know when I would arrive? In ordinary times, the eighty-five-mile trip would take three hours, but these schedules almost always ran late. There were buses going from Yajiang to Litang, but Zhaxi had instead put me in a seven-passenger minivan. The driver had a lot of experience, he reassured me, and I would be guaranteed a seat.

As soon as we left Yajiang and began to climb higher into the mountains, it became immediately apparent that I had made a big mistake. The driver was a fool and his vehicle no better. He stopped after an hour to douse the brakes with water in order to cool them and was barely able to restart the van. The plastic container he occasionally swigged carried the name of a local brand of hard liquor. It had snowed the night before and we had slipped twice on the swerving, icy mountain roads.

As long as we were traveling upgrade, gravity provided a safety factor. But now we had reached the high point, MOUNT JIANZIWAN. ELEVATION: 15,285 FEET. Several vehicles had stopped at the peak, including a bus bound for Tibet. The mini-van driver scattered a handful of confetti with Tibetan writing on it, a traditional prayer offering when reaching the mountain peak. That wouldn't be nearly enough to brake a skid on the steep descent.

The bus driver was putting on snow chains. The van driver said he would do the same. But instead of chains, he took out a few lengths of weathered nylon rope. A deep dread over-whelmed me and, with a fellow passenger, a writer from Shanghai, I bolted for the bus. When the van driver balked, I gave him half the fare.

The landscape had begun to change. We were now moving into grazing territory: yaks, sheep, and horses dotted the high plains. Dancing in the back of my mind was what I would find when I got to Litang.

The "bus station" in Litang proved to be little more than an open stretch of barren, frozen earth at the edge of town. The still, dry air was much colder than it had been in Yajiang. I could feel it in my lungs. First, I needed to find Litang. Then, I needed to find the Communist Party. I started to walk.

Before I had walked more than a few hundred feet, I noticed a Nissan SUV cruising the streets in the fast-fading, late after-noon sun. Two smiling guys in their twenties and a driver with a beard. Was I the foreigner coming from Yajiang?

My face lit up.

Relieved, but tired and disoriented, itinerary decisions nevertheless needed to be made right away. In Wang and Pu's village, I had gotten a first feel for agricultural homesteads. What I wanted now was to see the wide-open, high plains. You had to travel well out to see really wide-open ranges and big herds, the two who welcomed me said, but right here, not far from Litang Town, you could get an idea. The bearded driver turned off the macadam road and, fearlessly, drove right into a semi-frozen, marshy pasture, where several dozen yaks were sniffing shoots of short-stalked pasture grass from clumps of snow as the last slivers of light arched over the frozen highland plains.

We got back in the SUV and, after a stop to pick up the Party secretary and mayor of Jiawa Township, we headed for Kaniang, one of seven villages in the township, where I would spend the night at the homestead of Zhagen Aduo. Once off the main road, we bumped over, around, and through frozen clumps of earth until finally pulling up within walking distance of Aduo's compound.

The layout of Tibetan homes was by now becoming familiar: through the doorway, across the packed-earth first floor, where a grown porker snorted 'Good evening'; up the steep stairs to an anteroom where carcasses of a pig and cow hung from the ceiling; and into the main living space, about the same size as I had seen in Yajiang. Aduo's house was as well appointed as Wang and Pu's, but the dimly lit room withheld its artistic secrets until morning light.

Often in China, local Party and government leaders greet a visitor and then disappear, never to be seen again. Here, in Litang, though, the grassroots officials were local Tibetans: more forthcoming, less intent on impressing you with their position. The Party secretary, Luorong Pengcuo, said he would have his secretary write up the basic information about Jiawa Township and give it to me in the morning. Of the 1,820 people in the seven villages in Jiawa Township, seventy-seven were Communist Party members, only a tad under the five percent national norm. He was doing his job.

The consonants in the Tibetan phrase for "Thank you," *Ga dzren che*, were giving me fits. I replaced it with "*Zhaxi de le* [May auspicious days greet you]," which rolled off the tongue like yak butter.

What began to sink in about this household, as bowls of noodles and vegetables were brought to the low-legged table near where we were sitting, was that there were no women. Aduo, fifty-seven, had four sons, ages nineteen through thirty-two. Only the oldest, Luorong Yapi, who had two sons of his own, had married. Aduo's wife had died. That made seven males. Luorong Yapi's wife was up in the hills, several miles away, standing watch over the family's forty head of yaks. The dirty dishes, including a half-eaten plate of the ubiquitous cow intestines, remained on the table until morning.

Aduo's was a good place to visit because, although his homestead was designated "agricultural," in fact it was mixed. That the family also ran a herd of cattle made it easier to understand both lifestyles. In Aduo's village, numbering 470 individuals, 20 of 63 households had both farming and herding operations. The mix was preferable in this terrain. Low summer temperatures ruled out growing warm weather crops such as tomatoes and corn, but cabbage, turnips, potatoes, and highland barley supplemented the meat and dairy products that their animals provided.

WITH THE LOCAL PARTY SECRETARY, the mayor, and the county liaisons arranged by Party Secretary Yang Suping now on their way back home for the night, communication with Aduo and the other family members became more cumbersome. We were now almost two hundred miles west of Kangding, on the fringes of Chinese China. The farther west one traveled, the less standard the Chinese would become. But Aduo and the others were warm-hearted, and we gradually found our common tongue.

The mayor had been candid about the pre-bed washing habits of the family when I asked. "Some washed," he said, "some didn't." In any case, the regimen—first face, then hands, then feet, using a minimal amount of boiled water in a basin—was the same across rural China. But the outhouse situation—the need to walk down a steep flight of steps, in the dark, past a glaring pig—made it treacherous until you knew the routine.

Aduo was protective. He guided me down the stairs, eased me outside the main door to the large courtyard, and pointed to the open area in front of us. In fact, there wasn't any outhouse; *sui bian*, anywhere, was fine. Then, he backpedaled a few discreet steps to observe my needs. When they became clear, he went back inside the house and returned with several pieces of toilet paper which, again discreetly, he handed me and then quietly backpedaled again until matters were concluded.

The evening's entertainment was a VCD (video CD). MTV's influence was everywhere, even here on the high Tibetan plains: slapped-together graphics, melded with Tibetan song and dance. The outstanding question was why the lyrics on the screen were written in Chinese instead of Tibetan. The answer pointed to illiteracy and the mighty weight of Chinese culture. Tibetans yearned to be themselves...yet yearned to join the mainstream. 4.8 millions Tibetans, 1.3 billion Chinese.

"LENG BU LENG, ARE YOU COLD?," Aduo asked solicitously, the Sichuan component of his accent showing through. It was already in the low 20s and temperatures would fall into the teens or lower during the night. There would be no supplementary heat in the house until morning. Aduo had brought two thick, cotton quilts, assorted blankets, and a sheep fleece to the bunk bed, one of several along the wall, where I would sleep. Before turning off the light, he attached a long string to the light bulb switch in the center of the room and attached a weight to the end of the string. He positioned the weight on the table next to the bed. If I needed the light, all I had to do was pull on the weight. Next to the cord, he placed a plastic bowl.

Shifting sleeping positions during the night was an exercise in weightlifting...But I wasn't in the least cold.

By the time I awoke the following morning, Aduo was already busy vigorously sweeping the living area with a broom. Outside, a niece of Aduo's, wearing an ankle-length, plaid woolen skirt, had just finished sweeping the courtyard clean. She was rinsing her rag mop by the well. The hygiene wasn't quite as loose as it had first appeared. On my way to the outhouse, I met a mule. Or was it a donkey?

It was to be expected that my home stays would be arranged with one of the better-off families in the village. But a sense of perspective was almost always available a short walk away. Just behind Aduo's compound was a much more modest homestead. The building contained only one floor. The inside area to the left was reserved for storage and animals; the area to the right, where multicolored blankets were neatly piled, was reserved for sleeping and eating. In time, this family would no doubt add a second floor, but the simplicity of the window frames, the hallmark of Tibetan architecture, indicated that the home would never rival the lavishness that Aduo's revealed in daylight.

The fascination here was not the interior design, but a young woman in her mid-twenties who addressed me in English. Many in China study English in school and are often eager to try their skill. But Wangmo's English had a cultured Indian ring to it. Her story was different. In 1999, she had traveled overland to Dharamsala, India, the exile base of the Dalai Lama. There, for three years, she had studied not only English, but Tibetan. She had returned to teach Tibetan language in a neighboring village. As to how and under what circumstances she had reached India, she would only answer, "I don't know." Tibetan could be studied in Ganzi Prefecture and certainly in Tibet proper. But maybe it wasn't the right Tibetan, spoken by the right people. Some at least, her story told, were making great efforts to invigorate Tibetan culture.

One of Aduo's four sons, Dengzhu Zeren, twenty-six, was a Buddhist monk at the local Rila Monastery. He was home on vacation. He invited me into the adjoining room, which was sunnier. It contained a lavish display of Buddhist art including a representation of Sakyamuni, the original Buddha, who lived twenty-five hundred years ago and whom all Buddhists strive to emulate; a photograph of the Dalai Lama and another of the Panchen Lama; photographs of more recent leading Buddhist clerics; elaborate Buddhist artwork in the lotus flower motif; and decorative vessels and vases. Somehow, amidst all of this joyous color, several Pepsi Cola bottles had been recruited to hold synthetic flowers.

Dengzhu Zeren had joined the monastery at eighteen quite voluntarily and now, eight years later, was a fully ordained lama. The qualifications were basic, he told me: (1) one had to be at least eighteen years of age, (2) have an ability to read and write Tibetan, and (3) have an understanding of the basic texts of his denomination, the Flower Sect. His motivation, he said, was to become a *bodhisattva*, an enlightened reincarnation of the Living Buddha who chooses to remain behind and help others reach his state of awareness.

There are five Tibetan Buddhist sects, known popularly as the Yellow, White, Red, Black, and Flower Sects. They are so-called because of the color of the outer garments and hip sash followers wear on ceremonial occasions. Of the five, the Yellow Sect, from which the Dalai Lama emerged, has the most adherents.

Back in Kangding, I had had a brief encounter at the Jingang Temple with a disillusioned monk also by the name of Zhaxi Ciren. Just twenty-one, Zhaxi had been at the monastery since he was thirteen and felt trapped. Given a choice, he probably would have left the monastery. His day began at 6:00 A.M. and revolved around study. It left him stone bored. His salvation was his palette of pastels and a work in progress that stood on an easel next to a small sanctuary of Buddhist figurines. Zhaxi's artistic impulse was my introduction to the rich Tibetan artistic tradition.

Zhaxi expressed no great interest in his calling, but there was no way out. He had no skills, couldn't speak Chinese, and had nowhere to go should he leave. More than anything, for him the monastery represented security.

Dengzhu Zeren of Litang, on the other hand, seemed at peace with his choice of vocation. His broad smile told his story. The difference might have been that Dengzhu Zeren had a welcoming family to return to periodically.

Their Buddhist faith was the anchor of Tibetan life, many said. That surely required an extended stay to verify. Especially for those with activism in their blood, becoming a Tibetan monk had its risk. But if the numbers of monks, with their flowing tunics, in the streets of Litang was any indication, it was a risk many were willing to take.

Soon after getting up, Aduo's other sons and grandsons piled chunks of wood and other building supplies into a cart attached to a two-wheel tractor and headed off a few miles north to the yak camp. There, preparations were underway to move the family herd of forty yaks from higher up in the hills to lower ground where the winter temperatures would be warmer and the pasture thicker. By the time I arrived, they had just about completed a roughly crafted wooden shed with thatch roofing that would keep out the snow and rain. What appeared to be a stone fence enclosed the area, except that it wasn't made of stone. Unlike eastern Ganzi, rocks are scarce in Litang County. Retaining walls were fashioned from chunks of sod and earth—of unlimited supply.

This camp was where Aduo's daughter-in-law, Gecuo, would spend the winter and spring watching the family's yak herd. She had been doing this for six years. If her sun-leathered face and broad, muscular shoulders were any sign, she was one tough cowgirl.

IF MOST OF THE HOUSEHOLDS IN JIAWA TOWNSHIP seemed to have tolerable standards of living, they still fell far, far short of what the Communist Party considered to be "well-off": a per capita income of $800 per year. The average per person cash income in Jiawa was just $50, Luodengba, the mayor of Jiawa, explained. For the most part, the villagers were just sustaining themselves. They were neither helping to expand the economy by marketing products, nor stimulating the economy by purchasing products produced by others. Their consumption was minimal.

Levels of wealth in rural China cannot be compared with levels of wealth in China's cities. That complexity became sharper in Heni, a township in the western part of Litang County made up of eleven villages, 2,258 people, all of them herdsmen, nomads.

The topography here was different from where Aduo's family lived. These were the high plains: long stretches of open grassland, some of it marshy, interrupted by hills rising several hundred additional feet. After a two-hour ride, we pulled off the road into a clearing where seven black tents, spread over several acres, were elaborately anchored to secure them from howling winds. The cattle were up in the hills and would be brought down in the evening. The entire space was strewn with yak pellets.

Here the average yearly income was higher, about $85 per person. But this figure was deceptive. The herdsmen owned no land and grew no crops, resulting in higher food expenses. But they were freed of the time and cost of maintaining a homestead, and with it the comfort of living in a real house. Life was little different here than it had been five hundred years ago.

There were seven people in the first tent: the father, Sechiuma, fifty-four; the mother, Djoma, fifty; three unmarried sons; and two unmarried daughters. In rural China, minority couples are permitted three children, Chinese families two. The Party secretary, sitting on a rug on the dirt floor just across, couldn't deny that family planning standards were lax in this part of China; the evidence was right before our eyes.

The inside of the tent was a clutter of all the necessities of life: pots and pans sitting on a stone hearth, sacks of grain in the corner, giant chunks of yak butter wrapped in cloth waiting to be taken to market, animal skins, articles of clothing, cow intestines, and three carcasses (two sheep, one cow) hanging on wooden poles. A generator powered a light bulb and a television set. The entire tent reeked of smoke—from the fire, fueled by cow dung, that provided heat for warmth and cooking, and from chain-smoked cigarettes.

By nomad standards, Sechiuma, illiterate as was the rest of his family, was a wealthy man. He had more than 120 yaks, more than 60 sheep, and 10 horses that would do him proud during the summer festivals held in Litang. Each yak would sell for anywhere from $125 to $300. In any year, depending upon the family's cash situation, he would sell as few as two or three or as many as seven or eight. From cattle sales, from yak butter, from wool, from the fine yak fleece used to make bedding, yearly family income could range from $1,100 to more than $2,000—$300 per family member. Added to this was the government subsidy, which varied from year to year. A tidy sum, compared to Tibetan homesteaders who worked the land. The premise for this type of life was a willingness to wave all modern comforts.

A walk across the plain brought me to the other extreme: Tibetan nomad poverty. In place of the abundance in Sechiuma's tent, there was a feeling of meager living. The tent was smaller, the material articles of life were sparse. With only fifteen yaks, there would be less butter to sell in town. Slaughtering a yak for food would be a much weightier decision. Selling part of the herd would transfer this year's cash problem to the next. The yearly government subsidy was what made life possible here.*

---

* Subsidies for nomads vary considerably depending upon family wealth. Rich families sometimes get nothing. The average grant is $40 to $50 per year per person, though not every family member necessarily receives a share. In a family of five, for example, three might receive subsidies totaling $150.

An invitation was extended to spend a night in one of the tents. For the hosts, it would have required no more than fitting an additional body on the rug floor. Finding the outhouse would require no assistance. But temperatures would fall into the single numbers at night. The cold, the ever-pervasive smoke, and the thought of sleeping with three carcasses crimped the idea.

THERE WAS AN INTERMEDIATE STEP between the totally nomad existence I had just seen in Heni and the purely pastoral life of Wang and Pu in Yajiang. Tibetan herdsmen normally observe a two-season pasture rotation: a summer-fall camp up in the mountains and a winter-spring camp on lower ground. In some cases, the semiannual trek requires four to five days on horseback, covering a distance of twenty-five to thirty miles. In other cases, seasonal grazing grounds are within a few miles of each other.

In either situation, the government was encouraging families to live in permanent communities during the winter-spring rotation. This made it possible for the children to go to school. Zhagalazha Village's winter settlement, in existence since 1991, has the look of a traditional Tibetan village, with the exception that the houses are much closer since no land is apportioned to grow crops. Doji, twenty-nine, head of a modest household with twenty-three yaks, twelve sheep, and seven horses, had already begun to talk the talk of Chinese villagers, citing—in Communist style—the "five necessities" of a winter settlement: (1) a house, (2) electricity, (3) a television set, (4) a hothouse where young animals could be protected in winter, and (5) a winter store of hay to feed the animals when winter pastures proved too sparse.

Zhagalazha, a half hour south of Litang Town, provided the perfect rotation situation. Its winter-spring grazing ground was little more than a mile from its summer-fall grazing ground. This unusually ideal situation allowed the older people and children to remain in the permanent settlement the year through. The traditional grazing patterns that families had observed for generations made widespread implementation of winter camps with permanent housing difficult.

A LAST MISSION REMAINED IN LITANG. Sitting next to me on the bus in from Chengdu to Ganzi Prefecture a week earlier had been a young woman in her twenties. She was particularly well made up, with meticulous attention to her hair. You could tell that she took special pride in the way she looked. She answered a cell phone call just before the bus departed Chengdu, and the animation in her voice and the excited expression on her face as she talked were appealing. Eight or nine hours and 220 miles lay ahead of us, and I was looking forward to having someone to chat with.

She opened a book—a reader, another plus—as the bus began to roll, a translation of Jane Austen's *Sense and Sensibility*. When she looked up, I initiated the usual small talk, eliciting the basics: She had just spent nineteen hours on a train from Gansu Province and was headed for Litang. She would overnight in Kangding and resume her journey first thing in the morning.

The next time she looked up, I continued probing. I asked her to write her name in my notebook. *Wu Yali*. She was Tibetan. There were a lot of Tibetans in Gansu. In Litang, she said, she sold sewing supplies from a street stand. Then she fell off to sleep.

To travel hundreds of miles from Gansu to a remote place like Litang was curious to say the least.

Thirty minutes later, Wu Yali awoke from her nap and, eyeing an empty spot across the aisle, quickly changed her seat. That irked me because, on the floor, just under her new seat, sat a mutt, and a particularly ugly one at that, by the name of *Hei* (Blackie). Blackie belonged to a chain smoker in the seat in front of me with whom I had already had words over his trail of smoke. To abandon me, *for a dog*?

A week had passed, and I was now in Litang Town.

Litang was a small place: fifty-three thousand people in the entire county; twelve thousand in the county town. If the Communist Party couldn't find Wu Yali, no one could. I enlisted my two Tibetan Party contacts, Wang Pei and Angwang Qupi.

We started to walk the streets, asking for a notions shop, for the people from Gansu, for someone by the name of Wu Yali.

Litang Town wore a coat of many colors. You could find almost anything here. General merchandise stores sold items as diverse as scarves and yak butter. (Butter, it seemed, was everywhere.) On the next corner was a group of herdsmen selling raw sheep wool. Litang Town was where the villagers and nomads we had visited marketed their goods for cash.

On our way out of town to Zhagalazha Village earlier in the day, we had doubled back to an exceptional sight. A motorcycle-led convoy. The men on the cycles wore high fox-fur hats and leopard-skin tunics. Their sunglasses made them look like Hollywood was on location in Tibet. For a better vantage point, we circled ahead to their end point: the reception hall at a social activities club where a wedding reception was about to get under way. I, too, was invited. Tables were heaped high with every delicacy, enough for an army.

I made my way to the adjoining room to pay my respects to the bride and groom, each clad in golden-clothed robes with heavy beads around their necks. The bride wore broad golden bells in her hair, the same ornaments I had seen several days earlier in Yajiang. They were part of a family's treasure.

On a second try to get out of town, we passed three men in tatters. Every few feet they would stop in the street and, falling to their knees, genuflect to absolve their sins. They were members of the faithful on their way to Lhasa...by foot...a journey that would take them three to four years. A time-honored practice in Tibetan Buddhism.

Particularly distinctive of Tibetans is their dress and especially their hats. But walking the streets of Litang, it was impossible to single out any predominate style. Some of the hats looked like they came out of Dodge City, others like they might be worn by African chieftains. Leather, fur-muffed hats, like those worn in the Russian Army, were popular, but so, too, were hats with tufts of fur that did not cover the ears. Others wore scarves wrapped around their heads. Many just wore long hair, without any hats at all.

WE FINALLY RAN ACROSS SOMEONE who knew Wu Yali. She ran a beauty parlor, he said. That matched her attention to her appearance.

We congratulated ourselves on our detective work as we entered the Expert Beauty Salon: neat, moderately well appointed. There had been a notions shop, directly adjacent to her own, run by a relative from Gansu, said Wu Yali, dressed this day in a long, flowing, black skirt, with a multicolored sash around her waist. The shop had folded. Her story was getting ever more complicated.

She liked Litang. Hadn't required any time at all to get used to the altitude. Now twenty-seven, she was an experienced wayfarer. At sixteen, she had left junior high school in rural Gansu after the first year and spent three years studying hairdressing. Then, she had traveled south to faraway Guangzhou (Canton), where she studied cosmetology for one year. Returning home to Gansu, she worked for a while in an ink manufacturing factory. Because the salary was so low, less than $30 a month, three years ago she had decided to come to Litang, where she had opened up this salon. Rent was low, about $100 a month, and business was good.

Somewhere in her story was a tale of unrequited love. The novel she was reading on the bus, *Sense and Sensibility*, was similar to her own story, she said. That was why she wasn't looking for a boyfriend. Certainly, she had had many opportunities.

What brought her to Litang was what motivated the tens

of millions who formed China's "floating population." There wasn't much opportunity where she came from. The competition in China's largest cities was cutthroat. Her skills were ordinary; she wouldn't be able to compete. But here in Litang, among the hundred or so shopkeepers and tradesman from Gansu, she could find her place. They didn't sever their ties with their hometowns, these expatriates. As winter began to set its grip, and business, often conducted in unheated buildings or out in the cold, slackened, many of them shuttered their shops and went back home, to return in the spring. All told, there were some two thousand outsiders in Litang. Many of them, bolted security gates told, were away for the winter.

PARTICULARLY IN CHINA, where regionalisms are so diverse, generalization can be risky. Party Secretary Yang Suping was able to give me the broader picture when we met again, this time in Chengdu.

The differences between Tibetan life in western Sichuan and eastern Tibet, she said, were negligible. The food, the dress, the language were all similar. She accepted my observation that the influence of Sichuan language and culture, over and above the Mandarin culture that dominated all of China, constituted a further challenge to Tibetan life in Sichuan.

What was most intriguing to me was the possibility that the Tibetan part of Sichuan that I had seen, one of the areas of China farthest from Communist influence, was, by force of geography, one of the places best suited to implementing a core element of the Communist Party prescription for China's future: namely, the consolidation of land to facilitate modern, mechanized, large-scale agriculture.

Especially in the ranching areas west of Litang, livestock from different herds commonly grazed together in open pasture. Distinctive neckbands made it possible to determine ownership. To amalgamate the entire herd in a village, and give each farmer a share, would streamline the effort and eliminate the need for entire families to camp out in tents. It would also make it easier to market butter and other animal products.

To be sure, the days of subsistence agriculture were numbered. The pressure to earn hard cash to purchase tractors and fuel, build houses, power TV sets, inoculate herds, and outfit children for school would only grow. As long as they limited themselves to basic needs and no more, Tibetan nomad life was secure. But tractors and TV sets and most of the other items they would want to purchase were manufactured outside of Tibetan areas. Their prices would inevitably climb. Herdsmen, especially, needed to find their way to more and more cash. Scale ranching was the key.

But consolidating ranching operations, as easy as it was to achieve on paper, would challenge the entire traditional Tibetan way of life. Ninety percent of the work force would instantly become superfluous.

Yang Suping thought that within five years the transformation would begin. It was a challenge of first priority for the government.

"YOU ARE NOT SATISFIED," Yang Suping said with slight hesitation as we prepared to part.

I had once again gone fishing, trying to learn a little bit more about her as a person. To try to coax gray from black and white, I had asked her which of her accomplishments in six years as Party secretary and mayor of Kangding she was most proud.

"Making life easier for the people," was all the detail she had to offer. (One area was helping demobilized soldiers find work, I discovered independently.)

She slipped once in a while, telling me voluntarily that within the last year she had spent six months at the Central Communist Party School in Beijing (an indication that she was on the fast track), and corroborating that, in addition to tourism, her current responsibilities included propaganda, a key post at any level. But when I tried to learn a little more, she closed the door, repeating what she had told me in Kangding: "I don't want to talk about myself."

"It may be," I told her, "that in the future, as the system changes, you might have to open up a little. Perhaps I'm helping you prepare for that day."

She pressed her palms and fingers together and bowed her head slightly. A measure of thanks, I think.

China's Mountain People

□□□

OR AN HOUR ON THE BUS bound for Big Black Mountain,* Chen Menchu and I had been passing notes back and forth in Chinese to supplement his heavily accented Mandarin. Chen Menchu was an elementary school teacher in a remote rural village, and he was returning to the village after visiting his son, a junior high school student in the county town of Lüchun. All of the hamlets in the area were populated by the Hani minority, he clarified. "If you want to really understand village folk customs, get off the bus with me."

There followed a string of mild caveats.

"You aren't afraid of mountain roads, are you?" Chen asked, sort of off-the-cuff.

"*Bu pa*," I replied in the negative, assuming that the nine-mile journey ahead would be in one of the rickety, smoke-belching minibuses common to rural China. It was only after we got off the bus, astride the Zhe E River, in the middle of nowhere, one-third the distance to Big Black Mountain, that what was ahead began to emerge.

---

* *Da Hei Shan* in Chinese.

WHEN ONE SPEAKS OF THE MULTITUDES of China, he is most commonly referring to the Han race, constituting about ninety-one percent of China's population, which has dominated Chinese history through the ages. In fact, the most common Chinese term for the Chinese language—the great unifier of the Chinese people—is the Han language.

But the dominant Han aside, China boasts fifty-five official minorities, numbering over one hundred million people. Some, such as the Uighurs of the Xinjiang Uighur Autonomous Region in Northwest China, carry decidedly European characteristics, reflecting their Central Asian and Middle Eastern ancestry; others, including some Hui Muslims, are indistinguishable in appearance from the mainstream Han.

No place in China is better to learn about China's minorities than Yunnan Province, sharing borders with Vietnam, Laos, and Myanmar. One-third of Yunnan's population of thirty-five million is minority, and twenty-five of China's fifty-five minorities are represented in Yunnan—among them the Bai, Dai, Miao, Shui, Nu, and Hani.

In contrast to the fate of many members of the Bai, Yi, and Muslim minorities, the Hani people have so far successfully resisted becoming "sinicized"—morphed into Chinese. Living high in the mountains of southern Yunnan, they subsist, 1.25 million strong, in concentrated numbers largely outside the sphere of Chinese influence. (Another 110,000 Hani live across nearby borders in Laos, Myanmar, Thailand, and Vietnam.) Lüchun County, in Red River Prefecture,* five hours south of the Yunnan provincial capital of Kunming and bordering on Vietnam, promised authentic exposure to traditional Hani life, exempt from tourist influences that have turned some of Yunnan's minority people into performers and "culture vendors." Lüchun County, population two hundred thousand, is ninety-seven percent Hani, with twenty thousand living in the county town, and the balance in several hundred mountain villages.

---

* *Honghe Zhou* in Chinese.

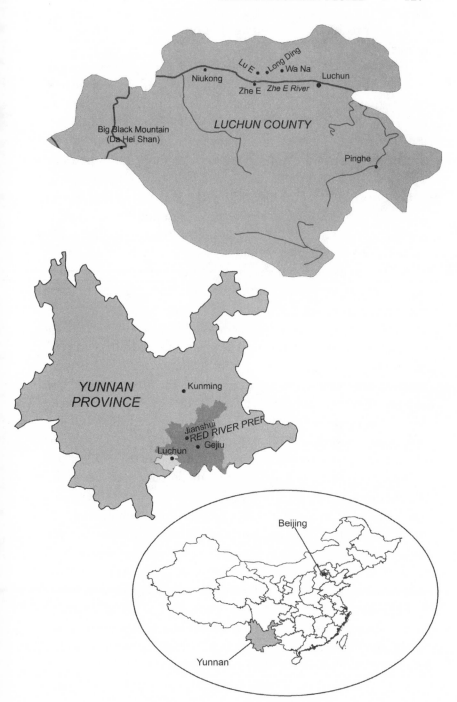

This has precluded the rampant intermarriage that has diluted other minority stock in China.

Getting from Gejiu, the seat of Red River Prefecture and China's tin-mining capital, to Lüchun Town, the administrative center of Lüchun County, entailed a full day's travel. As the crow flies, it is fifty-four miles between Gejiu and Lüchun. But snaking around mountain roads, many in advanced disrepair, that fifty-four miles stretches out to one hundred and fifty-four, taking up to nine-and-a-half hours to complete. One-fourth of the route, straddling the Red River, which flows ultimately into Saigon, is unpaved. So mountainous is Yunnan Province that a glance at a topographical map yields the image of a wrinkled tablecloth. Four buses leave Gejiu for Lüchun daily. But to ensure that they reach Lüchun without having to travel on perilous mountain roads after dark, the last of these leaves Gejiu at 9:10 A.M.

Ma Laran, squat, cranky, fiftyish, had met me—reluctantly, it was immediately apparent—at Lüchun Bus Station as an obligation to Liu Xingyuan, a superior in Gejiu in the Department of Industrial Development. Liu had specifically instructed Ma, a Hani, not to overmanage my visit. But Ma, a bureaucrat to the letter, knew no other way. With him was a friend, a member of the Communist Party Discipline Committee. That wasn't encouraging. Ma took me to a restaurant, saw to it that I had a bowl of noodles, then left me in a dank, partitioned area, announcing that he and his friend were going to another room to "eat and drink." I paid my 25-cent noodle bill and walked back to the Lüchun Guest House—one of Lüchun's best, I was told, at $10 per night.

The following morning, Ma proposed a day trip from Lüchun Town to Pinghe, a collection of Hani villages, where he had grown up. I explained to him my preference to travel alone, suggesting that he write a note of introduction for me; or as a compromise, that he allow me to stay in the village after he returned to Lüchun Town that night.

"*Buxing*. Unacceptable," he said, ruling out anything but a fully supervised experience. I dismissed Ma Laran and, asking at the bus station and around town, set out for Big Black Mountain.

AS WE WERE PREPARING TO GET OFF THE BUS bound for Big Black Mountain, Teacher Chen, himself a Hani, added a last-minute detail: the three-hour mountain journey ahead of us to the village where he taught would be on foot.

After a ten-minute rest, he led the way to a bamboo rope bridge over the Zhe E River to begin our trek to Lu E. A look to the north revealed a river valley meandering through hills of increasing height. The river was flanked by asymmetric vegetable plots, bounded by mounded earth. The "mountain road" we would travel was nothing more than a foot trail. One misstep on the rickety bridge could have taken Teacher Chen into the Zhe E River. But Chen, dressed in a pair of well-worn suit slacks, a green shirt with sleeves rolled up, and a pair of scuffed leather loafers, with a denim backpack on his left shoulder, proceeded as sure-footed as a Sherpa over the swaying bridge. This was a trip he made twice a month, and he was familiar with the terrain. I followed much more hesitantly, taking care to grasp the quivering bridge ropes while negotiating over the large spaces between the bamboo slats that comprised the bridge floor.

For much of the first hour, the terrain was flat or mildly inclined. We walked directly in the river bed, on well-worn foot paths a few inches above the river, and on the earthen dikes, a few inches wide, that demarcated the vegetable fields and retained irrigation water. From time to time, as dictated by topography, we crossed the river, hopping between protruding stones. The earth was firm, easing passage. Early on, Chen had freed me of my twenty-pound satchel, allowing me to use my arms for balance. He was of stocky build, with a slight paunch in the middle, balding in the middle of the forehead, with the first signs of gray. The added burden did not slow his brisk pace.

After an hour, the terrain changed abruptly and the path began to zigzag steeply upward, often at inclines of 45 degrees or more. The stretches of flat terrain became fewer and fewer. This sector was uninhabited; too steep even for terrace cropping. We came across an acquaintance of Chen's, in his twenties, headed to a nearby village. It was impossible to tell how well Chen knew this chap because, as I would soon see, even in the village lanes, where most faces are familiar, Hanis often barely greet their fellows when they pass them.

There were periodic breaks to catch our wind. But it fast became apparent that the Hanis, whose entire life is spent climbing steep mountain trails, often with heavy burdens strapped to their backs, were as fit as pack horses and as uncomplaining. Everything that came into the village was carried in on human backs. For those unaccustomed to altitudes above six thousand feet, an acclimation period was mandatory. Chen's acquaintance, twenty years his junior, took my shoulder bag and, hunching forward to square the burden, positioned the strap on his forehead. This was the traditional Hani way of bearing heavy loads, and freed the arms for balance. We passed a water buffalo, legs folded, passing the time of day just off the trail to Lu E. With planting still a few weeks off, this was the slack season for water buffalo, the closest the Hani came to mechanization.

As we neared the village, it became clear that the Hanis, and not the Hanis alone in China, were coexisting with nature only precariously. Teacher Chen and his acquaintance stopped to pluck and munch on some leaves (eaten as a pickled vegetable in the village) whose name in Hani is *atchi-la-tsa*. An acquired taste. What was curious was that virtually none of the surrounding vegetation had been browsed by animals, as would be the case in normal mountain habitat. Nor were birds plentiful. Most of the animals, Chen acknowledged, had been hunted into extinction. Most obvious was the sparseness of timber. Pine, sweet gum, chestnut, and oak sprouted here and there, but in minimal numbers. Water was plentiful in Lu E, so much so that it was safe to drink the water that streamed down the mountain without boiling (the norm in China). And with a mild climate and a maximum of frost-free days, growth should have been abundant. Yet, so aggressively did the villagers harvest any available tree growth, that dimension timber, a foot or more in diameter, was almost nowhere to be seen around Lu E. When he was a boy, Teacher Chen recalled, there were trees as thick as a man's chest. The Chinese monitored this problem, but policy and enforcement went in opposite directions.

Without seed trees, new tree growth was meager. And without tree habitat, birds could not thrive. Wood was the principal cooking fuel in the village, and the villagers harvested anything that would burn, to the extent that dead tree snags and fallen, decomposing boles, abundant on the floor of any healthy forest, and an essential part of the renewal cycle, were almost nowhere to be seen. Without decaying tree matter, forest fertility could not be replenished, and animals that found refuge in decomposing tree limbs could not thrive. In seeing to their immediate needs, the Hanis were compromising their future. But their imperative was the present: to provide fuel for cooking; and to slash woody vegetation, burn out the roots, and terrace the clearing to provide new cropland for an ever-growing population.

What could be seen in profusion on the slopes around Lu E was what the locals called *jiefang cao*, "liberation grass." The Hanis claimed that only after the Communists liberated China in 1949 did "liberation grass" appear. Now, literally and figuratively, its influence was everywhere.

By the time we reached Lu E village, two hours and fifty-five minutes later, Chen had outlined much of his life story. Born in the village of Si Jiao, almost within eyeview of Lu E, but several hours away by foot, Chen, forty-three, a graduate of the teacher's training college in Jianshui, had been teaching for twenty-one years. He had been transferred to nine different villages within the Niukong district in a space of nine years, before spending the last eleven in Zhe E district.

Chen's hope had been to be transferred to a school nearer to Lüchun Town, where he could be closer to his student son and where he could enjoy the cultural benefits of town life, including television, newspapers, and an opportunity to mingle with educated people who talked about things other than rice, cabbage, and manure. But that dream had been dealt a setback a year earlier when he had instead been transferred to Lu E, a village without electricity whose lanes and byways could not even accommodate a horse-drawn wagon. Chen's wife, also a teacher, was presently stationed in Niukong, thirty to forty miles from Lu E. Without roads, that translated into very few visits each year.

"You can hear the holler around the bend," say the Hanis about this pseudo proximity of village to village, "but to see the hollerer, you need to walk half a day."

TOGETHER, CHEN AND HIS WIFE earned about $185 per month, a respectable sum. But without the economy of a single household, that advantage was lost. About one-fourth of their income went to maintain their son in junior high school. And Chen used much of the rest to support and educate his sister's and brother's children, who were cash poor. Chen's dream, when he retired in seven years at age fifty, was to buy a plot of land on the outskirts of Lüchun and build a house on it, which he estimated would cost about $8,500. How he could ever amass such a sum, he had no idea.

Teacher Chen didn't have a home of his own in Lu E, a village of not quite one thousand, though he said he could have if he so wanted. Instead, he boarded with Zhao Niangma, a wiry, sinewy man of sixty with an unruly shock of black hair, and his wife, Long Weiyou, fifty-six, short like most Hanis, with sad eyes, and a facial expression that never changed. (Chinese women keep their surnames after marriage in China, and the Hanis follow Chinese practice.)

How Chen came to board here was not entirely clear. In part, it was because, alone in Lu E, separated from wife and son, Chen had no one to share with him the abundant housekeeping chores a house entailed. A preference not to strike physical roots in a place where he did not wish to remain was a second factor. For Zhao and his wife, whose children were no longer living at home, Chen provided a measure of companionship, and the status and convenience of having the village teacher, who could read and write, as a member of their household. Chen personally paid for neither his room nor his food, he said, though they well could have been subsidized by the village.

Zhao and Long had four sons. Two worked outside the village as tin-mine laborers, one attended senior high school in Lüchun, and a fourth worked the fields in the village. Of their three daughters, only one remained in the village. According to Hani tradition, a man and a woman with the same surname cannot marry. Since eighty of the ninety-three households in Lu E came from the Zhao line, daughters most commonly left the village, and brides commonly came from outside the village. Though the three generations of Zhaos did not live in the same compound, children and grandchildren visited often and frequently ate with the grandparents.

HANIS EAT JUST TWICE A DAY, at 9:30 in the morning and at 5:30 in the afternoon. That left some time for me to look around. During the peak farming season, this meal schedule provides several hours of daylight work time before breakfast and then a long stretch in the fields until dinner. For some in the village, it took the better part of an hour to reach their plots. Returning home for lunch was impractical.

What stood out immediately about the three-story Zhao house was that, while providing ample living space (several hundred square feet) by Chinese city standards, no sharp distinction was drawn between living and utility areas. In any one spot you were just as likely to find a brick as a banana. At one end of the main room, for example, where Zhao and his wife slept at right angles on two bunks with tightly woven straw mattresses attached to a wood frame, was a pile of earth used to replaster the mud-brick walls. In the adjacent corner, Farmer Zhao called attention to a duck resting on a bed of straw. He lifted the front end of the duck to reveal a clutch of incubating eggs just about ready to hatch.

Just over the raised threshold to the Zhao house (sufficiently high to keep the chickens out), to the left and right, were the dining and cooking spaces, with packed earthen floors. Next to the hearth area, where Mrs. Long was at work spooning beans, duck eggs, and the tofu Teacher Chen had brought from town into the wok, was a store of cooking utensils and condiments. The wok was recessed into slabs of chiseled stone that formed a counter. Zhao Niangma had forged the knives and cleavers himself in his ironwork shop. A small window, just several inches square, allowed some of the cooking smoke to escape. Most of it, however, settled in the wooden planks and rafters above, preserving the wood in the process, and imposing an ever-present smell of rancid smoke on the kitchen area.

Near the entranceway, where the lighting was better, Zhao was sitting and peeling bamboo sprouts with his cleaver for dinner. The peelings, destined for the ducks and chickens, were pared right onto the floor. Whether peeling, eating, chatting, feeding a baby, or smoking their ubiquitous two-foot-long, hollow bamboo pipes, the Hanis sit on round, calf-high, tapered stools woven from reeds—resembling upside-down waste baskets.

The Hani diet, unlike some of the other Chinese minorities, does not differ substantially from mainstream China. The staple is a particularly dry, rough-textured rice. Hanis consume several bowls of rice at every meal, supplemented with vegetables, eggs, and occasionally meat. (Zhao kept a store of salted, roasted pork on the second floor.) Without their rice, Hanis claim, they would feel "uncomfortable, listless." Breakfast and dinner menus are the same, with leftovers carried from meal to meal. Except for cooking oil, salt, and other condiments, the Hanis eat only what they grow. In Lu E, that translated into very little fruit.

Where Hanis differ from the majority of Chinese (themselves heavy drinkers) is that with every meal, morning or evening, Hanis consume three to four three-ounce glasses of forty to fifty percent home-distilled corn or rice alcohol. Unlike in most of China, where refusing to drink with hosts is considered an insult to the point of generating anger, for the Hanis, alcohol is more a dinner beverage, without strong social implication. The true tale is liver-based; but neither Zhao Niangma nor Teacher Chen seemed to be in any way less coherent after meals than before.

Halfway through dinner, after placing a long-necked bottle of honey on the knee-high dinner table for me to drink—an intended treat—Mrs. Long took time out to fetch four family ducks from the rice paddy where they spent their days. While his wife was bringing in the ducks, Zhao brought out some of his iron craft to show.

Just two or three minutes outside his door, on the main lane leading to the watering hole, Zhao had set up a work area, sheltered by a thatched roof, where he did his forging. His trade tools were very crude: bellows fashioned out of a hollowed log, an anvil mounted on a stout tree stump, and a handcrafted vise. But he fabricated high quality implements: hoe heads (75 cents), scythes ($1.00), and hatchets ($1.80). Most of these were sold or bartered inside the village. Zhao could make seven or eight of these in a day. These staples of village toil aside, Zhao brought out a handcrafted pistol and hunting rifle. They could be had for $10 and $25, respectively. These were crude firearms, reminiscent of museum pieces, but Zhao strutted a certain pride as he posed with the rifle slung over his shoulder, formation style. Only the many metal detectors on the road ahead kept me from making a purchase.

LIKE ALL FAMILIES IN LU E, ZHAO family income consisted of the food they grew plus the cash they could earn. Zhao was an above average farmer according to Teacher Chen, growing cabbage, cucumbers, potatoes, sorghum, bamboo, pears, chestnuts, peanuts, dwarf bananas, eggplants, greens, and *wu xuan* (eaten leaf and root). Some of these crops, such as the finger bananas he brought to my room one evening, were so seasonal or grown in such limited amounts as to be almost delicacies. And there were chickens, ducks, and a pig. But no dairy products.

Zhao had harvested five thousand pounds of rice—the main cash and food crop—the previous season and sold half of it. Since he owned the land, used his own seed, and spent nothing on fertilizer or pesticides, the $335 he earned was pure profit. Market-destined rice, as well as surplus vegetables, particularly cabbage, were sold at the weekly "market day," or *gan ji*, a fixture of rural life all across China from ancient times. Every Saturday, throughout the area, thousands of villagers, riding every conceivable conveyance, converged on the county town of Lüchun, or the district town of Niukong, to market whatever surplus they had to sell and buy what was not available in the village: rice, vegetables, eggs, thread, bed frames, puppies, kittens, brushes, chicks, underwear, hardware. When too heavy to haul on their backs, villagers sometimes carried goods destined for market to an intermediate drop-off point from where they were transported to market for a fee.

Market days, where villagers and townsfolk alike often fill every street space in the market town, are giant festivals bringing together every stratum of the population from every nook and cranny of the area. For the townspeople, these markets provide an open-air superstore; for the younger villagers, they offer a respite from the sameness of daily life; for the outsider, they present an instant window on the area. But market days also take a physical toll on the villagers, frequently requiring hours of tiring travel, and still longer hours spent squatting on an earthen curb. Not everything brought out for sale from the village finds a buyer; not every visit to the market town generates enough income to permit villagers to execute their shopping lists. Zhao Niangma preferred to stay in the village on market days and leave the selling and buying to others.

Cash income varied widely in Lu E, from as low as $4 or $5 per month up to $200. Zhao monthly family cash income came to $85 or $90, a bit above average for the village. It was the cash income a family could accumulate that would most decide whether and how long a child could stay in school.

FORMING A COURT AREA IN THE FRONT of the Zhao house were two wings that protruded from the main building. On the second floor of each wing, reached via two planks joined by logs to form a stepping ramp, were two sleeping rooms. The one that Chen gave up for me had a hole in the wooden floor, several spare bricks, and some tools. The crude bunk bed was made of wooden planks. There were no other furnishings, not even a stool. The room door had a lock, but it had no function, because a foot to the right, cut in the wood plank wall, was an opening wide enough to insert a hand to open the lock. The second sleeping room, across the courtyard, contained a wooden bunk and a small school desk (formerly used by Zhao's sons, now used by Chen for paperwork). The space under the dormers was used to store the charcoal Zhao used for his iron-work, tools, and a small boat (a curiosity, since there were no bodies of water anywhere near Lu E).

Moreso even than their layout, the single distinguishing characteristic of Hani homes is that they contain few windows. And those windows that do exist, mostly in the kitchen, provide ventilation rather than light. Zhao Niangma's home contained no windows other than the one in the kitchen. The reason offered was to provide security: so that outsiders could not see what was going on inside. This same function was provided by high courtyard walls in many Chinese farm villages.

Since Lu E had no electricity, the interior of most houses was cast in almost perpetual darkness. But, since the Hani language has no written form and few Hanis above fifty are literate in Chinese, they had no need for reading light. (Zhao Niangma could only write the name of one of his seven children when asked.) During the growing season, Hanis went to bed early and arose at daybreak, living most of their productive lives out of doors in daylight. Cooking fires provided most of the visibility needed for food preparation. For minimum light while chatting in the evening, for children doing homework, or to locate something in the dark, Hanis use candles and flashlights. Near his bed in the loft where Chen usually slept was a candle to read the magazines he brought back from Lüchun. They were stashed under his pillow. Lanterns fueled by kerosene would have provided better lighting than candles, but purchasing kerosene would have strained limited cash, and bringing kerosene in through the mountains by foot was a heavy physical burden.

I WAS UP THE NEXT DAY at the crack of dawn, preparing to accompany Teacher Chen to school. Morning washing in homes without running water follows a familiar pattern across China, and Chen was a schooled practitioner. He first filled an enameled basin with a small amount of water heated on the stove, then added just enough cold water to retain the heat. No more than two inches of water filled the basin. The face, hands, and arms were then thoroughly moistened and lathered with soap. With a wash cloth, he scrubbed soaped areas diligently, with special attention to the neck. The face and other soaped areas were then rinsed with the remaining water and the wash cloth rinsed, wrung out, and hung on the line to dry. Before bedtime, the same bathing ritual was followed with the feet and hair sometimes washed as well.

School would begin at 7:30 and run until 9:30. But before school an additional formality had to be understood. In most Chinese homes without indoor plumbing (reaching seventy percent or more), there is a family outhouse in the yard or, in built-up areas, on the street, serving several households. (Chamber pots take care of late-night needs.) In urban areas, the latrine is always enclosed; in rural areas, it may or may not be enclosed. In Lu E, Teacher Chen explained, formal outhouses had been abandoned. The pigs played havoc with them. He recited the Chinese couplet telling how nature's call was answered:

> Xiao bian, sui bian,
> Da bian, yuan yi dian.
> "Small business," anywhere,
> "Big business," well away from here.

"Well away from here," this day translated into the western edge of the village, past the schoolhouse, adjoining three gravesites. Unlike urban Chinese, who cremate their dead, much of rural China still buries its deceased. These graves, several years old, consisted of stones mounded around a raised bed of earth, with wild plants intentionally or unintentionally decorating them. It seemed irreverent to situate the "bathroom" so close to the graveyard, but the Hanis didn't see it that way.

It turned out that Teacher Chen had only given me part of the bathroom tale. Situated barely minutes from the Zhao compound, just to the left of their rice and vegetable plots, was a more traditional outhouse, surrounded by slats of wood to shield it from view. With wide gaps between the floor boards, and with a drop below of ten or more feet, this was a place for the nimble. (Chen was afraid that I would fall through.) Convenience aside, this location provided the Zhaos with natural fertilizer to augment the pig and buffalo manure that nourished their crops.

HALFWAY TO THE SCHOOLHOUSE, just as we were negotiating a narrow path between a village stream and a water-filled rice paddy, a melodious chorus was heard in the distance. It resembled a Gregorian chant in its precision, but with a sweeter tone. This was a call heard from schoolrooms across China just before the teacher arrives: elementary school students reciting from their readers in unison at the top of their lungs to a melody prescribed by Mandarin's four tones.

Education was what divided the villagers of Lu E. According to Chinese law, both elementary and junior high school are free and compulsory. But "free" does not include three school "fees": instructional fee, miscellaneous fee, and textbook fee, running $9 or $10 per semester. A serious sum to the poorest Lu E families, whose total cash income was just $4 or $5 per month.

ILLITERACY IS A SYMBOL OF POVERTY AND BACKWARDNESS, read slogans in two-foot-high letters all across southern Yunnan. There were no such signs in Lu E... and many nonreaders.

Teacher Chen estimated that, in addition to the eleven students registered for the first grade, there were seven or eight more who were not attending school. Lack of parent interest in education (especially for girls) was one factor (Zhao Niangma's eight-year-old granddaughter was one non-attender); cost was a second; China's population control policy, generally limiting minority rural families to three children, was a third. Trying to register an extra schoolchild was one sure way of informing the authorities that a couple had breached the child-limit policy. Each day, five or six children hung by the open doors of the schoolhouse or peered in through the barred but glassless windows. Some, it was obvious, were trying to meet the text with their eyes. Chen, who taught the third grade (sixteen students and a dog), shooed away those who lingered by the door;

the two assistant teachers, from inside the village, who taught the first two grades, were more compassionate.

Government financing from outside the village made possible a sturdy, four-room, brick schoolhouse with concrete floors. But the rooms were stark, with bare walls, and the crude wooden desks, each accommodating three students, had seen many years of service. There was no play area, not even the basketball hoop found at almost every schoolyard in China. What toys the children of Lu E had, they made themselves.

During most of the year, there was enough daylight to read by. At other times, students studied by candlelight.

The elementary school curriculum across China is unified, so the Lu E students, in theory, have the same learning opportunities as other children. Chen began the day reading from volume 6 of the language arts text. Recitation was in Mandarin, the official teaching language. Each student had his own copy. Because learning to read and write Chinese characters always lags behind acquiring vocabulary, even before they start to memorize characters, schoolchildren are taught to write in the Latin-character, phonetic transcription system known as *Pinyin*. Pinyin transcription is accompanied by a tone indicator above the word. A tone change yields a different meaning.

Periodically, Chen would explain a word or phrase—either in the Hani language or in Mandarin. Elementary education in Lu E, of necessity, is bilingual, with the emphasis on Mandarin rather than on Hani. Occasionally, Chen would chalk an equivalent meaning on the planks that served as the blackboard— the character for "black" to explain "dark," the character for "river" to explain "brook." I pulled myself into an empty, first-row desk next to a youngster with a reversed baseball cap (the current fad in Lu E) as Teacher Chen again reread the text and students went about practicing their penmanship. School children in Lu E would be exposed to the basics, but without television and without educated parents at home to help them, there could be no reinforcement.

At recess outside the schoolhouse, as I sat resting on a stone, every one of the students circled around to peer at me. To try to draw them out in basic conversation, I wrote my Chinese name in my notebook and asked them to write their own. As I got up to offer pen and paper to one of the kids, a few of them tried to "trick" me by moving the stone. A small breakthrough. But it took until the afternoon recess to get them to respond in larger numbers. Zhao Dezhe, Zhao Baifa, Zhao Sangao, Zhao Shengfu, and Li Cailong all found their way into my notebook, confirming what Chen had told me: that in eighty of ninety-three households in Lu E, the father was surnamed Zhao. These were children who not only had never seen a foreigner, they had rarely if ever met a Chinese. By late afternoon, when I was strolling through the village before dinner, some of them would call out my Chinese name, Ke Tianxi.

Though the Hani all take and use Chinese names in their daily life, the Chinese characters chosen sometimes set them apart from Han Chinese. A Chinese man, for example, virtually never uses the characters *ma*, meaning "horse," or *niang*, meaning "woman," in their first names, as did my host Zhao Niangma. Similarly, place names such as Lu E and Zhe E, likely rough transliterations for Hani place names, provide strange sound combinations in Mandarin.

Chen Menchu was an interested teacher. One of his goals before he finished his teaching career was to cultivate a few students who would graduate from college. But Chen was working against very long odds, the first of which was language. Chen himself spoke a very nonstandard Mandarin, and since, without radio or television, he was the only pronunciation model, his students, too, would learn imprecisely. The situation was marginally better in other villages with younger teachers who had learned more standard Chinese. Year by year unification through language in China—one of the outstanding successes of the Chinese Communist government—was moving ahead. But it would be a generation or more before Mandarin would penetrate China's remotest villages and bridge the language and culture gap.

For most children in Lu E, any education they were to receive would have to be absorbed within three years. Lu E Elementary School offered only three grades. For grades 4 through 6, students whose parents could afford it would have to board during the school week in the adjoining village of Long Ding, a two-hour walk away. And if they wanted to continue on to junior high school, they would have to board in Lüchun, entailing less frequent visits home and steeper boarding fees. All of this ran heavily against any single child ever graduating from high school.

"The cocks and the dogs can be heard from village to village, but you can go from life to death without ever seeing neighboring villagers."

SO ISOLATED WERE THE VILLAGERS of Lu E that few of them had ever heard of the Olympic Games, a Chinese obsession; few of them knew anything about soccer, the number-one sports passion in China; few were aware of the Taiwan issue. When I asked Zhao Niangma during dinner whether he had heard the name of the American president, he responded with the name of the only American president with whom he was familiar: Ni-ke-song (Nixon).

Zhao Niangma told me that he used to listen to the radio, but he gave it up when the batteries ran out. That, apparently, was a very long time ago. The only moderately current outside information the children of Lu E seemed to have was of pop tunes on the Chinese hit parade. Some who had traveled outside the village had purchased battery-operated tape recorders and cassettes.

Because the elementary school curriculum provides all children in China with identical content, humorous incongruities sometimes result. The afternoon session, which ran from noon to 1:30, opened one day with a lesson on the human body. It seemed like a good lesson, supported by a well-illustrated text in color, describing the various bones and joints of the body.

"If you exercise," Teacher Chen read from the text to kids who wouldn't know a beach ball from a volleyball, "your bones will grow longer and stronger." These were kids whose every day was exercise: stamina built by climbing steep mountains almost from infancy; strength built by carrying heavy loads on their backs; dexterity learned by straddling slippery berms between rice paddies almost from the day that they learned to walk. There were no playing fields, no sports teams, no exercise classes in Lu E. Nor were there many back problems.

I was interested in knowing whether the villagers, as a minority, felt economically or culturally discriminated against in any way. Abundant reports in China filter through of unscrupulous officials who squeeze China's peasants to the bone, exacting every conceivable levy from their meager existence. At the extreme, peasant exploitation has led to rioting. Speaking to Zhao Niangma at least, that wasn't the case in Lu E. He was taxed sixty-six pounds of grain per year. That to Zhao was reasonable.

As a community without electricity, without a road leading to the outside world, certainly Lu E qualified as poor, neglected. But though the villagers of Lu E had little more than their homes, their fields, their simple tools, and their animals, they were better off than many of China's other poor. They lived in an area with abundant water and a moderate, frost-free climate, relieving them of the need to use expensive heating fuels in winter and ensuring regular harvests. And they lived outside the earthquake belt that makes parts of Yunnan to the north an unpredictable place to live.

Their poverty lay not in their inability to sustain themselves at their present level, but in their financial inability to move ahead. For most families in Lu E, sending even one child to junior high school was too expensive; buying an extra pair of shoes or a dictionary was out of reach. And stepping up production to raise income on mountain terraces without mechanized equipment was impossible. It was difficult, watching villagers walking down the village lanes day after day, shovels and hoes slung over their shoulders, not to pause and ponder that preparing a field for planting, which millions of weekend gardeners in the West could accomplish in one or a few hours with a rototiller, could take a day or more in the village. Yet, it was also impossible not to reflect that the farmers of Lu E never knew the frustration of an expensive machine going down at a critical moment for lack of a 50-cent part or a $50 mechanic to install it. The machine they relied upon most was themselves. Unlike the competitive outside world, the Hanis were not a compulsive, nervous people. They flowed with the seasons year to year.

Cultural oppression is a more subtle matter. A curriculum geared toward majority Han Chinese being taught to an isolated minority could not escape anomalies. Among the subjects in the elementary school syllabus was singing, and all three classes (forty-six students this day) gathered in one classroom to sing with assistant teacher Zhao Zhoufa, twenty-six, who presumably had a better voice than Teacher Chen. Those who had no seats sat on schoolmates' desks. The song to be sung by Lu E's Hani children was: "Today Is Your Birthday, China." The kids had been through this song before, and the words were already copied into their notebooks.

One couldn't help wondering how a Hani kid, living in a secluded enclave such as Lu E, could extol at the top of his lungs a "motherland" with which he had only the flimsiest link. As if to be more Catholic than the Pope, assistant teacher Zhao, a Hani, carried the session ten minutes past the 1:30 dismissal time, enough to get in a tenth and eleventh repetition.

AFTER THE SESSION ENDED, I caught up with Zhao Zhoufa, slender like most Hani men and of medium height, and walked with him back to the village. Zhao's conversational Mandarin was even more limited than Teacher Chen's, but we got along. I asked him whether they ever sing Hani songs in class. He appeared not to understand, which might have been a response of convenience. So I repeated the question. "*Bu yunxu women*— They wouldn't permit it," was his simple reply. It would seem that in a curriculum for an officially recognized minority such as the Hanis, with a history stretching back at least fourteen hundred years to the Tang dynasty, there would be some room for Hani culture. But this appeared not to be the case. A totally China-oriented syllabus, together with the absence of any written Hani records, was the reason no one in the village I met had any idea how old Lu E was. (About two hundred years was the only guesstimate anyone would venture.)

I accompanied Zhao Zhoufa back to his parents' home, a mud-brick structure very much like the others in the village, and heard his story. He had scored one point shy in the entrance examination that would have qualified him to study for the same teacher's college teaching certificate that Teacher Chen held. Because he was a middle school graduate, however, the village made use of his education, with one important difference. Whereas Teacher Chen was paid a base salary of 20 yuan ($2.50) per day, Assistant Zhao received one-tenth that sum, 25 cents per day. Whereas Teacher Chen, by virtue of his teaching position, had a town residence permit, allowing him to live and work in Lüchun Town as well as in hamlets throughout the county, Assistant Zhao, classified as a peasant, was tied to Lu E.

Ever so slowly, almost as if he was trying to forestall the inevitable, Assistant Zhao Zhoufa walked into his room and painstakingly began to peel off his tan slacks. He folded them precisely and placed them neatly on his bed. His, too, was a room without windows. Since its walls were made of brick, the room appeared even darker than my room in the village, which allowed in slivers of light through cracks in the wood planks. Next, off came Zhao Zhoufa's pullover bearing a Hewlett Packard insignia, then his shoes and socks. His morning identity now on his chair, he picked up the pace and pulled on a set of dusty work clothes and the strapped plastic sandals worn by almost everyone in the village. The sandals, worn barefoot, solved the problem all in Lu E faced: a lifetime walking through mud and water. Redressing complete, Zhao Zhoufa was now ready to join fellow villagers in placing the last round of mud bricks in the firing pit.

THE OUTER SHELLS OF ALL THE HOUSES in the village were made of mud brick reinforced with straw. Only the schoolhouse and a few homes belonging to better-off farmers were built of commercially made, kiln-fired, clay brick and mortar brought in from outside the village. Cash outlay aside, without roads to accommodate even pack animals, anything that could spare the overtaxed backs of the villagers was to be embraced. Self-sufficiency was the ideal. Mud was everywhere to be found.

So fundamental was mud brick-making to village life that the ubiquitous brick pile was as much a constant of the village vista as the terraced rice paddies, the thatched straw roofs, the meandering creeks, and the ambling, grass-munching water buffalo. Hardly a family did not maintain a stockpile of bricks for ready repairs, and those contemplating a room addition or a new house for offspring began their stockpile long before building began.

The mud bricks were shaped in a wooden form and then stacked on their spines—sometimes in sheltered straw huts—to facilitate drying. When dry, they were positioned, layer upon layer, in circular pits ten feet in diameter and ten feet deep. When the pit was full, straw and wood that had been placed at the bottom of the pit were ignited through a tunnel, and the bricks allowed to bake for twenty-four hours. The bricks at the bottom of the pile, which received more heat, were sturdier (though less attractive) and thus more highly coveted.

Lu E's villagers farmed their land and managed their finances as individuals. But brick making, like house raising, being so labor intensive, was a collective undertaking. Labor swapping—first among family members, then among neighbors—was one of the chat topics after dinner over the bamboo pipe. Because the masonry skills of villagers varied widely, so too did the appearances of finished houses, which ranged from as elegant as well-pointed brick to primitive rustic.

IT WAS A TEN-MINUTE WALK from Zhao Niangma's house in the center of the village to the watering hole at the east end. Past Zhao's post-and-rail water buffalo stall with a thatched roof, twenty steps down an earthen lane, then a skip and a hop onto a slender board bridging a small stream brought you to the main passageway, where one day two untethered asses amused themselves close to where Zhao forged the iron tools that provided much of his income.

It didn't take many trips between Zhao's place and the watering hole to see all of village life unfold: school lads shepherding ducklings; a blossoming maiden leading a milking cow to its shed; a bushy-haired fellow in his twenties, on his way home from his plot, pausing to wash a muddy hoe and shovel in the stream.

Above and below were the rice terraces, rising some six hundred feet from the foot of the valley to the crown of the mountain above. Contoured by the swerves of the mountainside—sometimes as long and sleek as a carrot, sometimes as plump as an eggplant—these intricately patterned rice plantings, drawing on an agricultural engineering tradition two thousand years old, defined the Hani village. It was the abundant mountain water that had brought the Hanis to these mountains. "No matter how high you go on the mountain," say the Hanis, "you can always find water."

Most of the paddies in Lu E were still fallow with the sullen, brown look of winter, but a few sported the light green hue of slender seedlings. When they reached ten inches in a few weeks' time, these seedlings would be transplanted in paddies throughout the village for fall harvest. On occasion, a farmer could be seen in the distance carefully mending a fissure in the wall of his paddy. Every family worked for itself, but the interdependent, tiered system of agriculture dictated by the steep mountain slopes required that, in addition to bringing his own crop to harvest, he diligently keep the mud walls of his fields in good repair. A breach in his walls could affect all of the terraces further down.

DOWN THE LANE COMES A VILLAGER, *a handsome chap in a woolen jacket with leather epaulettes. Slung over his shoulder is a wooden plow, bowed, notched, and fastened with rope according to age-old design. Today or tomorrow or the morrow after tomorrow, he will hitch up his ox and, clad in rubber boots, guide him through a sodden field in a perennial spring ritual.*

A slouching woman, in her twenties or thirties or forties—not always easy to tell—prepares to step through the stream with a slew of crooked tree boughs harnessed to her shoulders. These were hacked—perhaps with one of Zhao Niangma's hatchets—from a thicket in the heights above Lu E. So tall are these limbs that from the rear they appear to be walking by themselves. The wood rests on a padded back shield, woven and stitched from banana leaves, worn across the shoulders, and fastened in the front. After the wood has had a chance to season, perhaps it too will form the bowed anchor of another plow, or the railing of a water buffalo enclosure, or the leg of a table, or the fuel for next winter's supper.

A hunched, laboring lady, wearing navy culottes decorated with silver border stripes, passes by, followed by a child of no more than ten or eleven. Blue is the traditional color worn by married Hani women in Lu E, often matched by a self-made navy kerchief, called a bao tou, *whose decorative pattern varies from village to village. (Unmarried women and men of all ages, on the other hand, wear common Western dress.) Harnessed on the hunched woman's back, stabilized by a sash across her forehead, are eighteen bricks. The child, mirroring her in posture, carries only four. A rough tally on the lane concludes that Hani women do most of the village hauling. The pace of activity is measured, almost as if by a metronome. Rarely is anyone seen rushing to complete a task. Ages ago the Hanis plotted their labor season by season. Now they are just following the blueprint.*

FOOT TRAFFIC ON THE PRINCIPAL VILLAGE walkway would have thinned significantly if the villagers were a bit more aggressive in solving problems. Lu E villagers were more fortunate than most in China in that they had limitless quantities of uncontaminated mountain water. But even though it was well within their engineering means, they had no system for piping the water to individual homes. So, several times each day, someone from the household, most often a woman, had to walk to a central water source (a pipe leading higher up the mountain) and carry back two pails of water suspended from a bamboo pole balanced on her shoulder.

Before I arrived, the pipe leading to the water source broke, requiring every water drawer to travel several hundred additional yards each time water was needed. A simple repair was all that was required, at most a new section of pipe easily available in Lüchun. But instead of dispatching one of the villagers to the county town immediately, a month had now passed. And just as likely another month would pass before that pipe would be fixed.

I NEEDED TO WASH OUT SOME clothes and, between morning and afternoon class sessions, Teacher Chen led me to the washing area at the edge of the village. Two plastic pipes fed water from higher up the mountain slope into a rock-strewn area amidst a clump of vegetation. The location, used for bathing as well as clothes washing, provided a small measure of privacy. A pregnant woman and her toddler were finishing up their washing, so we tarried in the distance to wait our turn.

Hanis change their clothes "occasionally," Chen said, which meant every few days or every few weeks. Clothes washing was too inconvenient a task to become a daily ritual, and most villagers had just one or two changes. When they did wash clothes, they went at it vigorously, using heavy lye soap, scrub brushes, and sometimes stones to beat out every grain of embedded grime. After he scrubbed each item for me—underwear, socks, shirt—Chen wrung it out and hung it on a nearby bush. That was my primer.

That afternoon, I returned to the washing hole with Chen for a more comprehensive lesson. Chen wanted to take advantage of a sunny day to wash his own wardrobe. He brought along an enameled metal wash pan, soap, and a spare set of outerwear.

In China's cities, the Western suit jacket sold with matching trousers is viewed as formal wear. Often the sleeve label is left in place to parade the status of the manufacturer. In the countryside, the suit jacket quickly becomes an ordinary jacket, worn even by laborers or farmers as they toil.

Methodically, Chen took off each garment, first lathering it, then scrubbing and pounding it in the wash pan before rinsing, wringing, and hanging it out on a bush or a boulder: suit jacket...trousers...shirt...tee shirt...socks. Next, he proceeded to scrub himself, including his hair. His undershorts, however, remained in place as he reached inside to finish the job. This is how the delicate issue of modesty was addressed in a public wash area.

As Chen went through his washing routine, we drifted into a little home-cooked philosophy. The villagers of Lu E are basically stoics. Resignation is their fundamental psychological prop. You could see it in the difference in facial expression between the children (who smiled like kids everywhere) and the adults. The older they got, it seemed, the more sullen they grew.

Teacher Chen in some ways represented the transition between dreams and resignation. As a trained professional, he enjoyed the possibility of career advancement. But now he was in Lu E, washing his clothes in a village stream and walking six hours every other weekend to see his son. "Dreams?" he asked rhetorically, reaching into his bottomless bag of Chinese aphorisms: "*Xin xiang er li bu zu...* People in Lu E, me, we all have dreams, but we don't have a way to carry them through." From the watering hole, we could almost see Teacher Chen's birthplace, Wa Na Township, across the valley. He hadn't traveled very far.

"Everyone has his own ideals," he mused. "*You chi, bu bing, jiu hao.* If you have food, if you remain healthy, that's good enough."

And, for the most part, the villagers were healthy, some living into their eighties and nineties. Twice a year a paramedic or nurse from Lüchun came into Lu E to inoculate the children. For common ailments, such as toothaches, there were traditional remedies ("the more bitter the better"). Most in the village had never seen a doctor.

As he finished up with his washing, Teacher Chen realized he had forgotten two necessities: a towel and a spare pair of socks. A few minutes in the open air took care of the former. He resolved the latter by putting on the wet socks he had just washed. They would dry in a few hours, he said.

We digressed to the question of myopia. I had noticed that no one in the village wore glasses. "Nearsightedness is very rare here," Chen wrote out on a scrap of paper. It would have been interesting to give the villagers eye tests.

An area of agreement with Chen at the water hole was that change was coming to Lu E. High on the hill, at the edge of the village, was a forty-foot, wooden stanchion supporting three high-capacity electrical lines. They came from Long Ding, the administrative village across the valley that handled the affairs of Lu E and five other nearby villages. (It was precisely this system of administration that ensured that no village in China—no matter how remote, no matter how backward—would escape oversight.) The electric lines had been in place for six months. Now it was up to the villagers to agree to pay the fees that would bring Lu E into the twenty-first century. That would be a slow decision.

To say that Lu E was without electricity was technically inaccurate. One family was ahead of its time. Word had it that they had set themselves up with a VCR. I followed the wires through the rice paddies to find water coursing through a two-inch pipe feeding a tiny turbine about the size of a small melon. Two thin wires, capable of carrying enough juice to power one small appliance protruded from the pint-size generator. I traced the lines back to the house to inquire about the VCR. The lady at the door, however, claimed ignorance. There was more to this story.

There was one person in Lu E who could have clarified for me more precisely the electrification plans for the village. And no doubt he could have provided more exact village statistics than I could get from talking to the *laobaixing*, the simple villagers. But checking in with the village head, who in Hani villages also often performed the quasi-religious function of *ru ma* or *ang ma*, meant checking in with official China, and that often paid negative dividends. There is hardly a village in China that the Communist Party does not reach.

There were about ten Communist Party members in Lu E. Those few who had joined the Party at the time of "Liberation" (1949) were illiterate. For the village head, joining the Party was a job requirement. For Teacher Chen (who had joined in 1995 and paid monthly Party dues of about 20 cents) and the others, Party membership was an expedient to job advancement.

ONE ENTERTAINMENT OPTION that required neither batteries nor electricity was an enchanting chorus that drew me out of the first stages of sleep past ten one night. The Chinese call this type of musical repartee *dui ge*, a staple of rural village life and particularly popular among China's minorities. Often, it takes place after dark, commonly between unmarried lads and lasses sifting through potential mates. Among the Hani, remaining single much past age twenty is taboo. I asked one of the villagers what would happen if someone reached twenty-two and just didn't want to get married. *"Impossible,"* he said.

It was the lilting, teasing, coy *dui ge* that grabbed at me that first night. In the nights that followed, I waited for these alluring chants to return...but in vain.

Here is how it might have played out.

A villager of means seeks to betroth a reluctant, comely miss. He enlists several clever young men to represent him in song. They pose four questions. If she fails to field any of them, she must agree to marry him; if she responds adequately, she retains her freedom.

> *Challenge 1*: What is round on the top and square on the bottom?
>
> *Repartee*: A *bamboo basket* is round on the top and square on the bottom.
>
> *Challenge 2*: What is round on the bottom and square on the top?
>
> *Repartee*: *Chopsticks* are round on the bottom and square on the top.
>
> *Challenge 3*: What is round on the inside and square on the outside?
>
> *Repartee*: A *wood stove* is round on the inside and square on the outside.
>
> *Challenge 4*: What is round on the outside and square on the inside?
>
> *Repartee*: A *coin* is round on the outside and square on the inside.
>
> Freedom reigns.

AMONG THE HANI, *DUI GE* are also a prominent entertainment feature of the two yearly festivals, both celebrated according to the lunar calendar: the "Tenth Month" festival (the Hani New Year holiday), celebrated for six days, which also serves as the harvest festival; and the "Sixth Month" festival, celebrated for three to six days. Each holiday features elaborate drumming and other traditional music; fan and pole dancing; village-wide, open-air drinking fests; holiday foods such as roast pig; traditional Hani sporting contests; and festive holiday dress. Zhao Niangma's wife brought out a carefully folded, ankle-length tunic, worn under a bodice with precisely embroidered sleevelets, and fastened at the neck by an intricate silver brooch. This was her occasion-wear for weddings, funerals, and festivals.

THE TRIP OUT OF LU E was problematic. It was about two hours by foot from Lu E to Long Ding. Long Ding, the administrative village and a bit less populous than Lu E, was the end point of a dirt road connecting to the county seat of Lüchun. But it was entirely possible that no motorized vehicle would travel out of Long Ding that day. Teacher Chen had a sister in Long Ding, and he skipped the afternoon class to accompany me there.

It took forty minutes to walk down the mountain to the ravine that separated Lu E from Long Ding. Lu E's fields stretched almost that far. Midway down, we snacked on some wild orange berries called *huang pao*. Hani villages are typically situated on the upper third of the mountain, with fields above and below. That meant that some villagers had to walk two hours round trip every time they needed to tend their fields. Zhao Niangma's vegetable and rice fields, in contrast, were just a few minutes from his home. In a year, that constituted days or weeks of work time and energy saved. Some plots—closer, more sunlit, better irrigated—were choicer than others. How plot ownership was determined was one of the major political decisions of each village. Villagers are very precise about their ownership of even a single tree. Later that day, Teacher Chen would pinpoint for me a tree planted by a relative decades ago to which he had harvest rights.

The pattern of life in Long Ding was little different from that of Lu E. Teacher Chen's older sister, a solid-looking woman in her forties who projected pride in her carriage, was busy stitching the traditional Hani back harness, the *suo yi*, from banana leaves when we arrived. She was illiterate, Chen had told me. The village women, most with the traditional blue *bao tou* on their heads, were indistinguishable from the women of Lu E.

But there were important differences between Lu E and Long Ding. The forest surrounding Long Ding was lusher than in Lu E, permitting a cottage industry that manufactured wooden doors. The clothes washing area in Long Ding, close to the dwellings, was constructed of stone and served by a spigot, spelling convenience. Most significantly, for more than twenty years, Long Ding had had electricity, and for fifteen years television. Roads, even a dirt road, meant that goods could be trucked in instead of carried in. Long Ding had a small store where sweets, cookies, and household items were for sale. There were newspapers: *The Red River Daily* and *The People's Daily*. Long Ding had a basketball court. The children of Long Ding knew about Michael Jordan and the NBA. Many in Lu E had never heard of basketball.

Lu E would not jump into the age of electricity with both feet. Hanis are excruciatingly slow to change. That is a Hani survival mechanism. And without a road in and out, the value of electricity would be limited. But a look at Long Ding pointed toward where Lu E was headed. With the information intrusion electricity would bring, Lu E's youth would be less inclined to remain in the village, and the vitality of Lu E would be challenged. Relying on nothing more than a plot of land, one water buffalo, a few simple tools, and their own backs, Hanis could get along with a minimum of cash. Once they began to depend on electricity and the luxuries and conveniences it offered, the pressures of a cash economy were inevitable. Before Lu E became richer, it would almost certainly become poorer.

The distinguishing factors that permitted the Hanis to maintain their separate identity over more than a thousand years were easy to pinpoint: their Hani language; the dress of their married women, symbolized by their *bao tou* headwear and back harnesses; their isolated mountain life, physically separated from other peoples and outside influences. They practiced no unifying religion as did the Muslims of China. And, more so than most other minorities in China, Hani cuisine, based heavily on rice, was very similar to the cuisine of the majority Han Chinese. More than anything else, the fact that seventy percent of their small population lived in concentrated numbers in and around Red River Prefecture in southern Yunnan Province is what allowed them to endure. Modernization and integration did not bode well for the Hanis.

There was a young woman in Long Ding I met only fleetingly who symbolized the conflict between change and tradition among the Hanis. Her name was Li Yunmei and she had obtained a post-secondary school certificate in computers. For some reason, she had been unable to find a job and had returned to the village. Her dress: jeans, form-fitting top, immediately set her apart from the villagers. It was impossible to imagine her wearing a *bao tou* on her head or washing clothes in a stream. I asked for her name and she wrote down her beeper number as well: 127-005xxxx. *The closest phone to Long Ding village was a forty-five minute walk away.*

AS IT TURNED OUT, I could have had a ride out of Long Ding to Lüchun Town that night, but preferred to have one more evening in the villages. Chen agreed to accompany me to the next village, Wa Na, near his birthplace, which would put me a bit closer to Lüchun the next morning. To walk forty-five minutes on level ground was a luxury.

Hanis traditionally limit village size to between forty and one hundred households. Once a village is established, symbolized by the installation of a village head, new households cannot join. When village population begins to strain the carrying capacity of the land, villagers commonly splinter off, establishing a new village under a new village head. There were numerous hamlets in the area whose name was prefixed by "Upper" or "Lower," designating such splintering. With two hundred households and more than thirty-four hundred residents, Wa Na was far larger than most Hani villages.

The teachers at the village school in Wa Na, where Chen arranged for me to stay, were on average fifteen years younger than Chen. This was the closest the Hani came to an intellectual class. We had a wide-ranging chat around the card table that night. One of the legends Hanis like to repeat is that Hanis, migrating from Yunnan to Vietnam, Laos, Thailand, and Burma, eventually reached Japan, evolving into the Japanese people. The Japanese have different thoughts.

Teacher Chen had to be back in Lu E early the next morning or he would lose a day's pay. He could accompany me no further than Wa Na. The road from Wa Na led directly to the county road and then on to Lüchun. The problem was that the chance of meeting a vehicle before the county road was again nil. Chen drew for me a very detailed map in Chinese which he said would take me to a junction called *Er Hao Qiao* (Number Two Bridge). There, I could "catch a tractor" to Lüchun. It would take me two hours, Chen figured, to reach "Number Two Bridge."

Chen and I had walked through the mountains together for some seven hours. In my heart of hearts I had to believe that, without some assurance that I would reach my destination, he would not send me off alone on a two-hour mountain trek with a map that diverted three times through shortcuts before reaching *Er Hao Qiao*. There were sure to be other walkers on the road, Chen said by way of encouragement. Back in Lu E, Chen had given me a short course in the Hani language. If I ran off course, all I needed to say in Hani was "*Er Hao Qiao ga ma ha me li?* How do you get to Number Two Bridge?"

I jotted down the estimated time required for each of the seven legs on Teacher Chen's map so that I could at least monitor whether or not I was on course.

Rain in the days before *Qing Ming Jie*, the early spring holiday on which Chinese honor their family dead, is thought to be auspicious. With map in hand, two weighty shoulder bags, and a broken, borrowed umbrella, I set out in the rain and mud at 8:10 A.M. for Number Two Bridge.

I had memorized the details of the first leg: In about fifty minutes I should be reaching Wa Long Village. Right off the road, I would see the schoolhouse. One of the teachers in the village, I was assured, would escort me through the second leg, which would take ten minutes, and guide me to the first shortcut. The caveat was *not* to take the road after the schoolhouse, which led to Dong De. Right on his map, Teacher Chen had written a note to show to a nephew who drove a bus that left Lüchun every morning at 10:40. My rain-delayed departure had already made that connection impossible.

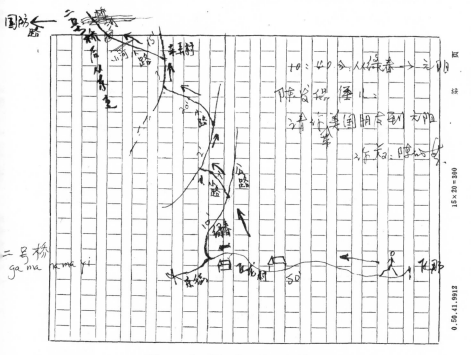

The road to Number Two Bridge

For the first twenty-five minutes, the road from Wa Na to Wa Long was flat, with just enough bare earth between puddles for me to keep up a steady pace. Just at the point that I spotted a mountain village in the distance that might well be Wa Long, a first fellow traveler passed me. In his thirties, I guessed, with a knit, collared shirt and plastic sandals on his feet, he carried a sheet of clear plastic over his head to shield him from the rain.

I tried to engage him in conversation but dialect made that futile. I was able to ascertain that he, too, was headed to Lüchun and that meant first to Number Two Bridge. In time, I was also able to learn that he had come from Si Jiao Village, where Teacher Chen had been born. As best I could determine, he did not know Chen.

Meeting up with my new road mate held two advantages: (1) I didn't have to keep looking at Teacher Chen's ink map, which would smudge in the rain, and (2) it compelled me to keep up my pace.

We passed the schoolhouse ten minutes ahead of schedule and took a nature break. It wasn't clear how soon after the school we were to take our first shortcut and I grew a bit anxious. But I was able to confirm from the chap with the plastic sheet that we were still on the road to Number Two Bridge. My confidence rose when a sign showed that we had avoided the "Dong De caveat." Shortly thereafter, we took our first shortcut, its narrow entrance shielded by shrubby growth. I wondered whether I would have ever found it on my own.

The public road from Wa Na to Number Two Bridge made descending S-turns around the mountain. The shortcuts connected segments of the public road, reducing the distance considerably. As we were completing the first shortcut, the rain that had slackened a bit began to pick up. The trails that formed the shortcuts grew steeper and more slippery. Monitoring Chen's map became impossible in the rain. So I took out a 10-yuan Chinese note and started to jot down the time of each road crossing. Seeing my growing shoulder-bag predicament, the chap-in-plastic relieved me of my lighter bag, improving my balance.

As we descended lower and lower, the trails grew more and more treacherous. My walk mate in sandals took each step with the certainty of a squirrel trapezing high in a tree. I struggled to match him. I began to search out rocks, pebbles, and fallen leaves, which improved traction; to shun mud as iffy; and to avoid glistening bare earth as trouble. I slipped several times, but remained on my feet. To that point, we had passed three or four travelers, all going in the other direction. One, I noted, was wearing glasses.

We headed into a long stretch of shortcut; toward what seemed to be the outer reaches of a village. Just then, as we were approaching a large rice paddy, I slipped and fell for the first time, coating my backside with mud. The day before, in Lu E, wanting to see up close the wood gathering that was such a basic part of Hani life, I had tried my hand at walking on the banks of rain-slickened rice paddies. Up was more sure-footed than down. But "down" was what was in store. Our shortcut to Number Two Bridge was taking us directly through village paddies. I slipped again, thoroughly laminating my blue shoulder bag with brown mud. Three Hani girls standing by with umbrellas giggled in unison, "Heh, heh, heh."

We continued for ten more minutes through the rice paddies, finally reaching a dirt road. It was 10:15. That tallied well with Chen's two-hour timetable. My scorecard for the trip: 5 slips, 2 near misses, 3 big errors.

There was a water spigot near the road, and I was prepared for a good long rest. But before I could even begin to wipe the mud from my windbreaker, a tractor came bouncing up the rain-streaked road. There was bus service on the road to Lü-chun, but it was these rough-chugging, two-wheeled tractors, hitched to metal carts, that provided the main transportation fleet for Lüchun County.

This tractor, shielded from the rain by a striped sheet of polypropylene, was already packed to the gills. On the cart bed was a load of firewood guaranteeing a sharp-edged, hour-long ride to Lüchun. Above, eight or nine people had already squeezed themselves into an area perhaps five feet by eight, toes finding crevices between the logs. There wasn't room for any more, not even one. Even so, it seemed unwise to pass up this 18-cent ride. As I squirmed into an opening, small potatoes began to dribble out from a passenger's fifty-five-pound burlap sack inside the cart. I stooped under the cart and retrieved as many as I could from the ground, well schooled in how hard-won each and every potato was on the Hani mountain slopes.

That accomplished, we lurched off in the rain for Lüchun Town.

Beijing 2008's
Dancing Logo

□ □ □

B EIJING 2008'S OFFICIAL OLYMPIC emblem—a stylized version of the Chinese character *jing* (from Beijing), centered over the words "Beijing 2008," with the five Olympic rings at the bottom—had just been released, and I paid a visit to the creators to learn a bit about the evolution of the design. Curiosity aside, there was the feeling that, unlike so much about fast-changing China, with four years yet remaining before the Olympics began, here was information in no immediate danger of becoming dated.

I expected to come away with a few draft sketches and some detail about what triggered each revision. But Zhang Wu, the head of the Armstrong International Corporate Identity Co., whose firm had submitted the winning design, was way ahead of me. Zhang, early forties, who had studied design at Beijing's Qinghua University and dug into philosophy and sociology on his own, launched into a ninety-minute PowerPoint presentation that spelled out, in intricate detail, nothing less than the evolution of Chinese culture. That was a very big subject.

He started out with two staples: *dao* ("the way") and *qi* ("essence"), which, in this environment, best translate as: "guiding principles" and "material implications." To each, he assigned

163

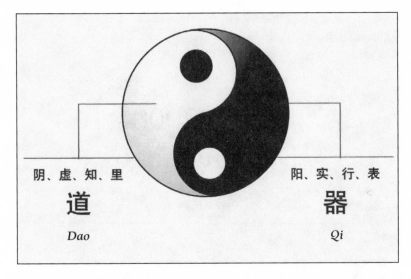

阴、虚、知、里　　　　　　　　阳、实、行、表

道　　　　　　　　　　　　　　器

Dao　　　　　　　　　　　　　　*Qi*

four properties. To *dao* he assigned subtlety, humility, knowl-edge, and inner thought; to *qi*, explicitness, reality, conduct, and appearance. Form is inherent in *dao*; *qi* is the execution of form. Through the five senses, the synthesis of knowledge and conduct reveals itself. Through the five senses, you experience Beijing's Olympic spirit.

The Beijing 2008 Organizing Committee had targeted three ambiences that would flavor their Olympic Games: an environ-mentally sound Olympics, a technologically advanced Olym-pics, a humanistic Olympics. The Beijing 2008 logo would be the most visible symbol of the Beijing Games. The emblem designers dismissed the first two focuses as overworked and decided on a *humanistic* Olympics as their thrust. Chinese cul-ture would serve as the guiding principle for the twenty mem-bers of their team as they modified their entry. That was a lot of weight to put on one logo, I remember thinking.

As my brain flooded, I asked Zhang if he could pick out from the mass of detail he had just presented, a few of the cen-tral ideas. Not to worry. "I'll give you the CD," he said. That complicated things further.

Zhang, his partner, Guo Chunning, and their group had

studied all of the logos of previous Olympic Games thoroughly. Before the Tokyo Olympics in 1964, they learned, virtually
all of the Olympic insignias depicted a recognizable landmark
or historical site, keeping their distance from conceptual ideas
that didn't trigger instant recognition. Intent on winning,
Zhang and Guo hedged their bets. In addition to the winning entry, which fell into the risky conceptual category, they
submitted five safer pictographic designs, including the Great

The six original entries

Wall, the Temple of Heaven, the Chinese knot (an ancient art
form used to decorate clothing, jewelry, furniture, and musical
instruments), and masks used in Peking opera.

In narrowing their focus for the 'Dancing Beijing' entry that
was to emerge the winner, Zhang and Guo decided that the
defining Chinese cultural icon was the Chinese writing system
itself. For millennia it had served as the cultural bridge with
East Asia, as well as the cultural wall between East and West.
The Korean, Japanese, and Vietnamese writing systems all had
their roots in ancient Chinese, which, once borrowed, inevitably carried along Chinese sensibilities.

The pictograph they chose to represent the Chinese writing system was the character *jing*, the common abbreviation for Beijing. They could have settled on a simple calligraphic rendering of *jing*, but decided on a seal version instead. The Chinese seal, for millennia the artifact through which Chinese have legalized documents, was one artistic level above calligraphy, they felt. Anyone could take a brush and scribe a Chinese character, but to chisel a three-dimensional character out of stone took special talent. Their seal would be red as have Chinese seals from antiquity. Red was auspicious.

As I plumbed for a logical evolution of the design in the wake of Zhang's elaborate presentation, Guo Chunning, whose idea it was to use the Chinese seal, confirmed that the final result was more random. Once the basic seal idea was accepted, he said, it became a matter of mix and match. Guo favored old-fashioned pen and brush work. The computer, though, could generate almost infinite combinations. And it was these that they sifted through, prompted by modification requests from the Beijing Organizing Committee and its panel of experts, on the road to the final design.

The *jing* character designating Beijing carried heavy baggage: it was to designate the location of the Games; it was to convey the fluid motion of the athlete; it mimicked the Chinese seal used for generations to legitimize official documents and works of art; it represented the unique Chinese writing system; its red color symbolized good fortune; its slinky lines were to convey the heroism intrinsic in the Chinese dragon, itself a composite of all higher animals—the mouth of a camel, the ears of a donkey, the horns of a cow, the eyes of a rabbit, the back of a snake, the scales of a fish, the paws of a tiger, the claws of an eagle. Whereas in the West a dragon connotes dread, in Chinese culture it connotes strength and stability.

It was the conflict between the dragon, the athlete, and the seal that prompted three stages of revision: the legs were not comfortable; the curl in the legs, suggesting the dragon, worked against the flexibility required by the athlete; ample freedom for the arms and legs was at odds with the aesthetics of the Chinese seal.

The English type for "Beijing 2008" underwent a similar evolution, from standard type to a stylized English font mimicking Chinese orthography. At one point, the designers asked three hundred Beijing elementary school students to write out the words "Beijing 2008" in English letters, hoping to inject a degree of playfulness into the design. It didn't work.

The Evolution of 'Dancing Beijing'

The parents of 'Dancing Beijing'

The first round selection

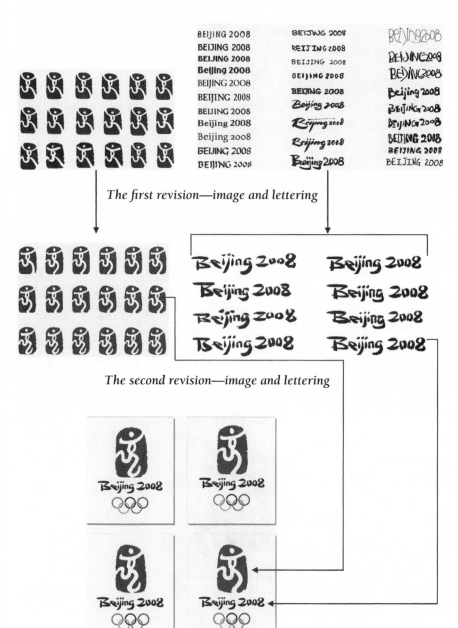

The first revision—image and lettering

The second revision—image and lettering

The final four

'Dancing Beijing'—the final version

The glitzy Chinese media effort to promote the Beijing 2008 emblem, whose licensing will generate over one billion dollars, suggested a slick packaging house working at the cutting edge of Computer-Aided Design. But Zhang and Guo's shop—a modest space in northeast Beijing—mirrors instead two guys, talented enough to lure clients such as Toshiba and Sony, but very much sleeves-up fellows, who saw an opportunity and dove in. Fame in hand, fortune remains ahead of them. BOCOG [Beijing Organizing Committee for the Games of the XXIX Olympiad] awarded them $25,000 as first-prize winners. Guo estimates that they spent about $100,000 in travel to former Olympic host cities and other expenses. Contest entrants were required to sign away all claims to their designs. Zhang and Guo cannot even use their winning design to promote their own business. When we first met, Guo Chunning said that he felt "extremely fortunate to have had this opportunity." But there was a murmur of discontent that he and Zhang would not be sharing in the licensing pot. By the time I spoke to him just before the 2008 Olympics, though, their achievement had become more widely known and that feeling had faded.

Back to the Coal Mines

□□□

A YEAR EARLIER, on the train to Zhuolu County in rural Hebei Province, northwest of Beijing, I met a forty-year-old fellow by the name of Zhang. He hauled coal for a living as an independent trucker. I was conducting a little informal political survey on the train, and he pulled me aside to get his two cents in. (To get him to open up, I promised I wouldn't write down his first name; there are tens of millions of Zhangs in China.)

His main line had stuck in my head: "Those Party Congress delegates, they are all a bunch of fakers. Politics doesn't have *anything* to do with our lives. What we care about is *money*. If you want to understand China, talk to the common people." I took down his number.

He must have fallen out of his seat ten months later when I rang him up from New York to take him up on his offer. Riding for a few days with a long-haul coal trucker, I thought, would be a really quaint thing to do. China is notorious for its coal mines. More people die in coal mines in China in a year—remaining stable in recent years at around six thousand—than in the rest of the world combined. Maybe Zhang could get me into the mines. I brought along a pair of safety goggles in preparation.

Zhang gave a "thumbs up" to the visit, but only when I called him from Beijing did he tell me that he was out of the coal-

171

hauling business, as were Liu and Li who worked with him. I decided to visit him in Xuanhua, a suburb of Zhangjiakou City, anyhow. On the train the year before, Zhang was sitting down. So I was somewhat surprised to find a bear of a man—maybe more teddy bear than papa bear, but bearish nonetheless—when I arrived at Xuanhua station for my potluck visit.

It didn't take but a minute for a first curiosity to pop its head.

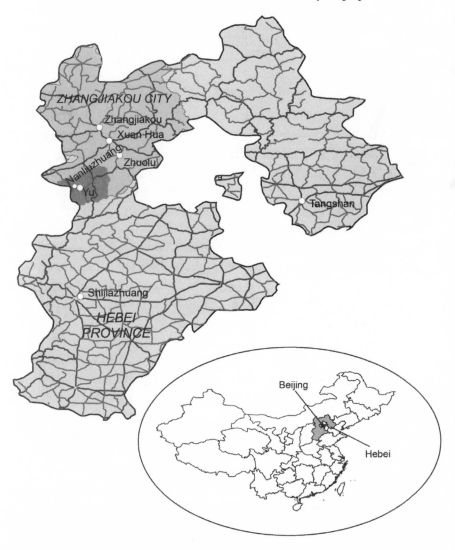

Zhang had a car, I knew. I had asked him about that before I came to be sure that we would be able to get around. Nevertheless, he brought along a friend of his who drove a taxi to the station. That was his way of introducing me to the fact that, although he had a car, it couldn't go anywhere. Since the car was ten years old, by law, he couldn't reregister it. The plates on the car were fake, he said. He could use the car around town because the police knew him, but we couldn't travel any distance with it. Hence, the taxi.

Zhang Guoqiang was very much about image. He was well groomed, without the shaggy sideburns common to mainland Chinese. Not someone you would picture around black coal. He registered me at the Xuanhua Hotel, Xuanhua's best, he made sure to let me know. When I had asked him on the phone what the hotel would run so that I would know how much cash to bring along (locally run hotels often only accept cash), he bellowed out the first of many *Ah, y-a-a-hs*, his signature expression of disapproval. In this case, that I, an American, should even concern myself with money.

Zhang was out to give me a splashy welcome and took me to the Lai Fu Restaurant. He knew the owner, another Zhang (unrelated), who was so enthralled by me and my Chinese that he ran next door to borrow a camera and invited me back to dinner the following night. Friends streamed in left and right. More often than not, Zhang Guoqiang introduced them as his brother, a common way in China to address friends.

"Your mother had a lot of children," I said.

Among the invited was Liu Bing, one of Zhang's two former coal-trucking partners I had met on the train the year before. Liu, much more sedate than Zhang, was genuinely amazed that I remembered his name. Actually, I had read it straight out of my notebook. On the train with Zhang the year before were Liu and Li. Fifty percent odds.

After dinner, Zhang and wife took me to the North China Music Bar, Xuanhua's biggest karaoke parlor (he again made sure to let me know), with nine spacious rooms. I flubbed my first attempt at a Chinese song, and they guided me to the English menu. Zhang and his wife loved to sing, but to hear me sing seemed to trigger even greater pleasure. In succession came "Love Me Tender," "To Sir with Love," "Old McDonald Had a Farm," and "Happy Birthday." Fortunately, the next day was my mother's birthday.

Twenty minutes into the evening, a girl in a white sweater was brought into the room.

"This is your girlfriend," announced Zhang.

She quickly nuzzled up to me. She looked about seventeen, well scrubbed, cute in manner if not in look. She was from far away, she told me. Liaoning Province. There was no work back home. My instinct was to get her story in detail. China's floating population is a big part of China's growth. But I had to face the fact that the body sometimes works at odds with the brain. I took a moment in between songs to tell Zhang's wife that I didn't require a "girlfriend."

"We didn't want you to be lonely," Zhang said when the news reached him.

From the owner of the North China Music Bar I learned that these girls, who received no salary, were brought in as a group by an agent. They were sort of like prostitutes, though singing and dancing with the customers was the main part of their work. Because of the sometimes seedy nature of the job, local girls rarely took such work in their hometown.

NEIGHBORING DATONG, not far from Inner Mongolia, is China's coal center. Most of the state-owned mines are located there. But there were hundreds of smaller, privately owned mines in Yu County, two hours south of Zhangjiakou City. Zhang had hauled coal for a year from Datong to Beijing and had also worked for three years for a coal prospecting company in Yu County. So, he could present the larger picture.

We headed seventy-five miles south to Yu County.

In the last decade, China has invested billions of dollars in developing a national highway system. The Xuanhua-Datong toll road had been completed within the year, halving the time between Xuanhua and Datong.

What is curious about these highways, virtually all of which charge hefty tolls, is that, outside of the larger cities, you rarely find passenger cars on them. The tolls, roughly comparable to American thruway levies, but coming out of much smaller pockets, are just too steep.

The traffic mix on the road told the full story. The lion's share of the trucks on the road was either laden with coal destined for Xuanhua or on the way back to Yu County to pick up another load. The traffic was so heavy with coal trucks at the Yu County turnoff that, after twenty minutes of waiting, we abandoned that exit for the next. I used the waiting time to home in on coal hauling-business realities, and to understand why Zhang was no longer in the coal business. Certainly, it had nothing to do with his talent behind the wheel. He was an expert, if at times reckless, driver whose foot rarely met the brakes.

As we traveled along the local roads in Yu County, passing through the market towns that hugged either side of the road, it was clear from the services offered that the entire pulse of Yu County revolved around coal: heavy motors to pull the coal out of the mines, tire and engine repair services for the big rigs that steamed through at all hours day and night, giant loaders to fill the trucks, and piles of wooden shunts used to shore up the mines. Maybe this was what West Virginia looked like sixty years ago was the thought. A cold, gray day, with temperatures in the twenties, framed the drab surroundings.

We pulled up at the Nan Liu Hotel in Nan Liu Zhuang Township for a pit stop and a bite to eat. This was not a tourist town. A step anywhere on the rutted road left a residue of black mud on shoe soles. Anyone stopping at the hostel had something to do with coal. A very few dollars got you a bed in a cold room with a hard stone floor and a television set shared by one or several others.

THE HUA ZUI COAL MINE outside Nan Liu Zhuang Township, like dozens of other private mines in the county, was where the process began. Just as we arrived, two men were carefully placing the last chunks of coal on a modest-sized hauler. At the mouth of the mine, like a choo-choo train at an amusement park, a string of eight dumpsters, pulled in tandem by a cable, was just emerging from a hole perhaps six feet in diameter. Each car could hold about a half ton of coal. When it reached the top, the string of steel carts dumped its load and went right back down again.

Every forty minutes the process repeated itself, day and night, summer and winter, 365 days a year, a coal-streaked foreman told me. He removed his blackened glove to shake hands, but his hand was every bit as black as his glove. Below ground, a crew of thirty, almost all farmers from the surrounding villages, worked with pick and shovel to load the carts. A second foreman inside the mine kept tabs on production: a gross output worth hundreds of thousands of dollars a year for this very average mine. For Yu County, business worth tens of millions of dollars per year.

The Hua Zui Coal Mine ran three hundred feet vertically and one thousand feet laterally into the hilly Hebei landscape. I itched to reach the mine floor, but it would have taken a colossal effort to talk myself inside the mine. In recent years, China's State Administration of Coal Mine Safety has closed several thousand private mines just like the one at Hua Zui as unsafe. (Heavy pressure from local governments, which exact large fees from the mines, keeps many more from being closed.) Under the best of circumstances, methane gas explosions, tunnel collapses, and flooding are an everyday reality. With so much money at stake, keeping a low profile is in the owner's best interest. Visitors are not welcome.

It was almost 4 P.M. and, on the road outside the mine, expressionless workers wearing hard hats walked deliberately to man the next shift. Their ages ranged from twenty to late forties. Some of them carried shovels over their shoulders; others led teams of mules on tethers. As more and more coal was dug out of the mine, the "coal field" at the bottom of the shaft became larger and larger, and the source of the coal moved farther and farther from the rail line that brought the coal to the surface. The mules hauled the coal from the coal fields deep in the mine to the rail line at the bottom of the shaft. Pay for the men who dug the coal in the mines was about $5.00 per day; for the mule masters, not much more. (The owner of the mine paid the master; the master took care of his mules.) For some of these farmers, renting out their mules provided reliable supplementary income to seasonal plow work in the fields.

The common chord among the workers, solemn, blank faces aside, was that all of them were thin.

Any of them—Wang, Zhang, Chen, Li—could have been pulled aside and the story would have been the same: danger and death without recourse. They mined because there was nothing else to do that paid as much as toiling in the deep black sea.

Once outside the mine, the coal was either loaded directly on trucks to be hauled to its final destination, or transported locally to coal yards, where the coal was sifted through giant screens to separate coal dust from chunks as large as good-sized turkeys. Chunk coal, at about $22 a ton, fetched almost double the price of coal dust.

The large chunks were then moved up conveyors and ground into uniform sizes for varied uses, much as stone and gravel yards crush stone for construction needs. Some of this coal was destined for industrial users, some would be bagged and sold for small-scale use, the rest would be crushed and molded into the coal briquettes marketed for home heating and cooking across China. Almost anywhere in China you can see vendors peddling six-inch round coal briquettes from carts that are drawn by horses or bicycle, or harnessed to their own backs. Through each briquette ran twelve holes, allowing the use of a standard tool to place the briquettes in the oven. The peddlers I met managed two or three dollars a day.

Whether in a pickup truck, a horse-drawn carriage, or a big rig, customers at the mines and coal yards had one thing in common. They all paid cash. There was no billing and no such thing as credit. At any hour of any day, a coal mine or station had to be ready to accept cash. That meant that there had to be someone on duty trusted by the owners. The temptation for sticky fingers was endless.

For the truckers, loading up was only the beginning. Anywhere on the roads out of Yu County you could see policemen (always at least two) at ad hoc weighing stations stopping truckers and levying fines for overloads. There were no scales. The police made their determination solely by the height of the load. They set a price, then haggled a bit with the drivers, who forked over the cash. Some of this cash reached the local government, some found its way to the pockets of the bosses at the police station, and the rest went into the policemen's pockets. Corruption? Call it a bonus for underpaid government workers.

About $125 dollars of a load worth $1,900 at the point of delivery went to fines, Zhang told me. Just a cost of doing business for the trucker, who was interested in heaping as much product on his rig as possible—as long as it moved and didn't blow an engine. The roads from Datong to Beijing were choked with coal-laden trucks that seemed to have stalled in the middle of the highway. In fact, they were creeping along, trying to maintain motion until they reached the top of the incline. It wasn't hard to see ahead a few years, as intercity passenger-car travel developed in China, when these slow-moving coal rigs would pose a real problem. Already, there were proposals that special roads be built for moving coal. That didn't seem a practical idea.

FOR MY HOST, ZHANG GUOQIANG, a profit of $7,500 to $9,000 a year was waiting after deducting fuel, fines, maintenance, and the cost of carrying his $50,000 hauler. That was a solid income in China.

So why was Zhang now off his rig? Certainly it had nothing to do with a shortage of work. Just a few miles from his house, in Zhangjiakou, stood one of the largest power plants in North China. Eight giant, mushroom-shaped towers and four towering smoke stacks spewed out exhaust, which cast a perpetual haze around Xuanhua. Their appetite for coal was insatiable. Working the longer Datong-Beijing delivery route that Zhang had plied was even more profitable.

Zhang claimed he had bolted from the business because the profit margin was too thin. But the thousands of coal haulers on the road pointed to another reason. It took a special breed to endure the filth, the boredom, the breakdowns, the endless days away from home. Zhang was more comfortable clean-shaven and neatly groomed. He picked his opportunities and had put away about $35,000 in the bank. (He expected equal candor about my assets.) Meanwhile, there was a steady income coming in. His wife, Jianli, an elementary school teacher by training, ran a betting salon afternoons for mahjong and poker players in a suite she had rented in Xuanhua.

Legality aside, this was a clean business. The winner each session paid her $12.50, giving her $350 a month income or more. That gave Zhang, who operated heavy dozers from time to time in the interim, the freedom to look for bigger fish. His partner in the coal hauling business a year earlier, Liu Bing, had found his more comfortable life in a clothing stand he ran in a mall in Xuanhua.

Many in and around Xuanhua had been lured by the coal-hauling call at one time or other. And just as many, it seemed, had abandoned it for cleaner pursuits.

Highway Dupe Foiled
in Jinning County

□ □ □

WITH THE DISPATCHER at Kunming's Long Distance Bus Terminal barking alluring destinations as far away as Vietnam and Tibet, I sought a more modest destination from the ticket checker at one of the gateways. I was looking for a trip that would take me south or west and bring me back by nightfall. Yunnan, in the southwest, is one of China's poorest provinces. But Kunming, its capital, a vibrant city of about three million, is uncharacteristically prosperous. I was looking for a less developed, more representative place to visit. The ticket checker put me on a bus marked "Kunyang."

A glance at the map and consultation with a Miss Peng in the seat ahead of me—a pert, short-haired woman, in her early thirties—revealed Kunyang to be the seat of Jinning County, located about fifty miles south of Kunming City. In addition to districts within its city limits, Kunming (like cities throughout China) administers several rural counties including Jinning, situated at the southern end of Kunming's largest body of water, Lake Dianchi.

China's buses, particularly those serving remote, outlying areas, often operate on loose timetables, departing only when

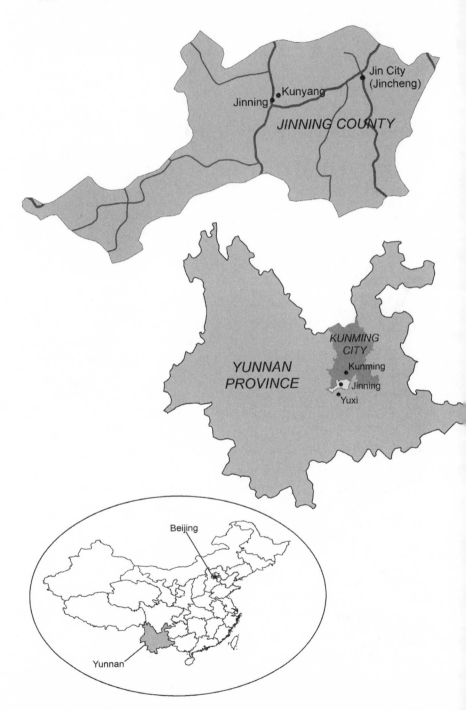

the bus fills up. The bus for Kunyang, seating nineteen, was more punctual than most, departing for the one-hour, fifty-minute trip just minutes late.

We soon reached the Kunming-Yuxi toll road. The chap next to me on the aisle—a nondescript, thirtyish fellow, with a soiled beige jacket and sparse, quarter-inch stubble on his face—provided an unappealing bus mate. So I passed up the banter that often makes riding China's buses so revealing, taking in instead the soybean and rapeseed landscape, interrupted occasionally by smoke-belching, government-run foundries and processing plants.

About forty-five minutes into the trip, with my attention entranced by the repetitive scenes that make so much of China look alike, heavy commotion erupted on the bus bound for Kunyang. The nondescript by my side had unsuccessfully opened a canned beverage, spraying liquid as high as the ceiling, and dousing me and several other passengers in the immediate area. The receiver of the bulk of the can's contents, the rider directly in front of the nondescript, wearing a weather-beaten leather jacket, was irate. He was making ferocious efforts to wrest the can from the culprit's hands. Eyes glazed, the nondescript resisted mightily, grimacing in anguish, as if his most precious possession were about to be taken from him. Unable to see the can's label, I assumed that he was a drunkard, desperately craving his can of beer.

When it appeared that the man in the leather jacket—a tall, menacing type—might strike the nondescript, I stood up and, stepping out of myself, told him to his face to back off. He relented for a while, then began to yank at the can again as the nondescript compulsively gulped down its contents. The beverage, I could now see, was Jianlibao, one of China's most popular soft drinks. The nondescript occasionally gestured wildly, but never uttered a sound, giving every appearance of being mute.

On his third attempt, the man in leather finally jerked the

aluminum can from the mute and poured its contents on the stairs directly in front of the exit door. He then bent the can in half, flexing it repeatedly until it broke. Reaching inside the bottom half of the can, he extracted a laminated slip akin in size to fortunes found in Chinese fortune cookies. After studying the slip for perhaps twenty seconds, the man in the leather jacket reached into his pocket and gave the mute what appeared to be about sixty Chinese yuan, $7.20.

Almost everyone on the bus felt certain that the Jianlibao Company had put prize tickets in certain soft-drink containers and that this one—scripted in blue ink—was a jackpot find. As the ticket passed from hand to hand through the bus, I caught the words "man's fate" on it. What seemed absolutely certain to me was that the tall man in the leather coat was exploiting the mute's feeblemindedness by paying him a fraction of the ticket's true value.

As curiosity grew among the riders, out of the blue a passenger in the rear seat took out a wad of money and passed it to the mute. Eager to enter the loop, I snatched the money from the mute's hand and counted it. The backseat passenger had upped the ante to 300 Chinese yuan, about $38. As I was taking the cash notes from him, the mute rubbed his thumb and forefinger together agitatedly, indicating that he wanted more money. Arms flailing, the mute then began to clamor for his ticket, grabbing at the man in leather. The ticket-holder threatened in return to slug the mute. Beginning to see red, with beads of sweat meandering around the lumps in my spine, I in turn stood up and, spitting epithets in Chinese, forcefully told the ticket-holder in the leather coat to return the ticket to the mute. The man in leather continued to seethe.

As emotions began to boil over, my gut reaction was to take out my camera and point it squarely at the tall man in the leather coat. He threatened to whack me. Ignoring his size, I wrinkled my brow and warned him to watch his step. Whereupon, I snapped the shutter a second time.

Thereafter, things evolved rapidly.

Apparently concerned about the ramifications of my photos, the man in the leather coat abruptly demanded that the driver stop the bus, whereupon he exited right onto the Kunming-Yuxi highway. The mute followed directly on his heels. The door closed and the bus had rolled no more than two hundred additional yards when the passenger in the back seat, who had upped the ante to 300 yuan, also ordered the driver to stop. He, too, got off on the highway shoulder, followed in step by a woman and a second man.

Yunnan dialect is said to be linguistically related to Mandarin. But what they do in Yunnan to vowels and inflection minimizes the relationship. I was fully in the dark as to what was happening.

Mr. Wang, in the seat ahead of me, a man in his mid-sixties, clued me in, interrupted from time to time by his clarifying wife. The five passengers who got off the bus were all in league. And the deaf mute wasn't deaf at all. To make sure that the "exploding" beverage can would cause as much havoc as possible, the "mute" had squeezed the can in the middle as he opened it, propelling its contents as far as it could possibly travel. (I neglected to ask Mr. Wang whether the bus driver, too, had a hand in the scheme.)

The objective of the five scammers was to bid up the offered price for the prize ticket to a moderate level within the ring, then entice a gullible outsider to come in and raise it yet further. The pickings were apparently lucrative enough for five people to spend their days riding the buses through Kunming's rural routes. Mr. Wang and his wife, who traveled often between Kunming and Jinning County, where they had a second home, had seen this once before. For the other riders, it was a first.

DUPES COME AND DUPES GO. An anthropologist at the Museum of National Minorities in Kunming pointed me towards a variation on this theme. In the "Small West Gate" section of Kunming, peasants from outlying districts were peddling Chinese medicine that claimed amazing properties. Working in teams as on the bus to Kunyang, they pumped up interest, hoping to hook an innocent. (Without an FDA to police drugs, when it comes to medicine, Chinese are especially vulnerable to drug scams.)

When I reached the "Small West Gate" section, seeking further information, the following ensued: (1) a banana peddler claimed no knowledge (after selling me two bananas); (2) a hardware merchant sent me to the Nanjiang Hotel; (3) a woman having her teeth attended to in a street-front clinic thought the amazing drug market had closed down; (4) a woman querying a policeman on Dong Feng Street opposite the Nanjiang Hotel confirmed the closure in a police sweep.

Such is the way with scams: once it was, now it wasn't.

Whether it was a group of peasants trying to pump up inflated interest in an "amazing" drug, a saleslady trying to oversell a "one-of-a-kind" item of clothing at an exaggerated price with the aid of a partner posing as a very interested customer, or a tout on Kunming's West Mountain heightening betting interest in a rope scam among Sunday frolickers with the assistance of a sidekick—everyone in China seemed to have their own scam variation to describe. Chinese are inveterate gamblers and miracle seekers; there always seems to be a compatriot lurking around itching to test them.

ALL OF THIS MIGHT HAVE TAKEN the sails out of the trip to Jinning County, if it hadn't proven to be such a quaint place to visit. Mr. Wang said that Jinning's history stretched back a thousand years to the Song Dynasty. How could I doubt him?

What set Jinning apart, according to Wang, was that it is the birthplace of Zheng He—a national hero with a legend-embellished past. Zheng He was a Hui Muslim with the birth name Ma Sanbao. ("Ma" is a particularly common surname among the Hui.) According to Professor Bai Yubao at the Museum of National Minorities, Ma Sanbao didn't put in much time in Yunnan Province. The Hui Muslims were traders, and, while still in his youth, Ma traveled to Beijing with his parents, where in time he became a favored eunuch in the court of the Ming emperor Yong Le and his successors. It was the Yong Le emperor who bestowed the name "Zheng He" on Ma.

Zheng He's claim to fame is that, between 1405 and 1433, in the name of building the reputation of the Ming emperor and recruiting tribute states, Zheng's flotilla of wooden ships made seven trips to legendary Xi Yang (which means "West Sea"). Zheng He, it is said, visited thirty-five Asian and African countries, including India, Ceylon, Siam, and Aden. Seven Chinese were reported to have reached Mecca. Zheng's voyages have come down to us as monumental maritime feats—he using a compass for navigation and employing sixty-two vessels and twenty-eight thousand sailors on his maiden voyage. Some of these ships were multi-tiered and several hundred feet long. Where fact ends and legend begins is highly speculative because primary historical records remain scant.

To get the emperor's reputation off on the right foot, Zheng He took along Chinese silk, porcelain, gold, silver, and tea to his destinations. He brought back spices, precious stones, and ivory, as well as giraffes, ostriches, and zebras. Whatever the truth quotient, Zheng He remains Yunnan Province's biggest hero.

Zheng He Park in Kunyang, a "recommended tourist site," but badly in need of weeding and delittering, hardly lived up to the name of the local hero. Ultimately offering a mediocre view of Lake Dianchi, it first provided an unimpeded view of a water tower.

Jin City, fifteen miles from Kunyang, the former county seat of Jinning County according to Mr. Wang on the bus in, proved a bigger find. In Chinese history class, they taught how, on market days, peasants from outlying areas would converge on the market town—as spokes converge on the hub of a wheel—with their crops and animals, returning home a few hours later with goods purchased from the proceeds. No doubt the reference was to a place such as Jin City. On Zhentong Street ("Crossroads Junction"), a lane stretching three hundred yards off the main traffic street in Jin City, almost every need was for sale in the open air: pears, apples, electric wire, bed frames (about $15), brooms, shoes (less than $2.00), fan belts, puppies, kittens, eggs, roosters, ducks (dead and alive), baskets, socks, hardware, pineapples. I bought an electric heater for $3.75. (Kunming—my temporary home—might be the "City of Perpetual Spring," but 31 degrees without heat at night was 31 degrees.)

As the minibus out of Jin City heading back to Kunming waited to fill, a cart hitched to a donkey across the road awaited passengers with closer destinations. The bus I boarded turned out to be a local, paralleling but never entering the toll road, stopping village by village. The scenes along the eucalyptus-lined by-way were images out of a documentary: oxen grazing in a field of rice stubble; water buffalo and ducks wallowing side by side in a pond; a two-horse cart hauling a load of straw plus a wife; a farmer bicycling to his field with a hoe across his shoulder.

A mother with a baby strapped to her back boarded the bus. No one got up to offer her a seat. As the passengers disembarked stop by stop—carrying scallions, foam rubber bedding, a yoke for an ox—the origins of Jin City's vendors and customers became clear. On Sundays in this part of Yunnan, all roads ran through Jin City.

The Chinese View of 9/11

☐ ☐ ☐

ONE OF THE MOST disillusioning aspects of the September 11, 2001, World Trade Center attack was the muted response of the Chinese government and the almost gleeful reaction of many mainland Chinese. Fearing ostracism on the eve of its entry into the WTO and cancellation of Jiang Zemin's upcoming APEC [Asia-Pacific Economic Cooperation] meeting with George Bush in Shanghai, China paid lip service to the American effort against terrorism, while stressing the role of the United Nations. In so doing, it sent a counter message to the Chinese people. In its finest tradition, the Chinese propaganda apparatus filtered the news—downplaying the human tragedy and concealing the sympathetic European consensus—directing Chinese to the desired conclusion: the terror attack was a natural outgrowth of an arrogant America that thinks it can manipulate the entire world.

I was clued into this by a very politically aloof Chinese physician friend from Beijing who had lived in New York for five years. In the days after the attack, she received upwards of a dozen phone calls from China. But what soon became apparent was that, while there was ample concern for her safety, there was very little compassion for those who had perished. "America ought to ask itself," said one friend in China, "why someone would hate the U.S. so much to do something like this."

My friend was flabbergasted. This Beijing caller was not a country bumpkin with six years of schooling, but a graduate of Beijing Medical University, affiliated with Beijing University, one of China's elite institutions. She was a fluent English speaker who had spent two years in the Philippines and was working for an American-owned clinic in Beijing.

That same night, my friend received a concerned call from a classmate in Canada who reported the same stone-cold reaction to the tragedy from her own circle in China. A week later, my friend spoke to a surgeon classmate calling from Shanghai who had just returned from a medical conference in Beijing. He reported the anti-American reaction of many of those at the conference. "Good hit! Good hit!" was one of the phrases he heard. A half year earlier, this Shanghai surgeon had completed a six-month study period in the U.S., where he had learned innovative surgical techniques that he immediately introduced to his hospital. His positive American experience had moderated his reaction to 9/11, which nevertheless still fell short of out and out condemnation.

The callousness of her friends and classmates back in China—almost all of them well-trained doctors, China's best—shocked my New York friend so deeply that she had no desire to speak to them for a long time. "What did this level of government disinformation and individual hardheartedness bode for China?" she wondered. Oddly, my friend noted, her generation of mainland Chinese, now in their late thirties, a generation reared on the sanctity of the almighty dollar, was far less humane than her parents' generation, which suffered through the Cultural Revolution of the 1960s and '70s.

None of this visceral hate for America is incidental. It is a direct outgrowth of a subtle and sophisticated brainwashing campaign, under the leadership of the Propaganda Department of the Central Committee, as old as the People's Republic. One may safely say that the most striking achievement of fifty years of Communist rule in China is not the eradication of poverty, but the brainwashing of its citizens. Left to their own thoughts, the Chinese government does not trust its own people to reach the correct conclusions.

Fluent in Chinese, when in China, I often watch the 7:00 P.M. Evening News, broadcast simultaneously across China. The last ten minutes of this newscast are devoted to international news. Whereas Chinese domestic news for the most part limits itself to presenting the achievements of the government, shying far, far away from anything that might offer a contrary view, the international segment at first glance offers some semblance of balance: famine and devastation in Africa, the Macy's Thanksgiving Day Parade, the ongoing conflict in the Middle East, the September 11 World Trade attack. Upon closer scrutiny, however, it becomes clear that what Chinese see is thoroughly filtered.

In the weeks leading up to the bombing of the Chinese Embassy in Belgrade in May 1999, for example, the Chinese were fed weeks of reports of U.S. bombing in Kosovo, with nary a line devoted to the war crimes of Slobodan Milosevic or the plight of the Kosovars that triggered the NATO campaign. The forced landing of the U.S. spy plane on Hainan Island two years later, in April 2001, after its wing was clipped by a pursuing Chinese fighter plane, received wall-to-wall coverage, with China stretching the definition of "territorial waters" like a rubber band to win over its people. Absent was the fact that the Chinese pilot who died in the incident was a "hot dog" who brought his death upon himself by getting perilously close to the U.S. reconnaissance aircraft.

So it was with 9/11.

All of China saw the Twin Towers burn and topple, but they heard little of the suffering of innocent civilians, of the bravery of firefighters, of the volunteers who traveled thousands of miles to lend a hand, of the millions of flags that graced homes and automobile antennas coast to coast, of the consensus across Europe that terrorism had to be fought at all costs. Chinese knew about the random and miniscule looting that took place in shops under the Trade Center, but little about the mounds of floral wreathes placed outside dozens of firehouses across the city, or the people who waited three to four hours to donate blood. The Arab/Muslim factor to be sure was made short shrift of, because China's traditional stance favors the Arab world; except that China had no qualms about buying weapons from Israel or quietly enlisting Israeli expertise on countering Muslim terror threats in Northwest China.

Many urban Chinese have access to computers these days, and hooking up to Internet chat rooms is a favorite pastime and source of information. Except that the government monitors and closes down any chat room that presents dissenting views. Thus, the proliferating disinformation, after 9/11, about an impending U.S. nuclear attack against not only Afghanistan, but also Iran, Iraq, Pakistan, and Libya. The thrust: the U.S. was planning a world war.

Not that the Chinese people aren't interested in the truth. They just don't have the information. A Shanghai classmate of my New York physician friend spent an hour on the telephone eager for the facts. From Chinese news sources, he said, he had no conception of how many perished in the WTC attack.

The explanations for Chinese indifference/hostility to the September 11 tragedy are easy to pinpoint: (1) xenophobia, China's one-hundred-year historical legacy of occupation by Europeans and Japanese, (2) simple jealousy. But what perpetuates this diminished sensitivity is a skewed education and information system that deprives every Chinese of one of his most fundamental rights: free access to information upon which to base his conclusions. Without this information, China—even as it prospers materially—remains a third-world information-age nation.

It is interesting to note that, try as the Chinese government does to control the minds of Chinese inside and outside of China, there are limits. The Chinese language television program in New York, SinoVision, is orchestrated by the mainland. Reports supplied by China Central Television are routinely aired; rarely if ever is there a report from Taiwan. During the Hainan Island spy-plane incident, relying on CCTV footage, SinoVision gave full vent to the mainland position and only scant attention to the American perspective.

When it came to the World Trade Center attack and the U.S. military campaign against Afghanistan that followed, however, SinoVision virtually abandoned mainland footage, relying instead on their own camera teams or international reports to show what all Americans were seeing. Chinatown abuts the Wall Street area and tens of thousands of Chinese compatriots were affected in limb and livelihood. To imply to the Chinese residents of New York that their shared plight was the fault of the American flag under which they live would be to mock the very viewers whom the station serves.

Resurrected History: The Mysterious Jews of Kaifeng

□ □ □

S CARCELY AN HOUR HAD PASSED following my arrival in Kaifeng, a city of about eight hundred thousand in Central China's Henan Province, when a serious hitch developed. The gatekeeper at the Kaifeng Museum informed me that the museum, which I had detoured 120 miles to see, was closed. In September, an armed band had stolen $60 million worth of artifacts. Most had been recovered—from as far away as Macao—but the museum was not yet considered secure. I spent most of the next hour with Li Kexiu, fifty-seven, a heavy-breathing, chain-smoking archaeologist who had worked at the Kaifeng Museum for thirty years—cajoling, imploring, presenting my case to see the third-floor exhibit.

Finally relenting, Li Kexiu returned to the resident Public Security officer who had refused to authorize my entry initially. Minutes later, the officer, arriving by bicycle, met us at the museum entrance with a heavy ring of keys and led us through three steel vertical gates to the third floor. There, under glass, sitting like orphans in an empty display hall, were two stone tablets—five and seven feet high, thirty inches wide, and five and four inches thick respectively—that traced the mysterious history of the assimilated Jews of Kaifeng.

ANYTHING SAID ABOUT THE FIRST APPEARANCE of Jews in China is conjecture. Between the seventh and twelfth centuries, speculation holds, groups of Jews, traveling overland along the old Silk Road through Central Asia, settled in Northwest China, with smaller numbers advancing further east into the Chinese heartland. Separate migrations from Persia and southern Asia brought additional groups of Jews to China's coastal cities by sea. Among cities mentioned as hosting early Jewish communities are Luoyang, Xi'an, Dunhuang, Hangzhou, Yangzhou, Ningbo, and Kaifeng.

Only the Kaifeng Jewish community left behind a written record, in the form of five inscriptions, chiseled on three stone tablets erected in the synagogue compound: the first tablet, dated 1489 (front) and 1512 (back); the second, 1663 (front) and undated (back); and the third, 1679 (back blank). The first and third tablets are housed in the Kaifeng Museum; the second has been lost. Though all inscriptions have weathered almost beyond recognition, their contents have been preserved through rubbings and copying.*

The 1489 and 1663 inscriptions are the most revealing.

The 1489 inscription, "A Record of the Reconstruction of the Synagogue," traces the religion of Israel (the "Correct Religion") to Abraham, Moses, and Ezra. It describes Jewish postures while praying and lists seventy clans of Jews as having come to Kaifeng from India. The narrative takes pains to fit Jewish concepts into cumbersome classical Chinese: way (*dao*), purity (*qing*), truth (*zhen*), ritual (*li*), worship (*bai*). "The Way [God]," it notes, true to Jewish belief, "has no form or figure, but is just like the Way of Heaven which is above." Except for the local custom of fast-

---

* The Chinese texts for the three tablets and their English translations are given in *Chinese Jews*, by Anglican bishop William Charles White, a missionary, originally published in 1912.

ing four days each month, the 1489 tablet mentions no specific holidays or religious practices, not even the biblically inspired "sinew plucking" dietary practice that was to inspire one of the common Chinese descriptive terms for Jews: *Tiao Jin Jiao* [the Sect that Extracts the Sinews].

The 1489 stone tablet details the building of the first synagogue in Kaifeng in 1163 and its four reconstructions. Kaifeng was a former Imperial capital that reached its greatest glory

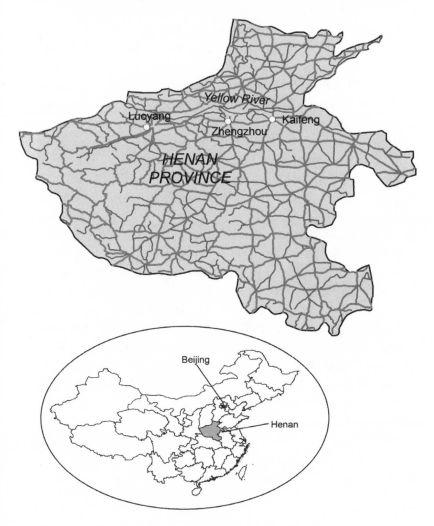

during the Song Dynasty, between 960 and 1127. It sits on the flood plain of the Yellow River, and much of its periodic destruction has been due to water. The 1489 narrative points to an organized community and notes acquisition of a copy of the *Scriptures of the Way* (probably, the Torah scrolls) through contact with Jews in Ningbo, along China's east coast. The detailed naming of members of the Kaifeng Jewish community in the 1489 and subsequent inscriptions make it possible, through comparison with local gazetteers and histories, for later researchers to piece together scant biographical information on the most prominent of Kaifeng's Jews. Ai Jun, for example, who passed the provincial civil service examination in 1447, was named chief secretary of the Prince of Dezhou Prefecture.

The 1663 inscription adds details on Jewish worship, specifically mentioning the Yom Kippur fast day. Its focus, however, is the reconstruction of the Kaifeng Synagogue following the Yellow River flood of 1642. According to estimates, this flood reduced the population of Kaifeng from 380,000 to 100,000, and the number of Jewish families from 500 to 200.* Nevertheless, the community banded together to salvage and restore the water-damaged Hebrew Torah scrolls and to rebuild the synagogue according to its original ornate design.

With their numbers greatly diminished, the assimilation of Kaifeng's Jews accelerated during the next century, and formal community life came to an end. By 1850, the synagogue had badly deteriorated. Thereafter, the synagogue buildings were dismantled, and the building materials sold (mostly to Muslims, who used them to construct the Great Eastern Mosque). By the time Dr. W. A. P. Martin, an American missionary-educator, visited Kaifeng in 1866, all of the synagogue buildings had disappeared.

---

* The cause of this flood remains unexplained. Some contend that it was the work of rebel Li Zicheng, who broke the dikes of the Yellow River in order to destroy Kaifeng City. Others say that it was an attempt by the Ming government to stem Li's advance. Most scholars believe that Li Zecheng had nothing to do with it.

In 1912, Bishop William White purchased the 1489/1512 and 1679 tablets (the first standing at the edge of a muddy pool on the former synagogue site, the second found built into the wall of a nearby house) on behalf of the Canadian Church of England. The tablets were transferred to the compound of Trinity Cathedral in Kaifeng. After rumors that White planned to remove the tablets from China resulted in a local uproar and the jailing of the most prominent Jew, Zhao Yunzhong, agreement was reached to grant custody of the stones to the bishop and his successors with the stipulation that they never be allowed to leave Kaifeng.

WITH CHINA ENGULFED IN A WAR of resistance against Japan and in civil war in the 1930s and 1940s, and then sealed off by the Communists in 1949, outside interest in Kaifeng's Jews waned. Only in 1980, as China began to thaw, did foreigners again visit Kaifeng in search of Jews. With the establishment of a quasi-diplomatic Israeli presence in China in 1990, followed by formal diplomatic relations in 1992, Kaifeng's Jews again became an active topic of interest. By then, two additional generations of memories had faded.

MUCH OF WHAT IS KNOWN about the recent history of Kaifeng's Jews originates from a 1980 survey by the then-curator of the Kaifeng Museum, Wang Yisha, reproduced in part in Sidney Shapiro's book, *Jews in Old China*. Wang identified seventy-nine Jewish-descendant families, a total of 166 individuals, still living in Kiafeng. An inherent difficulty is that Wang worked with a narrow data base and blurred memories. As subsequent inquirers revisited Wang's subjects, they ran the risk of inspiring embellished recollections. This limitation aside, Wang Yisha gave an identity to the community of Jewish descendants in Kaifeng. Most of the descendants, I found, knew of Wang Yisha, and through him have met other descendants. Following Wang Yisha's trail through the lanes of Kaifeng yields surprising insights and curiosities.

Much of Wang Yisha's information came from Zhao Pingyu, a former official at the Kaifeng Municipal Tax Bureau. The Zhaos are one of five remaining clans—Li, Zhao, Ai, Jin, and Shi—in Kaifeng that claim Jewish roots as documented by Wang. Formerly, there were said to be eight prominent Jewish clans, and Kaifeng's Jews were known as "the eight clans with seven surnames." A sixth clan, Gao, has moved to Xi'an in recent years. According to one of several interpretations, two lines of the Zhang family comprise both the seventh and the eighth clans. The Zhang clan name is not currently claimed by any of the descendants. They are said to have later converted to Islam. Because the surnames adopted by the Jews of Kaifeng are all common Chinese family names, however, surnames by themselves provide no strong evidence of Jewish ancestry.

Zhao Pingyu was said to live in the area of the city where the old synagogue used to stand, the current location of the People's Number 4 Hospital. The two landmark streets with a Jewish connection in this part of Kaifeng, a walled city of shops and basic one-story homes set in courtyards, are Northern Teaching the Scriptures Lane and Southern Teaching the Scriptures Lane. (Until the late 1800s, they were called Northern and Southern Sinew Plucking Religion Lanes, reflecting the Jewish dietary practice of removing the sciatic nerve and blood vessels attached to it from the hindquarters of kosher animals that had been observed in the past.)

When I inquired about Zhao Pingyu on Northern Teaching the Scriptures Lane, the initial response was: "He isn't home." When I reached his courtyard, his wife, Cui Shuping, a full-bodied, sixtyish woman in a blue tunic, was busy shaping dumplings. She clarified. Her husband had died a month earlier.

Like almost all Jewish descendants over the last hundred years, Zhao Pingyu had married outside the Jewish clans. (Since Jewish lineage is passed along maternally, almost certainly none of the descendants carrying the names of the six remaining clans could be termed Jewish.) Cui Shuping's connection to Judaism had been through the periodic visitors who sought out her husband, through the two Chanukah candelabra that flanked the picture of her late husband, and through the wood model of the Kaifeng synagogue her husband had built. Her five daughters, she said, were interested in going to Israel. She spoke vaguely of plans to open a Jewish museum and produced a sign etched in blue plastic that a tourist had sent to her. In Hebrew, English, and Chinese, it read: TEACHING THE TORAH LANE S.

Of the descendants interviewed by Curator Wang, Shi Zhongyu, born in 1922, who lived in a courtyard on Behind the Hospital Street, retained some of the most vivid childhood memories of his Jewish past. His father, he recalled, would dip a brush in red pigment and rule a line on the paper couplets that Chinese traditionally paste on their doors at the late-winter Spring Festival holiday. This was possibly reminiscent of God's request that the Jews in Egypt daub their doorposts with lamb blood so that, in the course of punishing Egyptians, God would "pass over" Jewish households. Shi Zhongyu also recalled an insipid lamb soup, an apparent Passover adaptation, that his family drank at the time of Spring Festival. Both customs had since been abandoned, he said.

Shi Zhongyu, a retired administrator with the Bureau of Industry and Commerce, claimed to never have eaten pork. This would make him unique among the Jewish descendants, most of whose families had been breaching this cardinal principle of Judaism for generations. The most astonishing discovery about Shi Zhongyu, though, was his ID card. Under the category "nationality," it carried the curious designation JEWISH DESCENDANT (*You Tai Hou Yi*). Shi, with some of the other descendants, had requested this change in 1980 and, though "Jew" is not included among the fifty-five official minorities in China, the request was honored, giving Kaifeng's Jewish descendants an official religious status granted nowhere else. Previously, the descendants, who are physically indistinguishable from other

Chinese, had all been included among the ninety-one-percent majority "Han" Chinese. A consequence perhaps of the publicity it received, the practice of stamping JEWISH DESCENDANT on Kaifeng ID cards was discontinued in the mid-1990s.

Shi Zhongyu belongs to the last generation of Jewish descendants with active memories of their heritage. His son, Shi Xinguang, in his mid-forties, a computer analyst for an engine factory, had only the vaguest knowledge of Jewish custom. Though he knew of the Jewish Sabbath, and listened with deep interest as I chanted the Friday evening blessing over wine in Hebrew, he knew nothing about the Jewish fast day of Yom Kippur. Until recently, Shi Xinguang said, Judaism had in no way influenced his life. Neither his son, he told me, nor his nephew (to whom I put the question directly) had any feelings about their Jewish ancestry.

When in 1993 I met in Beijing with the then-Israeli ambassador to China, Abe Sufot, just before traveling to Kaifeng, he mentioned his own visit there in May 1992.

He had been told at the time that there were no Jews in Kaifeng and no effort was made to introduce him to any of the descendants, though it was common knowledge that the Jewish descendants had met with delegations of foreign Jews many times in the past. Ambassador Sufot's visit was restricted to a viewing of the stone inscriptions at the Kaifeng Museum. Knowledgeable in Chinese, Ambassador Sufot found himself boxed in by politics. Israel wishes to remain at arm's distance of any charge of proselytizing, which would not play well in officially atheist China.

Shi Xinguang's perspective was that when Ambassador Sufot came to Kaifeng, the descendants requested permission to meet with him and were refused. His interpretation is that the Chinese government feared that Israel would try to organize Kaifeng's Jewish descendants.

Thus, despite a heightening awareness of their past, and the establishment of several research programs about Judaism in various cities in China, the one to two hundred Jewish descendants of Kaifeng, the group at the core of this interest, remained without the patron needed to restrike their roots. As to plans among the descendants to deepen their knowledge of their Jewish heritage, Shi Xinguang replied that they had no idea how to begin.

What remained unanswered, as I left Kaifeng, were the fine details as to how some of the Jewish descendants, after so many years of virtual assimilation, had suddenly come to seek formal identity as "Jewish Descendants." Shi Xinguang, whose Jewish awareness has come only within the last year or two, was unable to offer an explanation.* And speaking late at night in a dimly lit room with his father, Shi Zhongyu, who is hard of hearing, was difficult. There were hints that some of the Jewish descendants saw declaring themselves Jews as an avenue to a better life inside or outside of China.

When I brought up this curiosity to Ambassador Sufot upon returning to Beijing from Kaifeng in March 1993, he directed me to Professor Zhao Xiangru, a researcher at the Institute of Nationality Studies of the Chinese Academy of Social Sciences in Beijing. I had met Zhao, I recalled, at a Jewish New Year dinner for foreigners living in Beijing a year or two earlier. Speaking only Chinese, he appeared uneasy and out of place. In the interim, he had risen in stature.

Zhao, who is originally from Kaifeng and claims Jewish descent, highlights the difficulty in resurrecting history when

---

* Professor Xu Xin of Nanjing University, the ranking Chinese academic authority on Jews and Judaism, has delved incompletely into the evolution of the official status of the Jewish descendants in Kaifeng. In 1953 and again in 1980, he explains, the issue of whether or not to designate the Jews of Kaifeng as an official minority was considered in Beijing. The conclusion was that since there was nothing distinctive about the Jewish descendants in language, looks, and customs; and since most of the middle-age and younger descendants were indifferent to a change in their status, there was no need to alter it. He doesn't address how, despite counterdirections from Beijing, a number of the descendants managed to have their nationality designated as JEWISH DESCENDANT on their ID cards.

personal interests intervene. Since he now specializes in the history of the Jews in China, and had recently lectured on the subject at the Ben Zvi Institute in Jerusalem, Zhao should have been able to offer the background behind the JEWISH DESCENDANT identity card curiosity. Instead, he took a very cautious, bureaucratic route. "You must understand my position," he answered, and referred me to his research institute for formal permission to speak to him.

Zhao Xiangru, the most visible of China's Jewish descendants at the time, appeared to be trying to milk his Jewish ancestry to carve out a professional niche for himself. To do so, he had chosen to embellish history. His claim, well publicized in world Jewish funding circles, that there are currently two to five thousand Jews living in China is, as he surely knows, preposterous, given that, for generations, almost all Kaifeng men identified by surname as Jewish had married non-Jewish women.

WHEN I MET WITH THE ISRAELI AMBASSADOR to China, Dr. Yehoyada Haim, in Beijing in 2006, he reported no knowledge of the current state of the Jewish descendants in Kaifeng. In his four years in Beijing, he said, none had ever approached him. He had visited Kaifeng once and had met the mayor, but had not met any of the descendants. He recalled the tablet display as shabby and unimpressive. He did concur that in a country such as China it was entirely possible that the government in Kaifeng had given strict warning to the descendants not to approach the Israeli embassy in Beijing or consulate in Shanghai. To avoid charges of meddling, the Israeli government does not encourage its diplomats to seek out the Jewish descendants. Nor does Israel encourage support by nongovernment Jewish organizations, a source of unending frustration among the descendants.

WERE IT NOT FOR THE CONSTANT FLOW of Jewish tourists to Kaifeng—three to four hundred annually—Kaifeng's assimilated Jewish community would have remained little more than a curi-

ous relic. In 1999, that changed. A Finnish Christian foundation took an interest in the case of Kaifeng Jewish descendant
Jin Guangyuan, a director of a machine factory, who, with his
wife and their teenage daughter, was interested in going to Israel.
Even with Finnish sponsorship, the Jin family's path was far from
smooth. The designation JEWISH DESCENDANT that Jin carried on
his ID card was valuable documentation that would allow him
and his family to settle in Israel under Israel's Law of Return.
But, with a change in ID card policy in Kaifeng in 1996, Jin's
card now categorized him as "Han Chinese," requiring validation
from China's Ministry of Foreign Affairs that he was a Jewish descendant. He was able to receive that validation in Beijing.

Once they arrived in Israel via Finland in 2000, the Jin family faced further obstacles thrown up by Israel's Ministry of the
Interior, and at one point faced deportation. The family's proc-
lamation of being Jewish aroused distrust, because their spon-
sor was a Christian foundation that was also underwriting a
portion of their living expenses in Jerusalem. Their conversion
and integration into Israeli society was smoothed by Shavei Israel, an organization that specializes in bringing remnant Jewish communities to Israel. The three members of the Jin family
completed their conversion and now hold Israeli citizenship.

A fourth Chinese came to Israel in the summer of 2001 through
an American connection. While leading a group of American
Jews on a Far East study tour in 2000, Rabbi Marvin Tokayer,
a U.S. army chaplain who later served as the rabbi of the Jewish
community in Tokyo for eight years, was referred to a Chinese
college graduate in Kaifeng who was to be the group's guide. Im-
pressed by his eager and unending questions on Judaism and
Jewish tradition, Rabbi Tokayer arranged for Shi Lei to spend a
year in Israel at Bar-Ilan University, studying Judaism and learning Hebrew. Shi Lei, then twenty-three, followed his one-year
Jewish studies program at Bar-Ilan University with one-and-a-
half years at a yeshiva, the Machon Meir Institute of Jewish Studies in Jerusalem. Shi Lei, it turned out, was the son and grandson

of Shi Xinguang and Shi Zhongyu, the two Jewish descendants I had met just by chance in Kaifeng seven years earlier.

Shi Lei found himself unsuited to Orthodox yeshiva life, decided not to undergo formal conversion to Judaism, and returned to Kaifeng in the fall of 2004. A month after he left Israel, Shi Lei received notification from Israel's Ministry of the Interior that his application for Israeli citizenship had been approved. He would have been the first Kaifeng Jew to receive Israeli citizenship without going through the conversion process—an important precedent. Under pressure from the Jewish descendants in Kaifeng, Shi returned to Israel eight months later to claim his citizenship. Since he had been out of the country and stated that he did not want to live in Israel, however, the Ministry of the Interior reviewed Shi's case more closely and ultimately decided not to grant citizenship.

Today, Shi Lei operates a travel agency in Kaifeng and works as a tour guide. He also teaches Hebrew and English to a small group of Jewish descendants. Shi Lei and his father have turned his late grandfather's house into a modest museum for his tour groups, which—through artifacts and photographs—give visitors an overview of the recent history of the Jewish community in Kaifeng. Shi Lei's unwillingness to work more closely with his fellow descendants has left some in the Kaifeng community deeply disappointed.

WHILE SHI LEI WAS IN ISRAEL, a fledgling revival began in Kaifeng of far greater significance than the symbolic emigration of four Kaifeng Jewish descendants to Israel: the rebirth of a Kaifeng Jewish *community*. The modest stream of foreign Jews to Kaifeng through the 1990s gave the Kaifeng descendants (currently numbering five hundred or more*) a stronger link with

---

* The Jewish descendants of Kaifeng have traditionally considered their line to be transmitted through the father. Thus, a male Jewish descendant's daughter's child would not be considered a Jewish descendant. However, in recent years that designation has broken down; many of the descendants now originate from the mother's side.

their past, but no sense of community. Many visitors left books, Purim noisemakers (*groggers*), and Chanukah tops (*dreidels*). But, unable to read Hebrew or English, these remained nothing more than ornaments. That changed with the arrival of an American Jew—a teacher at Kaifeng University—who, from the fall 2002 until May 2006, set up a community center and organized classes in Jewish culture, history, and religion meeting four to five times per week. As their numbers grew to more than fifty students, they rented meeting space in Kaifeng. They also began to meet for Jewish holidays and on Friday evening to usher in the Sabbath. Over one hundred attended the Kaifeng Passover *seder*.

As many of the descendants corroborate, without "Di," as he is known in Chinese, there would be no Jewish community in Kaifeng.

In July 2005, Michael Freund, the chairman of Shavei Israel, visited Kaifeng with two Israeli rabbis. As a result, in January 2006, under Shavei Israel's sponsorship, four women in their early and mid-twenties left for Israel, where they completed the conversion process. Two are now studying at Jerusalem's Hebrew University. A second group (two teenage girls and one boy) arrived in Israel in November 2006. Michael Freund feels that the rekindled interest in Judaism in Kaifeng presents "an opportunity that we cannot and dare not allow to be missed." The ten descendants from Kaifeng now leading Jewish lives in Israel not only strengthened the Kaifeng connection with Israel and with the larger Jewish world, they also opened a pipeline of information and inspiration flowing in both directions.* The contradiction is that those from Kaifeng who choose to live in Israel are those best equipped to help the Jewish community in Kaifeng grow.

---

* See http://www.youtube.com/watch?v=Emmy82tFT30 for a clip of a January 2008 Chinese-Jewish wedding in Jerusalem.

IN MARCH 2008, I SAW HOW FAR the Jews of Kaifeng had come in a decade. At sundown on Friday evening, some thirty-five people (most in their forties, no old people) gathered at their second floor meeting room, off of Southern Bookstore Street. Shi Mingxia covered her head and recited the Hebrew blessing as she lit the Sabbath candles. Her son, Yage, twenty-two, one of five or six in Kaifeng able to read Hebrew well enough to pray, then recited, in Hebrew, the *Kiddush*, the blessing over wine that commences the Jewish Sabbath. As is the custom, the participants then filed silently to the wash basin to rinse their hands, those able reciting the Hebrew blessing. The Sabbath challahs were then salted, the proper blessing recited, and the bread passed around the table for each person to break off a piece. Feeling that their weekly gathering needed more religious content, Gao Chao had recently begun to read, in Chinese, a passage from the Bible—this night a portion from Leviticus detailing what foods Jews may and may not eat.

The biblical passage on the dietary laws pointed up the contradictions a minuscule community of Jews faces in reviving its past. At this stage in their renaissance, there was no practical way for them to observe the dietary laws. Everyone in the community brought a dish to the gathering and the meat on the table, mostly chicken, was not kosher. But they did not eat pork (the meat staple in China), and a good number of them had given up shellfish.

And there were other signs of revival. Gao Chao told me that he had given up the Chinese New Year customs of shooting off firecrackers and placing Chinese *duilian* [couplets] on the sides of his house entranceway.

"These aren't Jewish customs," he said matter-of-factly.

A Mayo Clinic Prelude
with a Double China Twist

□ □ □

A YEAR EARLIER, on an inauspicious Sunday at the beginning of October 1996, I made the biggest mistake of my life. The bushel box of Empire apples that the customer pulling up to our roadside stand wanted was already outside the truck, ready for sale. But this was the shortest crop of the '90s and the box on display was overpacked for appearance's sake. So I reached inside the Blazer and swiveled a forty-two-pound box of Macouns out of the way with extended arms at a contorted angle in order to reach a standard-size box of Empires. All of this to pull in an extra buck or two.

The "pop" I felt in my lower back should have been a minor event; as in the past, three or four days of immediate rest would have cured the injury. But, alone on the state road, with five hundred pounds of apples already outside the truck and no possibility of reloading, I pushed on. The thought of abandoning the apples never crossed my mind.

Eleven months later—after visits to two internists, two neurologists, an orthopedic surgeon, a physiatrist, an anesthesiologist, and an osteopath; two MRIs confirming minor to medium disc herniations at two levels and one set of flexion-extension X-rays; an epidural steroid injection, two sterile saline trigger point *injections, electric stimulation, analgesics, muscle relaxants, anti-inflammatories, and oral steroids—I was still without diagnosis.*

FACED WITH PROLONGED DEBILITATION, with no recovery in sight, even the coldest rationalist is prone to acts of desperation. So it was, just hours before the beginning of the Jewish New Year, that I received a call from a Chinese friend whom I had known for quite a number of years. I had told her over the preceding months about my back problems, and now she was calling to let me know that her friend, Dr. Sun, whom she described as a surgeon, could help me. He was free to come to my apartment that afternoon or the next day. Further, I didn't have to worry about paying him; he was her friend (implying weighty obligation in Chinese culture). I wanted to postpone this appointment until after the holiday, but the idea of a trained doctor—a surgeon—coming to my house to help me was irresistible.

Not ten minutes later, Dr. Sun was on the phone letting me know that he was on his way.

I should have asked Dr. Sun about his credentials, but a surgeon could not be ignorant. He spoke in Chinese, so I didn't know that his English was in fact quite poor. I knew that, on the side, Dr. Sun was peddling shares in a get-rich-quick, pyramid-style scheme, and later learned that he saw me as a stepping stone into English-speaking America. Still, a trained surgeon coming to your house is nothing to sneer at. I was more than willing to accommodate Dr. Sun's motive in return for expert medical advice.

After reading the history of my case that I had prepared earlier in Chinese, Dr. Sun gave me a perfunctory leg raise and leg tuck test, concluding that I didn't have "disc hernia." Thereupon, he began a vigorous pressure-point Chinese massage. The massage was so rough that the pressure on my left and right buttocks caused me to scream. I should have told Sun to stop, but I was so mired in frustration and desperation that I was determined to take anything Dr. Sun could dish out—almost as if the more pain I could tolerate, the greater the curative effect. That he could actually harm me, I had somehow stashed away in deep consciousness.

Before Dr. Sun left, I asked him gently about his credentials (he was, after all, still the friend of a friend; "face" was involved), only to learn that he didn't have any. Although in the U.S. since 1987, he had not passed any of the three-step U.S. Medical Licensing Exams. He had attended Second Beijing Medical University and worked as an internist at Chaoyang Hospital in Beijing (a second-rate institution). For eight years, he said, he had worked in New York as a "private researcher" for Dr. Hiromi Shinya, Chief, Surgical Endoscopy Unit, Beth Israel Medical Center. In place of his own business card, he gave me Dr. Shinya's card. Nowhere—here or in China—had Dr. Sun trained in Chinese massage, which, he told me, he performed in Dr. Shinya's office.

Whether any of this was illegal, I did not know. What was severely misleading at the least was the Beth Israel Hospital name tag "Dr." Sun wore, identifying him as "Sun, Jianheng, M.D., fellow." A fellow in American medical parlance is a fourth or fifth-year resident, a licensed physician in advanced training. Almost any patient reading "Dr." Sun's name tag would conclude he was a licensed American physician. When I called Dr. Shinya's office to ask about Sun, the secretary told me that she thought that Sun was a licensed physician.

For three days after Sun's massage, I suffered more than I had in several months, unable to walk, with sharp pain radiating down each leg. A few days later, my body returned to its pre-massage status. The treatment brought no benefit.

STILL TREADING MEDICAL WATER, I headed for the Mayo Clinic in Rochester, Minnesota, as a last shot. The letter of referral sent to the Mayo Clinic by my family doctor nine months after the injury summarized my condition:

> The patient continues to experience continual, de-
> bilitating, non-specific muscle spasms over his full
> body from toe to jaws. Spasms are minutely sensi-
> tive to body position. These spasms radiate from the
> left hip and the area on the right side above the iliac
> crest. Because of muscle constriction at the hips,
> through the buttocks, and up the back, the patient
> is frequently unable to stand or sit. Manifestations
> vary constantly. Original numbness in the left great
> toe continues.

After ten days of evaluation by five different Mayo doctors,
I emerged with little more than a vague diagnosis of "fibromy-
algia," an insurance code condition defined no more precisely
than "generalized muscular pain and fatigue." Even regarding this vague Dx there had been no consensus among Mayo's
doctors.

AS SOMEONE WHO HAS SPENT a good portion of his life studying China, it was assumed by all who offered well-meaning
advice that acupuncture would be one of my first recourses.
Even my dentist, Dr. Wiggs, contributed his two bits. However,
consulting with a Chinese M.D. friend here who had studied
acupuncture in medical school in China, I concluded early on
that, without a specific focus of pain, acupuncture would be
of no benefit to me. Delving further, I learned why so many
Americans swear by acupuncture in the case of lower back
pain. As medical texts document, in eighty to ninety percent
of lower back injuries, the patient stands a chance of recovery
no matter the nature of the treatment (i.e., in time, he would
have recovered anyhow).

Able to plug into the ex-pat Chinese medical network in the
U.S., I learned of numerous Chinese who, exploiting unde-
manding licensing requirements here, have set themselves up
as acupuncturists. Often, their medical training in China had
nothing to do with acupuncture. (In China, separate degree

programs are offered in both Western and Chinese medicine.) Just as often, they had no medical training in China at all. Their most valuable asset in this $500-million-a-year business is their Oriental countenance. May the ailing beware!

A SECOND CHINA TWIST

At about the same time that I was applying for evaluation at the Mayo Clinic, I sent four detailed pages, in Chinese, outlining my condition, together with MRI reports, to Dr. Huang Gaoqu at the National Sports Research Institute in Beijing. The National Sports Research Institute is attached to China's State Sports Commission (now the General Sports Administration of China), and its doctors treat many of China's world-class athletes, not a few of whom have disc problems. My main questions to Dr. Huang, whom I knew from time spent with China's Olympic softball team, prior to the Atlanta Olympics, were whether she had ever encountered full-body spasms such as I was suffering and whether acupuncture was an effective remedy.

Dr. Huang's response, after consulting with two senior doctors well experienced in trauma and rehabilitation, outlined the traditional Chinese non-surgical approach to disc problems. They included weighted traction, massage, and vigorous back-strengthening exercises. Nowhere in the prescription was acupuncture. Most helpful was her view that coercing spasms—forcing unresponsive muscles to perform normally despite constriction—was useful in breaking spasms. Sit-ups, which most U.S. doctors had recommended against, were an effective back-strengthening exercise, she felt. This was important to me because, after almost a year without systematic exercise, my muscles had begun to atrophy. Fifty sit-ups and one hundred push-ups had been part of my daily regimen since teenage years. This was what had allowed me to do heavy physical work my entire adult life.

As helpful and supportive as were Dr. Huang's insights,

never in my deepest thoughts did I envision that, five months later, on New Year's Day, 1998, I would be arriving in medically backward China to try to cure a condition that America's best specialists could not even diagnose. Other considerations aside, how could I make a twenty-hour voyage to the other side of the world when I couldn't even sit down at a table to eat breakfast? My inconclusive visit to Mayo and an about-to-expire, business class, frequent-flier ticket on Japan Airlines to China (which offered twelve-position, easy-chair seating) were what nudged me in China's direction. What sealed the decision was the realization that unless I began to use my body vigorously and succeeded in restoring it to normal function, regardless of the discomfort, the physical life—farming, exercise, hard work—that defined me would come to an end. Winter in New York was no place to work a reluctant body back into shape.

Dr. Huang's thought, when she met me at Beijing Airport, was to admit me to a Beijing hospital belonging to the State Sports Commission, where I would go through several weeks of traditional Chinese back rehabilitation treatment. This, pending a medical evaluation she had arranged with Professor Ren, a trauma expert.

My own plan was to travel to Kunming in the south of China and, through contacts, spend three weeks at the Haigeng Sports Training Center, the largest of twenty sports bases where China's best athletes train. There, for $15 to $20 per day for room and board, I could swim in the Olympic pool, receive massages, and participate in some of the National Softball Team's dawn-to-dusk training drills as they prepared for the upcoming world championships. I was prepared to give my body as much work as it could take, reassured by the tested premise that any exercise that left me feeling no worse after completion was beneficial. Remaining in a hospital in Beijing, which can be fiercely cold in January, held little appeal. But I would be foolish to reject hospitalization if that was the collective Chinese medical recommendation.

Two days later—without waiting, without waiting room, without forms, without signatures—Dr. Ren studied the MRIs and X-rays that I had brought from the U.S. His examination was far more vigorous than similar exams I had been through at home, as he flexed, pushed, tugged, extended, and twisted my legs in an attempt to produce the type of radicular pain that would help isolate the source of my spasms. After the exam, he ordered a back X-ray from an oblique angle—a position my X-rays at home had not explored. (With MRI and CT scans much less available than in the U.S., and out of pocketbook reach for most Chinese, X-rays are relied upon in China, where more sophisticated imaging would be used outside of the country.) After considering all the findings, Dr. Ren came to the same conclusion as the American doctors: the massive, non-specific spasms and stiffness I was experiencing could not be explained by the unremarkable imperfections and degeneration imaged in my spine. He, too, had no diagnosis. He saw no value in hospitalizing me.

There was no charge for the examination or the X-rays. "At home, rely on your parents; away from home, rely on your friends," the Chinese like to say.

IN KUNMING, TWELVE HUNDRED MILES southeast of Beijing and known as the "City of Spring" for its year-round moderate temperatures, with assistance from Dr. Huang, I put myself on a strict program, mirroring the practice schedule of the Chinese National Softball Team. For over a year, I had spent an hour or more each day after rising just waiting for my hip and back muscles to adjust sufficiently to allow me to leave the house for morning walks. At the sports camp, regardless of how I felt, I awakened shortly after 6:15, put on four or five layers of clothing to accommodate the pre-dawn chill, and shortly before 7:00 joined the team in the pitch dark for thirty-five minutes of pre-breakfast practice.

First, there were three laps around the field, followed by five to ten minutes of stretching, then twenty minutes of endless wind-sprint variations—hopping, jumping, kicking, running backwards, running relays, running while describing arcs with each leg (clockwise and counterclockwise). The competitive element—not wishing to fall behind the players (all decades younger than me)—carried me through where I would have stopped on my own. The only exercise I passed on was the sprint with an automobile tire tethered to my midsection.

After breakfast, there was often a repeat set of warm-up exercises followed by softball drills. Each day, before lunch, often pushing through cramped shoulder muscles, I forced myself to swim 150 meters in the camp pool. After lunch, more drills until dinner.

After more than a year of almost complete inactivity, all of this brought intense muscle soreness on top of the constriction from the spasms. During the first few days, Dr. Dai, the team doctor, trained in traditional Chinese medicine, gave me a series of vigorous, Chinese-style massages. After three sessions, these were discontinued because he felt that, without being able to isolate a source of pain, they had no benefit. Thinking that acupuncture might be useful in relieving exercise-induced soreness and having seen Dr. Dai perform acupuncture, I had purchased four packages of throw-away acupuncture needles in Beijing. They remained in their packages.

Dr. Dai prescribed a Chinese root called *tian ma*, said to be useful for nerve and muscle conditions. My trip to the Kunming Pharmaceutical Company provided my initiation into the esoteric world of Chinese medicine. *Tian ma* was offered in a wide range of qualities, starting at $4.00 per hundred grams and ranging up to $13.00, making it a very expensive medicine and leaving open many opportunities for fraud and deception—a major problem in China with pharmaceuticals.

"How do I know which price level to purchase?" I asked Dr. Dai.

"According to your pocketbook," he answered.

Most people apparently purchased the lower grades, which came pre-ground at $6.00 per hundred grams. Gulping down one teaspoon of *tian ma* mixed in water three times per day was as disagreeable as swallowing three teaspoons of ground finger nails. I suspended the effort after three or four days.

Though the constricting spasms never relaxed their grip, and sitting on a chair to read a book remained a trial, three weeks of concentrated exercising in Kunming brought about a fundamental improvement in body flexibility and range of motion. I began to be able to do things that would have been impossible before coming to China, including day outings deep into the countryside on rattling buses and participating in the soccer games the softball team played from time to time as a conditioning change of pace. The price of continuously forcing my muscles was a weariness that compelled me to be in bed most nights by 9:00. Sleep remained the only posture in which my muscles could relax.

I left China just after Chinese New Year—the year of the Tiger—with no more knowledge about the cause of my condition than when I had arrived. What I learned in Kunming was that, except for heavy lifting (which Dr. Huang told me to avoid), stressful exercise could not exacerbate my condition. The harder I exercised, it seemed, the better my body functioned.

Updating my family doctor, Dr. Cohen, on my rehabilitation experience in China soon after returning, he asked me to translate the Chinese wish words I had given him before departing for the Orient.

"I yearn to once again prance in the field like a young deer."

Olympic Silver Medal Chronicle: U.S. vs. China

□□□

I T WAS PAST 10:00 IN THE EVENING, and I was speaking to Chinese shortstop Christie Liu on the telephone in her room at the softball Olympic Village. Women's softball was a first-time Olympic event in Atlanta in 1996, and the eight competing teams were billeted inside Fort Benning, just outside of Columbus, Georgia, the softball venue. There would be no terror threat here.

"Do you believe in destiny?" shortstop Liu asked in Chinese, trailing off with a sigh of despair. China had just defeated the Netherlands, 8-0, that morning to move to a record of 4-1. Pitchers He Liping and Liu Yaju had combined to pitch a no-hitter. Shortstop Liu had hit a home run. A victory the following night against Taiwan would put China into the medal round. But earlier in the week, in its only loss, China had fallen unexpectedly to Japan, 3-0, and according to the complicated Olympic softball competition rules, the first two finishers in the preliminary round would be guaranteed a bronze medal, while the third and fourth teams would have to play an extra game to win the gold medal. China's head-to-head loss to Japan, it appeared, would place China third.

Destiny or self-shaped fate?

The following afternoon, just before the team was ready to set out for Golden Park for its game against Taiwan, short-stop Liu had her answer. In remarkable fashion, Australia, which China had trounced soundly, 6-0, had just defeated the widely heralded, virtually invincible U.S. softball team, 2-1, in ten innings. American pitcher Lisa Fernandez, pitching a perfect game, had reached two outs and two strikes on the batter in the bottom of the extra-inning tenth. All of the sails had already been punctured for the Australians. In the top of the tenth, the U.S. had scored the game's first run when the Aussie centerfielder threw the ball into the stands in an attempt to nab a runner already standing squarely on third base. But Fernandez came up high and flat on a riser to number four batter Joanne Brown, and Brown hit the ball out of the park to give Australia a 2-1 victory, one of only a handful of defeats the U.S. had absorbed in international competition in the past ten years.

The Chinese team, which was holding yet another of its countless meetings in preparation for that evening's game against Taiwan when word of the U.S. loss came through, was rejuvenated by the news. "There is no destiny," shortstop Liu blurted out after the meeting. "There is only fighting spirit."

Fighting spirit had been a weak point for the Chinese team. For the past decade, despite a base of just two hundred softball players in the entire country, China had ranked within a step of the U.S., defeating them a year earlier in the pre-Olympic Superball tournament in Columbus. Yet, there was hardly a Chinese player who believed in her heart that a gold medal was attainable. That was the feeling the players carried with them during Olympic training in China; that was the feeling they brought into the Olympic Games.

In a debate in the athlete's dining room in Fort Benning with Chinese centerfielder Zhang Chunfang, after China's 10-0 thrashing of Puerto Rico, she could only defer to Chinese reality. In the Yen'an enclave in central China to which the Chinese Communists retreated under siege during the dark days of the War of Resistance against Japan from 1937 to 1945, Mao Zedong coined an aphorism: *Shi shi qiu shi*—"seek the truth," "be objective." That was the guideline the players cited. When the debate shifted to whether such protective caution served any useful purpose on the ball field, where reality is as often relative as objective, centerfielder Zhang drew out yet another Chinese saying: "If you get bit by a snake, you don't return to the well for ten years."

Even when the official media guide showed China to be equal physically to the U.S., centerfielder Zhang, China's Olympic hitting star at .394, and a blocky 150 pounds at 5 feet 6 inches, would not be shaken. "The U.S. heights are understated," she persisted. Pursued from a different angle, and asked whether they possessed an inner zeal to prove that they were better than U.S. shortstop and living-legend Dot Richardson and U.S. star third baseman Lisa Fernandez,* neither Chinese shortstop Liu, who hit two home runs and performed like a vacuum cleaner in the field, nor third baseman Tao Hua, who hit three home runs, could ever recall such compulsion.

"We want to win...but *objectively*, the U.S. is better." That was the unconcealed team consensus.

The Chinese carried the isolated training life they led in China right through the Olympics. The Americans were free to go to the Peachtree Mall for shopping, or to meet friends and family when they weren't playing or practicing. The Australians were out beer drinking at 3:00 A.M. The Chinese spent virtually all of their time in the Athlete's Village—gossiping, sleeping, and watching soap operas and the Olympics on TV. Head coach Li Minkuan preferred the isolation of Fort Benning, one hundred miles away from the hubbub of Atlanta. Without outside stimuli, it was sometimes hard to dream; but with too many diversions, the Chinese discipline that allowed

---

* When she was not starring as a pitcher.

222 ☼ CHINA MOSAIC

a country with just eight softball teams to buck the talent-rich, rah-rah-driven Americans might not hold up.

Only when China almost beat the U.S., losing 3-2 in the final preliminary game, did cracks in this inborn Chinese defense mechanism, deriving from absolute practicality and fear of losing face, begin to appear. Centerfielder Zhang was willing to give China a fifty percent chance. Shortstop Liu was talking about fighting spirit. Second baseman Yan Fang was talking about her ultimate Olympic dream. ("Their team trains six hours per day, six days per week," reminded U.S. coach Ralph Raymond after the game, anticipating the challenge ahead.)

A variation on the objective reality motif governed Coach Li's pitching strategy for the medal rounds. A victory against the U.S. in the final game of the preliminary round would give China first seeding; a loss might relegate China to third place, requiring China to play an extra game to win a gold medal. *Objectively*, only Chinese pitching ace Wang Lihong, perhaps the best pitcher in the world when she was on her game, and who registered more strikeouts than any other pitcher in the Atlanta Olympics, could defeat the U.S. It had been two years since the U.S. had last faced Wang Lihong. But to use her in the final preliminary would give the U.S. an added opportunity to become familiar with her baffling change-up. Further, Wang Lihong, already plagued with various injuries, had undergone an intestinal operation in March in which three inches of her colon had been removed. A bulldog, who previously could pitch two or even three games in a day at top form, she simply had not trained enough before the Games to recover peak stamina.

Facing the same situation, the Americans might have chosen to throw caution to the winds and gone with their best. Citing "objective reality," Coach Li chose the indirect route: first secure the silver against Australia with Wang Lihong, then go for the gold with his second best. "After achieving a bronze medal in the preliminaries," Coach Li told me the night before the semifinal against the Americans, "it would be *inappropriate* to end up with just a bronze in the medal round." There was an element of "face" here, mixed with Chinese practicality.

EARLIER IN THE WEEK, in the Athlete's Village, one of the Australian players had been trying to sell extra softball tickets they had to some of the Chinese players. (With a full house of eighty-five hundred at every session, medal-round tickets, priced at $32, were being scalped for up to $150.) "China doesn't have any fans," commented her teammate when there were no Chinese ticket takers.

The Chinese played all their games in China before empty houses. This too was a Chinese reality. "The crowd puts more pressure on the U.S. than on us," commented second baseman Yan Fang feistily to American reporters, supplementing her interpreter from time to time in English acquired during a scholarship year at Oklahoma City University where she was an all-American. "That encourages us."

LOOKING BACK, CHINESE COACH LI would probably have preferred that the heart-arresting, 1-0, semifinal, ten-inning loss to the U.S., if it had to be a loss, be concluded with less physical effort. With the score 0-0, U.S. runners on first and second, and no outs in the bottom of the seventh, Li Minkuan, smelling victory, modified his plan to save his best pitcher for the Australians. He brought in ace Wang Lihong, who got China out of the inning. The lingering question was whether the four innings she pitched in the loss to the U.S. would be debited against her stamina in the silver medal game against Australia the next day.

Shortstop Liu took to bed an American corollary to her "fighting spirit" after the 1-0 loss: "When the going gets tough, the tough get going."

Even in striking out ten Australian batters and giving up no earned runs as China defeated Australia 4-2 to win the silver medal, Wang Lihong struggled throughout, never finding her rhythm and throwing many more pitches than usual. But Coach Li's strategy had worked. With the silver medal (which would be worth $10,000 or more to each Chinese player) secured, China was now ready to contest the gold...without Wang Lihong in the starting lineup.

What China most feared, the players said again and again, was the umpires. This, too, was a perceived Chinese reality. Coach Li said openly that the umpires consistently worked against the Chinese. The U.S., he said, was in any case a deeper team than China. But to have to fight the umpires as well as the Americans was too heavy a burden. In the top of the third, in the gold medal game, on a double steal, China's Zhang Chunfang appeared to slide under U.S. catcher Gillian Boxx with the first run of the game. The video replay showed that clearly. Canadian umpire Carmichael called her out. In the bottom of the third, the Chinese withdrew their team from the field and protested for ten minutes that a two-run home run down the right field line by Dot Richardson of the U.S. was foul—to no avail. The U.S. added its third and final run on an error. China got back one of these runs in the top of the sixth.

2-3, 0-1, 1-3. Gold medal to the U.S. 1996 Olympic reality.

"Americans show their emotions outside; Chinese inside," second baseman Yan responded earlier in the week in the Village when we were exploring East-West differences. Yan Fang, who American shortstop Richardson dubbed "awesome," sobbed uncontrollably in the Chinese dugout for ten minutes following the gold medal loss.

Recapturing
Faded Olympic Glory:
Training for Beijing 2008

□ □ □

OUTSIDE THE CAMP, the eternal, placid pace of rural China was at play. A water bison tethered to a rope munched on green tomatoes. On mini-plots defined by mounded earth, leather-faced peasants planted soybeans, cauliflower, and potatoes in early March sunshine, taking advantage of southern Sichuan's frost-free climate. Others carried buckets of night soil, perched at the ends of long bamboo poles to distribute the weight. An ass, side-saddled with eighty-pound sacks of flour, bowed his head in resignation under the load. Puppies without collars frolicked in courtyards, while free-ranging mongrels of every description sniffed in search of the next generation.

But inside the Panzhihua Olympic softball training camp, at the southern tip of Sichuan Province, where twenty-two athletes and six coaches were cloistered, an intense drama, with subtle subplots, was unfolding: an attempt to regain faded Olympic glory. The sign outside the dormitory set the tone: Sweat Brings Glory, Hard Work Brings Results.

In preparation for the 2008 Beijing Olympics, head coach

Wang Lihong abandoned the Chinese team's traditional seven-day schedule, adopting instead a ten-day cycle, oblivious to weekends, which mirrored the Olympic softball competition schedule. Every conceivable game situation was drilled end-lessly: infield drills, outfield drills, toss batting drills, live batting drills, small ball practice (bunts and chops), base running drills, rundowns, pitching drills. You could cut the tension at Panzhihua with a knife.

During intrasquad games, Coach Wang occasionally stopped play to focus in on misplays: an unnecessary cutoff of a peg from right field by first baseman Yu on a single to right; a foot-work error by catcher Pan on a play at the plate. After each game, a statistical workup of the game was posted in the dor-mitory courtyard by the team statistician. Performance bonus-es of around $10.00 were given as incentives.

Days three, six, and nine in the ten-day cycle—morning and afternoon—were spent in the meeting room watching video tapes of the opponents China would face at the Olympics. Evenings from 6:30 to 8:30 on video days, Coach Wang ran a strength training regimen, orchestrated to Chinese disco mu-sic, turning the camp into a carnival for a few hours.

As before the 1996 Olympics, to augment the team's five pitchers, Rob Schweyer, thirty-two, a journeyman softball pitcher from Canada, was brought in to upgrade training at a salary of $4,000 a month. He could throw 10 to 15 miles per hour faster than any Chinese woman pitcher (who topped out at about 62 miles per hour), giving the Chinese hitters a good idea of what they would face in Beijing in August 2008 against the U.S. and Japan's top-gun hurlers, whose risers could reach 70 miles per hour. In a day's practice, Schweyer would throw as many as eight hundred pitches, a load that would kill any Chinese pitcher.

Under unrelenting pressure to assure a stellar performance by Chinese athletes at the Beijing Games that would surpass China's thirty-two gold-medal performance in Athens and position China among the elite sporting nations, the country's General Sports Administration draped an iron shroud over Chinese Olympic training. Virtually all journalist access was cut off. Around-the-clock uniformed guards, buzzing around like summer flies, monitored every step of anyone unauthorized to visit the Panzhihua camp. The goal was to filter out all distractions. Nevertheless, without the knowledge of the team leaders, transportation and lodging arrangements were made. "Going through the back door" is a time-honored practice in China.

If isolation was the goal, the Panzhihua camp, located on the outskirts of Hongge, a laid-back farm town eighteen miles from Panzhihua and hundreds of miles from the Sichuan heartland, provided it. Hongge's main attractions are its 4:00 A.M. wholesale vegetable market and its hot spring.

SOFTBALL IN CHINA IS A SPORTING MIRACLE. Hundreds of thousands of women play competitive softball in the U.S.; in all of China there are just ten adult softball teams, with little more than two hundred softball players. Yet, by carefully recycling superb athletes too short for basketball or volleyball, or a tad too slow for track and field, throughout the 1990s China consistently ranked within a step of the United States, climaxed by a silver medal at the 1996 Atlanta Olympics.

Thereafter, the team slowly began to fade: veteran players retired, without replacements in the pipeline. The provincial teams that fed the national team fell down in their recruiting task, their job made more difficult by changing China, which began to offer more career choices to China's youth. Parents became reluctant to put their only child on the precarious sporting altar. In 2000, at the Sydney Olympics, China finished fourth in softball. The General Sports Administration grew impatient and, for the Athens Olympics, brought in a Canadian coach, Shan McDonald, who didn't much like living in China and left after six months, content to add her fourth-place Olympic experience in China to her résumé.

With the Beijing Olympics on the horizon, in December 2005 the Sports Administration's Small Balls Department (which governs baseball, softball, field hockey, and team handball) pulled the rug from under head coach Wang Lihong, the pitching star of China's 1996 silver medal team, and replaced her with an American, Michael Bastian. Had the Small Balls Department done its homework, it would have discovered that Bastian had been at best a mediocre coach in the U.S., posting a record of 43-83 at Centenary College before resigning in 1998 to accept a coaching job in the fledgling Women's Professional Softball League. What the Small Balls Department should have known is that all of the top American softball coaches work at universities, none free to take a coaching position in China.

Longtime Chinese Olympic Coach Li Minkuan, at the helm of China's 1996 silver medal triumph and the architect of China's softball program, called Wang Lihong's replacement by an American a case of "blindly worshiping foreigners." In retrospect, Coach Wang, thirty-eight, a proud, independent woman with a three-gear demeanor that shifts from sweet to stern to acerbic—a Chinese softball treasure who could slice home plate into fractions of an inch in her heyday as a pitcher—felt that the softball team administrators "gave Michael credit for my accomplishments."

Indeed, tension between the team "leaders" (lingdao in Chinese) and the coaching staff is an eternal source of friction on Chinese teams. With little knowledge of the sport they administrate, they nevertheless have a strong say in training schedules, in selecting coaches, and in fixing the fifteen-man Olympic softball roster. (Just before the Panzhihua camp opened, a former assistant softball coach known for his brashness wormed his way onto the coaching staff against head coach Wang Lihong's wishes. At Panzhihua, he could be seen ingratiating himself—pai ma pi [ass kissing] in Chinese—with the dour team leader, Jiang Xiuyun, patiently running laps at her snail's pace, as he cemented his coaching staff ticket to his Olympic bonus.)*

In his year at the helm, high-profile Bastian, forty-five—a large, affable, well-groomed man, with a more than ample stomach, well-courted by the Chinese press—proceeded to undermine the work ethic of the Chinese national softball team.

First baseman Yu, the team veteran at thirty-two, told me that Bastian didn't have the team run in the morning, reduced strength training to once a week, and abandoned the traditional intensity of Chinese practices, which at times could see an infielder forced to field as many as one hundred balls in a row in order to groove footwork and sharpen reflexes. That found instant favor with many of the players, who at first cherished their unforeseen "vacation" practices and the chance to banter with Bastian in Chinglish. Yu Yanhong said that "Michael talked a lot but didn't drill the things he talked about." That his instructions had to be filtered through a translator didn't help.

In chats I had with him at the World Championships in Beijing in 2006, at the 2006 Asian Games in Qatar, and during the team's U.S. tour in the summer of 2007, Michael contended that Chinese softball was twenty-five years behind the times and that he wanted to turn the players into "thinking individuals who could make decisions, not robots." What he failed to grasp was that the Americans he had coached were all college-educated, while his Chinese players did not have even a decent high school education. It was precisely robotics that made Chinese softball possible.

America's top players surface through layers of competition like cream that rises to the top. China's softball players are handpicked for speed, strength, and dexterity, then judiciously hammered into softball players as a coppersmith molds

---

* Similar tensions were at play at China's Olympic baseball camp. The Chinese baseball bureaucrats felt that if they didn't use former major leaguers Jim Lefebvre and Bruce Hurst provided by Major League Baseball, they would take the blame. The Chinese coaches who ran the day-to-day training, on the other hand, doubted that foreigners could coach Chinese.

an urn. The Chinese realized early on that certain talents—world-beating pitching speed, a natural batting eye and wrist snap—emerge only from a large pool of talent, which they did not have. They could not be trained. So perfect conditioning and perfect defense, achieved through endless repetition, became the hallmark of the Chinese softball team. Bastian did not appreciate that premise.

What nailed Michael Bastian's coffin was a 10-7 semifinal loss to a mediocre Taiwan team at the December 2006 Doha Asian Games, relegating China to third place. Team administrator Jiang Xiuyun argued in Doha that adapting to Michael's "power hitting" philosophy needed time. By the New Year, that patience had waned, and Wang Lihong was back at the helm. Even then, Chinese face-saving marred the change, and Bastian was senselessly kept on as batting coach, where he continued to preach his barren power hitting formula. His ongoing presence left the team in turmoil, culminating in a Michael-or-me tantrum in Boston by Coach Wang before Leader Jiang. The tantrum bore fruit and, in September, Bastian was fired outright.*

THE ISOLATION OF THE PANZHIHUA CAMP and repetitive training routine made the Olympics seem a world away. That would change as the team broke camp at the beginning of March and headed to Australia for a tune-up tournament, followed by another practice round in the U.S. in May. By the time they settled in at the Olympic Training Center in Beijing for the last weeks of practice in June, with the "Bird's Nest" National Stadium (the site of the August 8 Opening Ceremony) within clear view of their dormitory rooms, that excitement would

---

* Even then, he didn't let go. Near the end of the Panzhihua camp, rumors spread through the camp that Bastian was nearby, though no one had seen him. Walking around Hongge in late afternoon, by sheer happenstance, I saw a large figure approaching. Bastian seemed to know everything going on at the camp, including the fact that there was no practice that day. He had slipped some of the players a few bats, he said, but not to tell Coach Wang. Six months out of his job, he still worked to maintain his connection with the team.

grow. For leftfielder Lei Donghui, this would be an unforgettable time: "To play in the Olympic Games for someone who lives in Beijing is really a special honor. It's the kind of experience I'll probably never have again my entire life."

Medal-winning bonuses running into the tens of thousands of dollars would also be special for these players, who are salaried at about $300 a month.

THE 2008 TEAM WOULD NEVER MATCH the 1996 silver-medal winners in talent. It had no stars. But that didn't put a repeat silver medal out of reach. If lead pitcher Lu Wei's recovery from "Tommy John" elbow surgery* (after the former Dodger and Yankee pitcher) continued on track, and the team played up to form in the preliminaries, China's pitching and defense would carry it to the four-team medal round, where it would likely face feisty Australia. It would take exceptional fighting spirit to overcome the Australians.

As with other team sports, fighting spirit has been a traditional weak point for China's softball team, well acknowledged by the players, who tend toward self-deprecation and Chinese realism (a legacy of Mao Zedong's "seek the truth"), a time-honored face-saving mechanism in China. At the Panzhihua training camp, I circulated among the players a Chinese translation of the previous chapter about the 1996 team's confrontation with Chinese reality, hoping to spur a reaction. "We all have fighting spirit," responded good-humored second baseman Sun Li in her Sichuan accent. The transformation was unconvincing.**

If Chinese spunk rises to the task against Australia, it would

---

* In this surgery, a tendon is harvested from the forearm or below the knee, then woven in a figure-eight pattern through tunnels that have been drilled in the ulna and humerus bones that are part of the elbow joint. It has a success rate of eighty percent.

** Chinese national swimming coach Feng Shangbao believes that it is the absence of passion, of the "hobby factor" as he calls it, that is missing in Chinese athletes, most of whom have been professionals since their early teens.

take an exquisite effort plus a solid measure of luck to get past Japan and ensure a silver medal. To beat the Americans and win the gold, it would take double measures of each.

China Goes to
the Dogs

□ □ □

"WE FOUND a *bee-guh-er*," the voice over the phone sang in Chinese at 7:45 in the morning. "He has long ears. Can you meet me under the bridge at 4:00 this afternoon to have a look?" The sterilization of life that accompanied the rise to power of the Chinese communists in 1949 brought with it an abolition of prostitution, opium use, and the unequal distribution of poverty. It also brought—for health reasons—a prohibition against dogs as pets in China's teeming cities. For the next forty years, the only Chinese permitted to keep dogs were China's peasants. Some were raised as pets; others to satisfy China's appetite for dog meat. Since the 1990s, though, as China loosened its noose around most nonpolitical areas of life, puppies have begun to pour into China's cities, to the delight of Jing Jing and millions of other Chinese children. Climbing prices reflect China's newfound affluence.

Intelligence about "nouveau riche" China's latest craze had reached me in New York in a letter from Sichuan in the fall. But in staid Beijing, I found on arrival, secrets emerge more grudgingly.

Fuchengmen Station, on Beijing's loop subway line, proved to be a stop too soon. At the next stop, a fruit peddler advised that the Guan Yuan Agricultural Market, which in the past had

233

offered puppy dogs, had been torn down for a new high rise. The present puppy location, she directed, was adjacent to the bird market at Xizhimen Bridge.

Colorful birds and aquarium fish are China's traditional house pets, and the bird market astride the Xizhimen overpass is an established business area. Dozens of vendors in outdoor stalls were selling canaries and parakeets in cages, cages without birds, birds without cages, and birdseed. But puppies were nowhere to be seen.

"What kind of a dog are you looking for?" a man straddling a bicycle—who later gave his trade name as Mr. "Puppy Sales" Xu—asked.

"An American dog," I answered, presenting myself as a Beijing-based businessman who dealt in industrial plastics.

"How about a Chinese dog?" he replied. And he zipped open his jacket pocket and out poked a pug-faced pooch just a few weeks old. "No," he preempted, "puppies don't mind spending their days in someone's coat pocket, $500."

"Something with longer ears," I said.

"How about this?" a colleague a few steps away by the name of Guo broke in. He opened a canvas bag and out peeked a tiny terrier.

Mr. Guo, starting to get silly, said he had a dog with an American passport. "If he has a valid passport," I said, "I will pay $500 sight unseen."

Mr. Guo, who, unlike Mr. Xu, sells dogs as a sideline, asked what kind of a dog I was really interested in. Without a clue as to how dogs other than Pekinese are called in Chinese, and not finding the picture I was looking for in *100 Famous Breeds*, the standard dog reference in Beijing, I started to describe a dog about a foot high, with five-inch ears, and brown, black, and white coloring. I needn't have worked so hard. *Bee-guh-er* was a working term in Chinese dog circles.

The discussion turned to whether or not I preferred a cropped tail.

"Dogs, especially beagles, don't like their tails lopped," I argued.

"They don't care," Guo countered.

"A tail is like a rudder on a ship," I retorted. "How is a beagle going to chase rabbits through the woods without his tail?"

If he could locate a beagle, Mr. Guo said, he would give me a call. The price would be $180, with or without. If I paid in American dollars, I could have it for $120. That was two hundred percent or more below the beagle market in China, I later learned. "Beware of bait and switch," a Beijing friend warned. "Because China as yet had no dog clubs that certify breeds," *120 Famous Breeds* (another standard reference) exhorted, "authenticating pure breeds can be a problem."

It is imperative when visiting friends in China to bring gifts. For Rong Rong, who runs a beauty parlor in Sichuan Province's Chengdu, I brought a necklace and a box of imported mints; for her seven-year-old daughter, Jing Jing, I brought a New York Mets baseball hat; for their one-year-old dog, Lan Lan—an almost Lhasa Apso breed, purchased for $450 from business profits—I brought rawhide dog chews and a rubber bone.

Most of China's big cities now have dog markets, but when it comes to dogs in China, few beat the bustle at the Green Sheep Palace Dog Market in Chengdu. On Wednesdays, the market draws dozens of merchants and hundreds of buyers; and on Sundays, ten thousand customers, little boys and little girls in tow, slither shoulder to shoulder through the aisles and lanes.

The Green Sheep Palace Market begins on the main avenue where mixed breeds—displayed in satchels, wicker baskets, bicycle baskets, and on ribbon leashes—are offered at the pavement's edge for $100 or less. Most are just a few weeks old; sometimes a complete litter is huddled in a box. Sellers are mostly working-class transients in their twenties.

The half-mile-long earthen lane, leading from the avenue to the main market, is where dog accessories—cages, baskets for sleeping, leashes, and dog food—are sold. With no domestic pet food industry as of yet, the most affluent Chinese feed their dogs off of their plates. One Beijing household was reported to spend $60 a month (more than some Chinese earn in a month) on feeding its dog. For many dogs in China, though, food is butcher shop "unconsumables," sold by weight out of bulk containers.

The more carefully bred dogs in Chengdu are sold by professionals in covered, licensed stalls. Here you can find better mixes at $500, Shih Tzus for $1,400, and Pekinese for $5,000. Many of these merchants are quite satisfied to sell just one dog per week. The stall area also includes imported dog perfumes and other grooming aides, imported dog food, and toys for pups. The most expensive dogs in China, such as an all-white breeding female Pekinese, are offered privately for $15,000 and more.

Local governments in Chengdu and elsewhere in China make little effort to regulate the health of dogs for sale. Dog licenses exist, but few purchase them. Chengdu maintains a publicly run pet clinic at the entrance to the Dog Market, where for $15 a puppy can be inoculated. But there is no monitoring, and most owners choose to save the fee. With little health supervision, returning home with a cuddly ball that later turns into a sick dog is not uncommon.

In fact, many new dog owners, eager to please an only child, have no idea at all what they are getting into. A few months after purchase, they unload their furry bundle at a steep discount. Rong Rong's sister, Li Li, bought a German Shepherd mix and parted with it three months later.

What happened?

"It grew," she said.

Many Chinese have as little as one hundred or two hundred square feet to live in. Further, with few open outdoor spaces or even empty sidewalks, China's dogs are rarely taken out for walks. Instead, they are trained to visit pans that are left for them in their cages or in a corner of the apartment. Accuracy isn't always the best.

With the pool of breeding stock still tiny, many Chinese pet dogs come from long distances. A woman in her twenties I met standing in front of one of Beijing's most chic department stores cradling a puppy in a basket had traveled thirty-three hours on the train to Beijing from Guangzhou. She had brought along four young pups, which she was selling for $100 each. When sold, she would return home. Her dogs came from Shenzhen, adjacent to Hong Kong. Other dogs come over the border from Russia. Still others are bred locally or in other parts of China. In today's money-oriented China, where almost everyone is angling to become an entrepreneur, breeding puppies at home provides an additional opportunity. Breeding stock is often what can be borrowed.

Lan Lan, the dog purchased from beauty salon profits, was unable to meet me at Chengdu Airport. Rong Rong, his mistress, who first clued me into China's puppy-dog rage from afar, said he was away on business, courting two girlfriends. He would be allowed home when posterity was served...and when he stopped shedding.

How Mousie Tongue
Became Mao Zedong

□□□

HINA HAS BEEN MAKING headlines again:

- The Chinese are working hard at engaging with the North Koreans on the nuclear issue.
- Big fry and small fry alike are being urged to understand just what the "Three Represents" represent.
- Internet cafes are all the rage.
- The Communist Party is patting itself on the back for reining in the SARS that its coverup helped to unleash.
- Beijing 2008 Olympic preps are rolling into high gear.

And...the street has it, *The Love Boat* is planning a return call to Shanghai next spring.

Of course, there has been the usual flood of satellite reports from China with the traditional mangling of Chinese names. But, if you've been paying close attention, you have no doubt noticed that something is different. Peking has all but disappeared. It is now Beijing (correctly pronounced Bay-*jing*—as in "Jingle Bells"—and, as silky as it may sound from Captain

239

Stubing or Tom Brokaw, incorrectly pronounced Bay-*jing*—as in *Je vous aime*. And, therein lies a rather perplexing tale, for scholars and citizens alike.

Chinese is a strange language. (One less-than-polite scholar even had the audacity to call it "a historical mistake.") Its words are made up of ideographs—pictures—most of which have long since ceased to hold any visual connection to the ideas they propose to graph. To help foreigners learn to speak—and eventually read and write—Chinese, various systems have been developed that enable Chinese sounds to be recorded in our own familiar Latin script. Unfortunately, none of these systems does a very terrific job. To our ears, Chinese has some extremely unpalatable sounds, and it is just very hard to represent them with English letters. An otherwise perfectly stable girl in Dr. Solomon's Chinese 1 class at Queens College, when asked to look in her book and speak aloud the transliterated Chinese word for the number "four"—*sz*—froze...and absolutely refused.

Until fifteen or so years ago, there was a muddled uniformity in transcribing Chinese into English. Journalists, travel agents, businessmen, and the like all used a somewhat similar scheme—a variation of the Wade-Giles system—to record Chinese names and places. Though most of them never learned that Chou was pronounced Joe, not Choe, at least they all mispronounced Chou En-lai's name the same way.

Then, all of a sudden, when Vice Premier Teng Hsiao-p'ing made his swing through the U.S., the media decided that they would switch over to the transliteration system used on the mainland: the Pinyin system. Improved clarity was given as the reason. So, overnight, the world over—on the *Today Show*, in *Time* magazine, in *The Wall Street Journal*, in *National Geographic*—the stars of the day took on new looks: Teng Hsiao-p'ing became Deng Xiaoping, Chao Tzu-yang became Zhao Ziyang, Hu Yao-pang became Hu Yaobang, and Mao's humbled wife, Chiang Ch'ing, became Jiang Qing.

Unfortunately, this abrupt transition brought with it some first-class confusion. TV reporters who had taken months to school themselves that Teng was pronounced "dung," which rhymes with "hung," suddenly began calling Deng, Doong. And anchormen who had long called the late Chairman Mao Tse-tung, Mousie Tongue, now felt a strong urge to call Mao Zedong, Mao Zee Dong, which rhymes with "gong." Taiwan stayed Taiwan, but Peking became Beijing. Shanghai stayed Shanghai, but Tientsin became Tianjin.

Now, I could give you legitimate linguistic reasons for all of this, but that would require a discussion of "dental" versus "labial," "fricative" versus "gutteral," "initial" versus "final." And we haven't even touched on "tone sandhi" yet. You would never have the patience.

So, don't expect this new system of writing Chinese names and places to improve our pronunciation of them any time soon. Besides, people seem to rather enjoy mispronouncing the next person's name. As one fellow put it: "Just because the other guy doesn't know how to pronounce his own name, doesn't mean that I have to mispronounce it too."

They Wiggle and They
Wriggle and They Squiggle
and They Jiggle...

□ □ □

SNAKE ALLEY—Huaxi Jie in Chinese—consists of a two-block arcade located between Kwangchow and West Hoping Streets in the West Gate district of old Taipei, not far from the Lungshan Temple and the Tamsui River. It is the center of Taipei's snake trade.

A proper snake story deserves an engaging beginning. But if you are at all squeamish, better skip the next two paragraphs.

THE SCENE VARIES FROM SNAKE SHOP to snake shop, each of which has cages of hissing snakes at the entrance. Usually, the snake vendor will first hang five or six snakes from a line. When the crowd around him is thick enough, he'll draw one of the snakes tight, slit it from end to end, and zip the skin right off. There is some dripping, quite a bit of wriggling, and an occasional dangling intestine.

The vendor then wrings the blood and whatever else comes out of the snake into a glass, adding wine, various potions, and sometimes a little venom. Next, he begins his pitch, goading the crowd and elaborating what a glass of the above can accomplish in very explicit sexual terms ("Do you have a problem? Does your wife

243

complain that…?"). While all this is going on, the snakes are hanging on display in various stages of life and death. Eventually, they end up in a pot.

Are you still there?

Though the custom of eating snakes as food has deep roots in Chinese tradition, precise folklore is hard to come by. Mostly, it seems, snakes were plentiful in subtropical southern China, and so the Cantonese, who have a reputation for adventurous eating, made them a part of their diet, as did the Hakkas and the Fukienese. From South China, the practice of eating snakes moved to Hong Kong, which is heavily Cantonese, and to Taiwan, whose non-indigenous population is drawn mainly from the southern part of the mainland. All seem to agree that, in addition to its libidinous benefits, snake meat stimulates the blood and therefore makes a good winter food, and that snake gallbladder (sometimes swallowed whole) is good for the eyes.

I pursued this in Snake Alley at the Asian Ginseng and Medicine Shop with Mr. Ong, a doctor of Chinese herbal medicine (his diploma was on the wall), who offered me ginseng pills, snake-penis pills, and Reborn Pills—the very best in aphrodisiacs—all at about $25 a bottle. To improve my eyes, he suggested a snake gallbladder capsule, and if that didn't work, turtle-gall grain pills. "They are *not guaranteed*," he stressed.

Snake Alley offers four types of poisonous snakes for the eating pleasure of its partially tourist, mostly native clientele. They are not inexpensive, ranging in price from $14 per pound for the small bamboo snake to $23 per pound for the hundred pacer—so named because if it bites you, you die within one hundred paces. Priced in between are the umbrella snake, worshipped by the Taiwanese aborigines, and the cobra. Snake farming does not appear to be a full-time job. Rather, farmers and aborigines living in rural mountainous areas trap and snare snakes living in the forests and turn them over to middlemen who market them in Taipei and other cities on Taiwan.

About ten restaurants in Snake Alley feature snake delicacies (there are several more snake restaurants in other parts of the city). All reach their peak of activity between 9 P.M. and midnight on weekends. We tried—correction, we *visited*—two of them. The Jin Dai [Modern] Restaurant at 48 Huaxi Street offers five items at $12.50 per bowl: poison-snake soup, poison-snake blood, poison-snake gallbladder, poison-snake venom, and snake semen. You can have the above from nonpoisonous snakes for $3.75 per bowl. Beverage? A bottle of snake wine— wine mixed with snake venom and semen. $25.

At the Ya Zhou [Asia] Restaurant at 55 Huaxi Street the menu is more popularly priced: snake meat soup at $2.50; and at $7.50 per portion, fried snake meat, roasted snake meat, snake sashimi (to accommodate Japanese visitors), and steamed snake eggs.

To refer to the above as "restaurants" might stretch the term. There is a definite carnival atmosphere to the entire deafening scene, with a microphoned barker at the entrance touting his wares and their virtues to the crow-necked crowd. (If you want to take his picture: $1.50.) Elsewhere on the street there are monkeys, tattoo parlors, and stalls where you can play darts and loops. Each restaurant does a hefty and varied take-out business: the Ya Zhou featuring dried hundred pacer to be ground into a powder and drunk with water at about $1.80 per ounce; and the Jin Dai featuring snakeskin handbags as well as snake pills.

A tasteful snake story deserves a fine snake soup recipe. Supplied by a reknowned Snake Alley chef who wishes to remain anonymous. *Untested*:

> Add Chinese black mushrooms, bamboo shoots, pieces of snake, all shredded, to chicken stock.
> Bring to a boil and simmer. Add corn starch. Some add shredded pork.
> Add pepper or other seasonings to taste.

How does snake soup taste? Florence Lin says it tastes "gamey and rough-textured." Sarah Spurdle says it tastes "tender, like chicken." Marsha Wagner says it tastes "fishy." Karen Yu says it tastes "good." So we have a consensus.

If you're still hungry, you might do better at one of the non-snake food stalls located in Snake Alley. At the A San Restaurant, they serve various preparations of local delectables including crabs, shrimp, shark, chicken feet, goose tongue, preserved eggs, as well as a "special egg wine." The featured beverage is mushroom tea (15¢ extra with honey). (Larger and still more interesting open air food markets—active between 6 and 12 P.M.—can be found adjacent to Snake Alley; at the intersection of Liao Ning and Xing An Streets in the center of town near Changchun Street; and, in the northern part of the city, at the Shih Lin market, near the Grand Hotel. Specialties include: barbecued sparrow on a stick, turtle soup, seafood sausage, vegetarian dumplings, rice noodles, seafood, and sticky rice cakes.)

Snake Alley is bisected by a cross street with a selection of one storied "parlors" graced by overly made-up young girls who appeared to be no more than fifteen. This is Taipei's "legal" red light district. (Its gaudy "illegal" red light district, almost all of whose establishments carry the euphemism "barber shop" in neon, and which all but disappear from view during the day, is located on Changchun and surrounding streets in the center of town.) Further along the street crossing Snake Alley is the Sexual Diseases Hospital. The snake potion-red light district-hospital progression apparently has its logic in experience.

A satisfying snake story demands a clever ending. So I went to the fortuneteller, one Mr. Yin, whose establishment was located not far from the brothels, for his advice. We got off to a bad start. He wanted $40 up front, citing his fifty years of experience at face reading, hand reading, and bamboo-rod reading. I told him I wasn't interested in being read; I just wanted to know how to complete my story, and that wasn't worth $40. He seemed insulted, but agreed that for $20 he would tell my friend's fortune and answer my one question. I came off second best, though. For his half of the $20, my friend learned that if he married now, his wife would die. He seemed happy to be spared the loss. As for me, the fortuneteller said that his responsibility was to reveal my fate, not to write my articles, and since I didn't pay him enough, he wouldn't tell me any more.

Saving One Chinese Face

□□□

THEN AS NOW, coming to the United States, even if it meant leaving spouse and children behind, remains the ultimate prize for a Chinese in his twenties or thirties. For a woman who wants to emigrate legally, and can't qualify to attend an American university, marriage to an American provides one of the best routes out. I had received my share of proposals.

The letter I received from Sharon Chen's parents, with two photographs, was a bit disarming. I had helped Sharon to get a softball scholarship at Oklahoma City University just as the Tian'anmen revolt was breaking out; this was couched as a favor to me.

> Ya'an, Sichuan
> April 25, 1991
>
> Respected Mr. Ke Tianxi:
>
> There is something which we have to discuss with you. Everyone in our family respects and admires you, particularly my niece, Li Meifang. She is twenty-six, a high school graduate, five feet five inches tall, nice looking. Both she and her parents are comparatively well off. She wants to be your lifelong companion.

Respected Mr. Ke Tianxi, you should have a trust-
worthy mate and a home blessed with a happy marriage. Our niece awaits your reply.

I declined.

But the following autumn, in the course of planning a visit to Sharon's parents in Sichuan, I rethought the matter and
wrote a note to Meifang. Perhaps I was being a bit devious.
For the principle appeal to me was not Li Meifang, but the
opportunity to understand how private business, just getting
started in China, functioned in a communist country. Meifang
ran a clothing store in Chengdu and was apparently quite successful at it.

No one could say that Meifang was not aggressive. Even before I had arrived in Beijing from New York, she had called my
hotel from Chengdu looking for me. A week later, she met me
at Chengdu airport, took me to my hotel, invited me to dinner,
and showed me the pandas at the Chengdu zoo and the other
local attractions. My plans were to stop off for a few days in
Chengdu, the capital of Sichuan, and then travel to Sharon's
parents' home in Ya'an, several hours away by rickety bus. I
had been to many of China's larger cities; the opportunity to
visit a secondary city, slower paced, with the look of old China, held strong appeal. Ya'an in particular had old-style, wood-
construction teahouses where the locals would while away idle
hours.

I wanted to visit Ya'an alone, content to muddle into the
unknown as the price of an authentic experience. But Meifang
and Sharon's parents had arranged that she would accompany
me to Ya'an, and there was no undoing the plan without being
outright rude. We walked the streets of Ya'an, took a day trip
to Meng Ding Mountain, went dancing, and tried fish hot pot,
a local favorite. In between, I tried to glean something about
small private business in China from Meifang,

As it turned out, Meifang was not Sharon's parents' niece

at all, but a family friend. There was some sense that Sharon's parents' principle interest in this match was a matchmaking fee they hoped to extract from Mei Mei, as Meifang was called. Her obvious purpose aside, Mei Mei had a stubborn streak of honesty, and it was our shared feeling that Sharon and her parents were both connivers. This proved to be our strongest bond. Mei Mei later told me that it was she, not the Chens, who had borne the hospitality expenses during my five days in Ya'an. Why she associated with the Chens at all was the open question. As someone who was just passing through, this wasn't something that I needed to delve into too deeply.

Meifang and I remained friends and, two-and-a-half years later, in February 1994, she arranged to visit Beijing, where she had never been. I agreed to show her around. There was something very quaint about a New Yorker introducing a girl from Sichuan to her nation's capital.

We made the full tour: Tian'anmen, where we saw the lowering of the flag, which takes place every day at dusk; the Forbidden City; the Great Wall, where I had to implore the guide to speak Chinese; the Temple of Heaven; the Summer Palace; and Beijing's shopping streets.

"*Baijing hen da*, Beijing is very big," said Mei Mei, giving Beijing the Sichuan pronunciation.

THE MORNING BEFORE SHE WAS to return home to Sichuan, Mei Mei took out an envelope. It contained seven X-rays and a seven-page hospital report written in Chinese. In 1990, in Chengdu, Li Meifang had been diagnosed with fibroma—a non-malignant tumor—of the jaw at one of Chengdu's largest hospitals. One-third of her lower jawbone, from chin to temple, had been cut out and replaced with artificial bone.

Soon after the operation, the synthetic jawbone cracked and began to shift. The Chinese doctor who performed the surgery scoffed at her complaints: headaches, dizziness, an inability to eat properly, difficulty with speech. "Your expectations," he said, "are too high." A canvassing of all the hospitals in Sichuan, a province of 120 million,* revealed no doctor who would help her, seeing perhaps no benefit in inheriting another surgeon's failure. Within the last year, the condition had worsened. Full of despair, Mei Mei asked me to take her X-rays and chart back to the U.S. and see if there was anyone there who could help her.

From a first look at the medical report I could understand only the barest outlines of the case. It was simply too technical. I sufficed with clarifying her history and current complaints, and having her rewrite illegible portions of her medical report to be deciphered later on with the help of a dictionary. Written cursively, Chinese can be maddening. I also took frontal and side-view photographs of her face, thinking that they might later be helpful.

Almost immediately upon returning home, I translated the hospital report and set out doggedly to speak to as many doctors in the U.S.—Americans or Chinese here for in-service training—as possible, in search of a remedy for Mei Mei's jaw. The need seemed urgent.

There are hundreds of Chinese doctors and medical researchers working in New York hospitals and in research centers such as Rockefeller University. I plugged into as many of them as I could find. But many of these Chinese contacts, who included virologists and hematologists, had only minimal information to offer. Sometimes it was the name of a hospital in China that was strong in oral surgery; sometimes they provided assistance in deciphering Mei Mei's medical record. On rare occasions, they reaffirmed information I had heard elsewhere.

Early on, I went to see Dr. Andrew Zeidman, an oral surgeon in Manhattan whom I had at one time consulted personally. Jaw reconstruction wasn't his specialty, but he looked at the

---

* Sichuan Province was downsized by about thirty million people in 1997, when Chongqing was designated an independent municipality under the central government.

X-rays and offered useful input. Zeidman was highly critical of the surgery, which he felt should never have been performed at all. Mei Mei's condition could be remedied, but it required major surgery, costing tens of thousands of dollars. Left alone, the lower right side of her jaw would collapse and she would be unable to eat normally the rest of her life.

Dr. Zeidman, like most American oral surgeons, did most of his surgery in his own office. But for more complex cases, he sometimes operated at St. Luke's-Roosevelt Hospital. By pure chance, in two weeks, he would be working with an exchange oral surgeon from China. He gave me the name of a friend at the hospital who had himself spent some time in Beijing. Dr. Brookstone turned out not to be the most amiable of sorts, but he was able to testify to the high level of Chinese oral surgeons and to link me up with the Chinese surgeon, Dr. Wu, who would be arriving shortly.

By the time I met Dr. Wu Jiang a few weeks later, I had spoken to enough U.S. specialists to understand that there was no way around surgery, that Mei Mei's condition was operable, and that the logistics involved in seeing this through to completion were daunting.

Dr. Wu was an associate professor at the School of Stomatology (dental and oral medicine) attached to Beijing Medical University, one of China's premier medical schools. He was to spend three months as an exchange fellow in oral surgery at St. Luke's-Roosevelt Hospital in Manhattan. He spoke hardly any English, although he could read professional journals. Unlike the American surgeons with whom I had spoken, Wu had the time and interest to help, and was willing to go into great detail in his explanations. Wu Jiang's specialty was cosmetic surgery of the face and jaw, which dovetailed with Mei Mei's needs. He was to serve as my bridge, giving me the professional knowledge I needed to pursue Mei Mei's recovery and connecting me to the world of Chinese oral surgery. To bridge the language gap, I studied material from a Chinese text on facial reconstructive surgery to which Wu had contributed. In many cases, the English vocabulary was as unfamiliar as the Chinese.

Taking care not to overdo it, I missed no opportunity to befriend Wu. He loved jazz and I took him to the Blue Note in Greenwich Village. I took him to a kosher delicatessen for pastrami. I walked him through Harlem. I photographed his visits to Manhattan's most famous sites as a keepsake. I helped him with letters he needed to write in English.

AS I WAS BEGINNING to understand something about jaw reconstruction, I was also beginning to understand how licensing limitations influenced surgical decisions. The doctors I spoke to when I began my search were oral surgeons. In this country, oral surgeons are dentists. Their surgical sphere is limited by law to the area above the neck and below the eyes. And this colors their surgical approach. Mei Mei's replacement jaw could be constructed using a cadaver's jaw, which would be shaped and then filled with marrow taken from her own body; or it could be fashioned directly from her hip bone. The latter holds distinct medical advantages over the former. But because an American oral surgeon's license does not permit him to take a hip graft from a patient, a separate surgical team is required. Thus, many oral surgeons opt for bone bank material, making the operation simpler. In Mei Mei's case, it wasn't the method of choice. In China, where dentistry is a medical specialty, oral surgeons are free to take their bone material from any part of the patient's body.

With so many approaches to rebuilding Mei Mei's jaw, I found myself getting into intricacies of anatomy and surgery about which I had no right to an opinion. Yet, Mei Mei depended on me to sift through the options and make a recommendation. Mei Mei prided herself on her looks, and it seemed that a cadaver's jaw would be easier to shape than a piece of her own pelvis. However, cadaver bones—dead tissue—only serve as a construction mold until the body can regenerate a fully living jaw. And, the process of absorbing the dead bone and regenerating new bone was sometimes less than perfect.

Yet, using the patient's own bone material involved, in effect, a second operation. I had to judge the impact that a hip graft would have on Mei Mei's ability to walk (minimal, it turned out). The jaw was a hefty piece of bone. I needed to understand how a thin slice of hip bone could take the pounding of a jawbone. Anything Mei Mei might ask me, I wanted to be prepared to answer. I sifted through the knowns and unknowns as I fell asleep each night. It was a weighty load.

The jawbone that needed to be replaced was comprised of two parts: the horizontal "body," from which the teeth grow, and the vertical "ramus," which connects to the side of the face. Some surgeons who advocated a hip graft from Mei Mei's own body proposed to cut this boomerang-shaped replacement jaw in one piece; others in two pieces.

The vertical portion of the lower jaw connects to the side of the skull at the temporal mandibular joint (TMJ). A bony knob, called a *condyle*, attached by connective tissues, sits inside the socket of this joint. In Mei Mei's case, the joint had been destroyed during the first surgery and could not be rebuilt. It took much thought for me to accept the fact that a reconstructed jaw could function without a new joint. But it could. That the reconstructed condyle would in time reintegrate with surrounding soft tissue was the reason.

And there was the issue of the hardware—plates, screws, wire—used to secure the reconstructed jaw. Inferior materials used in her first operation in China were part of Li Meifang's current problem.

While I was striving to understand the surgical possibilities for Mei Mei, I also had to keep her abreast. She had recently opened a notions boutique with a partner in the Tibet Hotel in Chengdu, which had a fax machine. But Mei Mei knew no English, and I had to simplify complex medical terms, then translate them into Chinese. All the while being careful not to crush her spirits. Some of these faxes ran several pages. Our phone and fax contacts were so focused on Mei Mei's jaw that we dispensed with "Hello, how are you?"

Karen Kane, a friend of mine interested in China, put me in touch with a friend of hers by the name of Xu Ling. Xu Ling was a graduate of the School of Stomatology at Beijing Medical University—the same school Dr. Wu had attended. She was completing a course at the School of Dental Medicine at Stony Brook, on Long Island, in order to qualify for an American license. Xu offered to take Mei Mei's X-rays and history to the head of oral surgery at Stony Brook for analysis. An additional question was whether there were centers in the United States that would be willing to perform this surgery without charge. The tens of thousands of dollars needed for such an operation were well beyond Mei Mei's means.

Dr. Allan Kucine, trained at Columbia University, the acting department head at Stony Brook, had reams of useful information on all the surgical approaches to jaw replacement. And, if a hospital could be found, he was willing to offer his services free of charge. That seemed a gift from heaven. But as generous as it was, there were two problems with his offer. First, he proposed to use a cadaver's mandible rather than a hip graft which, it was becoming clearer and clearer as I spoke to expert after expert, was the preferred method. Second, he had performed only a handful of such operations, which was unsettling.

Dr. Wu Jiang, the visiting Beijing surgeon upon whom I was relying more and more, provided my most daunting dilemma. During my conversations with Xu Ling, I found out that she was a former classmate of Wu Jiang at Beijing Medical University. Wu, she said, had been a political stooge who had snitched on his classmates. (Then, even more so than now, the Communist Party was everywhere, and stooges were their eyes.) Further, in her words, he had been allowed to practice medicine even though he repeatedly failed the qualifying exams. "If a patient is given six months to live," Ling said about her classmate, "with Wu, he would have six days." This revelation caused me days of anxiety. There was no way to double-check the charge. Dr. Wu was my only direct link to the world of Chinese oral surgery. In the end, his detailed knowledge of the intricacies of the surgery Mei Mei needed forced me to reject the characterization of incompetence. But the doubts raised about him prevented me from asking him to perform the surgery himself.

Shortly thereafter, I spoke with Steven Roser, the head of oral surgery at Columbia-Presbyterian Hospital in New York. Roser was an objective source of information, because he was one of the few oral surgeons who held both M.D. and dental degrees. Among the surgical options, Roser leaned heavily toward a hip graft. He also felt that this was not an operation that should be performed by a surgeon who did only one or two such procedures a year. Roser surveyed for me the medical centers and surgeons that could handle such an operation, but made it crystal clear that he had no interest in this case. Among the doctors he mentioned was Walter Guralnick of the Harvard School of Dental Medicine and Massachusetts General Hospital. Guralnick had been to China many times, he said.

The Guralnick lead came at a time that my support network among American doctors was beginning to crumble. In particular, my relationship with Dr. Zeidman, who had made the crucial connection for me with Dr. Wu, had turned sour. His was one of the few private offices in New York that had a machine that could duplicate X-rays. I had paid him $3.00 or $4.00 each; perhaps a bother, but no loss. Now, I needed more copies to circulate among surgeons. He balked. "You're on a mission," he said, without a tinge of sympathy in his voice. "I don't want to be involved." Seething, I peeled off $100 in cash and left it with the receptionist with a pointed note.

ZEIDMAN WAS RIGHT ABOUT ONE THING; I was on a mission.

Other doctors were less acerbic than Dr. Zeidman, but no more supportive. During a low moment in my odyssey, I asked my old family physician, Dr. Steiner, how he would handle Mei Mei's case if he were in my shoes. "I would walk away from it," was the response.

As it happened, Walter Guralnick of Harvard, semi-retired, had spent extensive time at the School of Stomatology of the West China University of Medical Science in Chengdu, Mei Mei's hometown. What Mei Mei did not know through her years of suffering was that mere miles from her home worked one of China's top three jaw reconstruction surgeons, Dr. Wang Dazhang. If she mentioned his name, Guralnick said, he was sure Dr. Wang would see her.

Conversations with Dr. Wu and Dr. Guralnick finally convinced me that arranging an operation in the U.S. was too difficult. Finances aside, the surgery would require a stay in the U.S. of several months while the jaw healed, with follow-up in case of complications. The logistics were impossible. China's top oral surgeons, Dr. Guralnick said, were the equals of America's best. He was sure that Mei Mei could get the care she needed in China. This did not comfort Mei Mei, who was exhausted from her experiences with Chinese hospitals. But for me it sketched a path to a successful conclusion. Chinese doctors in all disciplines rely on their contacts with American hospitals to provide advanced training. Increasingly, Chinese medicine follows the American model. A request from the U.S., and particularly with an endorsement from a surgeon at a top American hospital, would be hard to ignore. That became the core of my strategy for arranging treatment for Mei Mei in China.

After two months of intense searching, it would have been almost theatric if it had turned out that Mei Mei's answer lay just minutes from her doorstep. But her visit to Dr. Wang did not leave her encouraged. Dr. Wang could perform the operation, but would use a rib graft for the entire procedure. He could not guarantee the cosmetic result. When I called back Dr. Guralnick for his reaction to Dr. Wang's diagnosis, he said that normally at Mass General, when a half-mandible was needed for a case such as this, they used a hip graft. This did *not* mean, Guralnick said, that Dr. Wang didn't know how to take a hip graft. He had seen him do it many times.

Wang Dazhang, age sixty, Sichuan's most famous oral surgeon, had developed his skills during the Cultural Revolution when physical beauty was not a priority, when for a woman to wear makeup and perm her hair was to risk being tagged a counterrevolutionary. It might well have been that the techniques Wang had perfected gave secondary importance to the cosmetics so vital to an attractive woman in 1990s China. Durability and beauty didn't always move in the same direction.

Things were becoming exceedingly complicated and quick resolution in her hometown would have simplified the matter greatly. But I could not push Li Meifang into surgery with a doctor who foresaw a mediocre cosmetic result. Despite the trauma that lurked under her skin, cosmetically, all the surgeons agreed from the head photos I showed them, her outer appearance had not suffered. The thought of losing her looks petrified her.

Dr. Wang's hospital in Chengdu, Beijing Medical University Hospital, and the No. 9 People's Hospital in Shanghai were the three possibilities. Both Dr. Guralnick at Harvard and Dr. Roser at Columbia had recommended Dr. Qiu Weiliu in Shanghai. Dr. Guralnick called Dr. Qiu "a superb surgeon," but neither Mei Mei nor I had any connection with Shanghai, no friends or relatives who could ease the recuperation. The advantage with Beijing was that Dr. Wu, who would soon be returning to China, worked there and could coordinate both personally and professionally. Dr. Wu had mentioned several times that, aesthetically, his Beijing hospital did prettier operations. A weighted judgment to be sure, but something that stuck in my mind.

I express-mailed a summary of her case, copies of her X-rays, and the photographs I had taken of Mei Mei's face in China to the deans of the departments of oral and maxillofacial surgery at the hospitals in Beijing and Shanghai. Everything was written in English. Chinese, who often seem in a perpetual struggle to show that they are as good as foreigners, liked to be stroked by outsiders. Communicating in Chinese would have diluted the effect.

Professor Zhang Zhenkang's response from Beijing Medical University could not have been more gracious or honest. He expressed confidence that, using a hip graft from Mei Mei's own body, her function and appearance could be improved. But he took care to note that because her previous operation had destroyed the local anatomy, reattaching the muscles that play important roles in chewing might be difficult. Living conditions in the ward, too, might not be as comfortable as in the U.S. If Mei Mei wanted to come to Beijing, they would take her case. Surgery like this in Beijing would run up to $3,000, a tenth or less of the cost in the U.S. Mei Mei could handle such a sum.

In trying to steer Mei Mei toward surgery in China, I needed to remind myself that whereas Beijing, Shanghai, and Chengdu were all just China to me, Beijing or Shanghai, where Mei Mei knew no one, were each a thousand frightening miles from her hometown. A conversation with Dr. Tom Albert, an oral surgeon from the University of Oregon, who had spent a year as a professor at West China Hospital in Chengdu and another year at No. 9 Hospital in Shanghai, and also knew Dr. Zhang in Beijing, reassured me that I had pinpointed for Mei Mei the best surgeons in China. And, by making my request for their help as a foreigner, I had ensured her preferred care. Although there were no guarantees as to the outcome, her chances for success were as good in China as they were in the U.S.

All of this should have made Mei Mei ecstatic; she would soon be getting the care she needed. But her fax after she returned from Beijing at the end of August didn't give me any rest. She had been examined by Professor Zhang, the dean, with whom I had corresponded; by Dr. Wu, whom I had cultivated in New York; and by Dr. Wang Xing, a senior surgeon to whom Dean Zhang had assigned the surgery. In their private discussion, Wu had given Mei Mei the clear impression that Zhang was much superior to Wang, and that she should make every effort to convince Dean Zhang to perform the surgery himself. Zhang had promised her only that he would be involved. Mei Mei implored me to request that Dean Zhang personally perform the operation. She told me that Dr. Zhang had shown particular interest in our relationship, implying that there was some mileage in stretching it to the hilt.

Seven thousand miles away, this put me in a quandary. It made no sense to me that Zhang would assign an inferior surgeon to this case with the outside world looking in. Perhaps, it occurred to me, Dean Zhang, nearing retirement, was no longer performing surgery. In any event, in trying to convince Professor Zhang to do the surgery, I had to be very careful not to alienate Dr. Wang.

Mei Mei would be returning to Beijing at the end of September for surgery.

August 30, 1994

Dear Professor Zhang:

I want you to know how relieved and thankful I am to hear that you were able to examine Li Meifang in Beijing yesterday and that she will be returning to your hospital at the end of September for surgery.

When I returned to the U.S. from China in the spring, I promised Meifang, with whom I have developed a very special relationship, that I would spare no effort to obtain for her the very best medical treatment possible. It wasn't an easy task. For, as I learned, there are five or six approaches to this surgery and each has its advocates. In the end, after consulting with fifteen or more doctors here, I was led to you. From past and present colleagues and students at Beijing Medical University, from discussions with Dr. Walter Guralnick of the Harvard School of Dental Medicine and Massachusetts General Hospital, and with other American oral surgeons who have spent extended periods in China, and from Li Meifang's own feelings, I have been led to the conclusion that you personally are the surgeon in China best equipped to perform Meifang's operation. Though I have no doubt that your protégés can offer her excellent care, my inner feeling is that your unparalleled expertise and skill, honed over many years, offer her superior prognosis for recovery.

I would thus be most appreciative if you could *personally* perform Li Meifang's jaw reconstruction surgery so that the promise I made to her can best be fulfilled.

I hope to be in Beijing in November and very much look forward to meeting you at that time.

With deepest gratitude.

HER FAX FROM BEIJING on September 30 left me with a still heavier feeling. It breathed real fear.

When she had visited Beijing a month earlier, Professor Zhang had put the success rate of her operation at ninety-six percent. Now, she wrote, she was hearing something entirely different. First, despite my plea, Dean Zhang was not going to be the operating surgeon. In their first pre-op consultation, Dr. Wang, who would be wielding the knife, stressed the uncertainty of the operation. Not only that, the first operation would concentrate on the structure of her jaw; she would have to come back in a year to fine-tune the cosmetics.

> Jon, I'm afraid. All along, I've been hoping that they could do this without cutting my hip bone. Now, they are saying that, even with the hip, they can't guarantee anything. The operation is scheduled for October 7th at 8 A.M.

A major factor in the pressure cooker in which Mei Mei found herself was the Chinese hospital system. Like many patients, she had entered the hospital more than two weeks in advance of surgery: to undergo pre-op procedures that could easily have been done on an outpatient basis and to claim a scarce ward bed.

I was caught in a maelstrom of emotion the like of which I had never experienced before. There was no phone in Mei Mei's room. To calm her, I had to go through the hospital switchboard to the eighth-floor duty nurse's extension—a never-ending trial. Further, the hospital was about to enter a five-day Chinese Independence Day lull during which it would be virtually impossible to reach anyone. Professor Zhang lived on the hospital grounds and I had his home extension. But getting the switchboard operator to ring him so that I could clarify the surgery prognosis was an exercise in persuasion.

I REACHED ZHANG'S WIFE soon after the fax arrived, and she told me to call two days later, on Sunday, at 9:00 A.M. Beijing time. With the twelve-hour time difference, I was having trouble keeping track of todays and tomorrows.

Without reaching Professor Zhang, I couldn't know whether his designated surgeon, Dr. Wang, was just trying to protect himself or if there had been some real reason for this change in prognosis. Another potential complication raised in Mei Mei's fax: she had just learned that her platelet count was low. If it stayed low, she might have to return to Chengdu without an operation.

By the time I reached Mei Mei in the ward the next day, October 1, her mood had zigzagged and my emotions were caught in the twist. Now, she said, "If Zhang thinks I need two operations, I'll have two operations." But the contradiction in prognoses continued to weigh heavily on me. What if the operation didn't work?

I reached Dean Zhang's wife the next day, the 2nd, and she seemed kinder. Dean Zhang, she said, would like to speak to me about the problem at 9 A.M. on the 5th from his office. I called Mei Mei with the news. She accused me of playing doctor. She was on an emotional roller coaster, and I was being dragged along on the ride.

I reached Zhang's wife on the 4th just to confirm the telephone appointment with her husband the next day. Now I learned that he would not be available on the 5th after all, or on the 6th or the 7th either, because he had to attend a joint conference with a German delegation. How then was he going to participate in Mei Mei's operation on the 7th? She said to call his office on the 5th and if Zhang was not there, he would leave a message for me.

Counting the minutes, not to be a second late or early, I dialed Dean Zhang at precisely 9:00 A.M. the next day. Dr. Wang, the surgeon for Mei Mei's operation, and not Dean Zhang, answered the phone. He didn't paint nearly as gloomy a picture as had Mei Mei. A second operation would be needed *only* if she wasn't satisfied with the cosmetics. In any event, it would be minor. The bigger concern was her platelet count. The original surgery date had been cancelled pending reexamination the next day. A low platelet count prevented the blood from clotting normally. If the condition persisted, several months of treatment would be needed before she would be fit for surgery.

Two days later, I found a message on my answering machine. Her platelet count had risen and the operation would take place on October 10, three days later than scheduled. For the first time in weeks, I had a weekend with nothing urgent to pursue.

A FEW HOURS AFTER THE OPERATION, I reached Dr. Wang on the phone with my heart pounding. The news was positive. The five-hour operation had gone smoothly, and Wang was hopeful that Mei Mei's jaw function would be restored, though he would only know after the wire had been removed two months later.

After pursuing her treatment on an almost daily basis for six months, I wanted to share this victory. But I had no way to get in touch with Mei Mei. She would be confined to bed for a week while her hip healed. I relied on Dr. Wu to keep me up-to-date. When she was finally able to reach the phone ten days after the operation, it was almost impossible to understand her through her wired jaw. By the time she was discharged from the hospital on October 29, she was able to walk without a limp. "We are rather satisfied," was Dr. Wang's appraisal when I spoke to him on the phone before her discharge.

IT WAS WITH A MIXTURE OF EXCITEMENT and trepidation that I went with Mei Mei to see Dr. Wang when she returned to Beijing six weeks after the surgery. Dr. Wang would remove the wire from her jaw and the success of the operation could be evaluated. I felt that I wanted to celebrate with Mei Mei this greatest of victories, but the opportunity never came. Tending to her healing hip and eating through a straw had taken the smile from Mei Mei's face. To add to her worries, the Tibet Hotel in Chengdu would not renew her lease, and she was in the process of liquidating the equipment. At least one worry, however, was instantly removed when I saw her. The surgery had had no negative impact on her good looks.

With Mei Mei now an outpatient, we had to climb the eight flights of stairs to reach the ward and Dr. Wang. Only doctors or current patients could ride the elevator.

Dr. Wang removed the wire and declared the operation a success. The jaw, he said, was straight and the occlusion (the meeting of the upper and lower teeth) was normal. What worried me more than the tightness of her jaw, which would loosen with use and exercise, was that her lower jaw seemed to move up obliquely rather that vertically when she opened her mouth.

The next day, we brought the X-rays Dr. Wang had ordered to Dean Zhang Zhenkang. His was not exactly an "independent" opinion, but still a worthy one. Dean Zhang was particularly concerned with the excessive tightness of Mei Mei's jaw muscles. They opened just two centimeters (three-quarters of an inch). If this did not improve to three centimeters within a month's time, he said, there was a problem. The urgency with which he set up her reexamination with Dr. Wang for the next morning conveyed his concern to us.

By the next morning, Mei Mei's jaw had loosened somewhat and she was a bit less agitated. In reconstructing her jaw, Dr. Wang had taken a rectangular piece of bone from her hip, then cut it into two pieces longitudinally, placing them at right angles, and attaching them using stainless steel wire. The new jaw segment was then wired to the portion of her natural jaw that remained. The grafted jaw had knitted well, the X-rays showed. No further teeth had been extracted. Dr. Wang noted that the new joint on the right side of her face was lower than its original position. This contributed to the oblique direction in which her jaw traveled. But no further surgery would be necessary.

For me, the fact that, through persistent legwork, a patient seven thousand miles away, on the brink of medical catastrophe, could be mated with surgeons capable of building her a new, functional jaw using a part of her own body remained a miracle. For Mei Mei, though, the imperfections in the movement of her new jaw, and the fact that she considered her teeth to be misaligned, continued to weigh on her.

There was no celebration.

FIFTEEN MONTHS LATER, Mei Mei finally found her American mate and moved to Colorado to join her new husband. Time had not diminished her complaints. In her view, the surgery result was less than satisfactory. So, as much for my own piece of mind as for hers, I brought her East and set up an appointment with Dr. Guralnick (the oral surgeon who had convinced me that China was the best place for Mei Mei's reconstruction surgery) at Massachusetts General Hospital.

"This is a good jaw," Dr. Guralnick said. "If I were showing slides before and after, I would be happy to show these slides." The results, he said, were well above average. He recommended no further surgery.

He considered the diagonal travel of the jaw to be quite normal given the difficulty in reestablishing symmetry in the newly grafted jaw and in reattaching the muscles. As I looked back over the correspondence, this was something Dean Zhang at Beijing Medical University had pointed out clearly at the time he offered to do the surgery.

As we walked along Boston's Freedom Trail following the visit, I felt my own sense of liberation and ecstasy. Mei Mei far less so. In looking in the mirror each day, she was seeing what had been and would never be again. I, on the other hand, was looking at what had been, and would never be a worry again.

The Great Wall Scam

□□□

*T*HE FREEWHEELING, unregulated thirst for money
that has accompanied China's unprecedented prosperity
has brought with it unparalleled fraud and corruption.
Among the most vulnerable prey are local Chinese tourists. Chinese newspapers report regularly about heightened anti-
fraud surveillance and scrutiny. But Chinese dismiss these measures
as dull-toothed. In 1993, China launched a year-long campaign to
stamp out corruption. By 2008, it was still in full force.

*A January 1993 Beijing Evening News dispatch picked up the
story of a tourist from Fujian Province by the name of Guo, one
of a party of forty, who boarded a "One Day, Five Sites" excursion
bus headed for the Great Wall.*

> ...En route, the "guide" suddenly demanded 30
> yuan...Without choice, a number of tourists paid.
> The few who refused to pay were not allowed off the
> bus. When the bus returned to Qianmen Station, the
> point of origin, several young thugs emerged who
> cursed and beat them. Guo was knocked onto the
> ground unconscious.

EVERY DAY, THOUSANDS OF CHINESE from outside the city—*wai
di ren*—flock into Beijing. Some are "peasants" without city
residence permits who come to Beijing from nearby counties

or distant provinces in search of work. Others are free-mar-keteers and businessmen from other provinces working for government-owned companies who come to the capital to buy and sell. Many are tourists and honeymooners who come to see China's most famous sites. At the top of their lists is always the Great Wall at Badaling, fifty miles from Beijing—the recon-structed segment of the six-thousand-mile-long, brick and stone barrier first built more than two thousand years ago to keep out rampaging nomads. Even without English language translation, 15 yuan ($2.50) was a bargain price for a day's out-ing to the Great Wall and four other tourist destinations.

Several months later, when I got off at Qianmen subway station looking for a bargain fare to the Great Wall, a pleas-ant-looking woman, about thirty, was waiting on the subway platform to meet me, just as the kiosk vendor outside Beijing Station, who had directed me to Qianmen Station, had prom-ised.

"Great Wall"? she asked in Chinese, and presented the same gilt-edged Chinese business card introducing the excursion I had been shown at Beijing Station.

Once outside Qianmen Station, the "welcomer" walked with me for one block, whereupon she introduced me to a second woman she said would be my guide for the day, and asked for 15 yuan for the tour ticket.

"First," I said, "I would like to see the bus."

She explained that she couldn't walk me all the way to the bus, which was two blocks away, because she had to go back to the subway platform to meet more "guests." I relented when she agreed to show me her ID card: Zhai Lijun, No. 0119124. The ticket, No. 0039809, bore the name of the Beijing Long Distance Bus Company (a state-owned business) and was fur-ther stamped with the seal of the Beijing City Transportation Administration. It carried no date and no ticket price.

The minibus I soon boarded, seating eighteen, promised a comfortable journey to the Great Wall, and when it filled, we began to move without announcement. After meandering through the streets of Beijing for fifteen minutes (covering a distance that turned out to be less than two miles), however, we suddenly pulled up to the curb and were asked to disembark and board a larger bus seating about fifty. This bus had seen many trips, and the battered rear door had to be roped closed. I alternated with a fellow back-seat passenger from Qingdao, on China's East Coast, in propping a foot against the door to keep out the early spring draft. Still…a great deal to the Great Wall for $2.50.

How a bus company is able to run a day tour to the Great Wall, complete with stringers all over Beijing, greeters at subway stations, minibuses and big buses—all for $2.50—became clear only after the third tourist destination. At the first stop, we visited the Beijing Literary Theme Park, which, using animation, electronic music, and in-the-flesh guides, recreated more than forty scenes from four Chinese classics: *Dream of the Red Chamber*, *Journey to the West*, *Chronicle of the Three Kingdoms*, and *The Water Margin*. The Beijing Literary Theme Park was off the theme of the Great Wall, but entertaining at the outset.

The second stop took us to the tomb of the sixteenth-century Ming emperor Wan Li, one of thirteen Ming emperors buried here. The third stop, the Nine Dragon Amusement Park, had nothing to do with the Great Wall, with literature, or with history.

No admission tickets had been mentioned at the first two sites. We simply followed the tour leader. At Nine Dragon, tickets were distributed before entering the amusement area, with no payment asked. Without tickets or ticket prices, it was easy to conclude that admission was included in the tour price. With choices and prices presented at the outset, there would be those who might choose to skip this destination or that. There might even have been a consensus to omit the theme and amusement sites.

By the time one of the guides strode down the aisle for the first time to collect 60 additional yuan from each tour member, three sites had already been visited. It would have been very difficult to refuse to pay.

The reason the Nine Dragon Amusement Park (whose promise of a Disney-like multimedia experience through the tunnel of time ended with the promise) was included in the tour, even though it stole valuable time from the Great Wall, was that it was expensive. It cost over $5.00—fabulously dear for modest Chinese budgets. The ticket booth sign provided for group purchases at a discount, but full price was asked from us after the fact by the guide strolling down the aisle. At discounts of up to thirty percent, kickbacks aside, the tour operators pocketed not just the $2.50 tour-ticket price, but profits on admissions tickets as well. We had all paid out 75 yuan—$12.50—to this point.

Only when we reached the Great Wall did members of the tour—a placid cross-section of middle-class China that had been content to that point to suck oranges, munch watermelon seeds, and nibble on sausage sticks—become outwardly agitated. The guide had already announced that admission to the Great Wall (which included the right to climb the wall) was fixed at 16.50 yuan. But moving down the aisle, she asked for 21.50 yuan. The extra yuan, she explained totally unruffled when explanations were demanded, was a *mandatory* hygiene supplement. Actually, as we were to learn later when we queried the attendant at the Great Wall ticket office, it was a ticket to a separate exhibition, having nothing to do with the Great Wall, called "The Secret of Life." Making its purchase a condition for admission to the Great Wall added further profit for the company and brought the tab for tour members to almost $17.

The tour bus did not stop at the footpath to the Great Wall, but at the cable car (ride fee: 15 yuan; 10 yuan more if you wanted to ride down instead of walk; total tour fee: 121.50 yuan or $20.25.

Out of wisdom that they had already milked the cow dry, or because there was no rake-off in it for them, the tour escorts made no attempt to sell cable-car tickets to tour members. They simply contended that the cable car was the only practical way up the Great Wall since the sun was edging lower and lower in the sky. Only when a dozen hot-mouthed tour members refused to buy cable-car tickets and menacingly surrounded the guide were they taken by bus to the footpath where they were able to climb the wall without additional fees.

That evening, riding the subway back to my hotel, I noted in a front-page story in the *Beijing Evening News* that that same morning public security teams had carried out a sweep of the Qianmen area, detaining twenty-eight illegal tour buses, and apprehending fifty-one ticket touts working in concert.

Bus No. 00046 (Beijing license plate 52050) had evaded the sweep. It did not carry the name of the Beijing Long Distance Bus Company printed on the tour ticket, but of the Macao-Hong Kong Taxi and Bus Company. Like dozens of similar "tour buses," it had been leased or sold to private tour operators. The batch of bogus tour tickets issued in the name of the Beijing Long Distance Bus Company had either been purchased or printed without authorization. Even a seasoned police-beat reporter (which China did not yet have) would have been hard put to sort out all the details. Our tour guide, who had swung her head left and right to avoid being photographed, had insisted that she feared nothing.

ELEVEN MONTHS LATER, AMID RECURRENT rumblings from Chinese tourists, the atmosphere was friendlier. But the tour-business framework remained comfortably intact: the greeter at the Qianmen train station, still playing up the Great Wall and downplaying the lucrative amusement sites; the handoff outside the subway station from greeter to ticket seller; the little bus and the big bus. The bus fare remained 15 yuan. The tour bus, the "guide" stressed without being questioned, was *government*-owned. She didn't mention who owned the tour company and was unable to produce a business card. As before, the profit lay in the sale of admissions tickets. I got off the little bus and never boarded the big bus.

A full-amenities day tour to the Great Wall—including bilingual guide, air-conditioned coach (with closing doors), all admissions, hotel-point pick-up and return, a sit-down restaurant lunch, and enough daylight to see the Great Wall—I later learned from the tour desk at the Hotel Beijing-Toronto where I was staying, would have run little more than $30.

Riding Beijing's Buses

□ □ □

MAYBE YOU REMEMBER the Ringling Bros. circus act in which a little yellow car pulls up to the curb, the doors pop open, and clowns start to pour out left and right. Eight, ten, twelve, fourteen...Just as it appears that the last passenger has surely emerged—I mean where could they put any more?—the rear seat folds back and two more clowns bounce out wriggling their rear ends. One of them opens the trunk and a boy steps out...with his younger brother...carrying a dog.

That's the feeling you get as you ride Beijing's buses and see it proved to your very eyes that two people *can* occupy the same space at the same time.

Certainly the preferred way to move around Beijing, if you are traveling on your own, is by taxi. And by our standard, taxis in China are reasonable—costing less than 50 cents per mile. There was a time in Beijing when, out of reach for locals, taxis were only available at a handful of hotels and other locations frequented by foreigners. And even at those locations, it was not unusual to have to wait thirty to forty minutes on a queue. By the 1990s, however, taxis were for everyone.

It is possible, it should be noted, even for a short-term visitor to go native and rent a bicycle at various locations around town. Careful! Riding merrily along to a Christmas party with a friend near the Beijing Language Institute one bitterly cold Sunday evening, I made a perfectly fine right-hand turn, *right into someone's rear wheel—zhuang che le*, they say in Chinese. Fortunately, he suffered nothing more than a bent spoke and was pacified by a pack of cigarettes and a smile. If you are not used to riding a bicycle in traffic, Beijing is not the place to learn.

Taxis and bikes aside, there will be times when, if you demand a little freedom, you will have to rely on public transportation. Beijing, a city of about seven-and-a-half million in the city center,* has a modern, two-line subway with a loop extension, and a light-rail line serving the northern suburbs. Three additional lines will be in place in time for the 2008 Olympic Games. For many destinations, however, there is no substitute for riding buses and trolleys.

The best thing about Beijing's buses is their frequency. Stand at the Tian'anmen bus stop (not far from the famous square where the May 1st and October 1st celebrations are held and the site of 1989 revolt) and you can watch the city's most popular lines (Nos. 1 and 4—which ply the length of Chang'an Avenue) pass every few minutes from 5:00 in the morning until 11:00 in the evening.

The first challenge, though, is to *locate* the bus or trolley stop, a problem because stops are often spaced one-half to three-quarters of a mile apart. (My second day in China, knowing little of buses or taxis, I found myself walking three-and-a-half miles from the center of town to my hotel, the Yanjing.) The problem is solved if you get yourself a copy of the *Beijing Shi Qu Jiaotong Tu* (Beijing District Transportation Map) and unsolved if you can't read Chinese.

---

* Augmented by a "floating population" estimated at up to four million—non-Beijingers, registered and unregistered, who come to Beijing to work. Administratively, Beijing is structured somewhat like New York City and New York State: Beijing City, consisting of eight urban districts, surrounded by ten rural and semi-rural districts, stretching out as much as one hundred miles from downtown Beijing. The total population of greater Beijing is 15.2 million plus the floaters.

There are so many people in China that, at least on the most traveled routes, there are no rush hours. The goal is not to get a seat, but to get *on the bus*...any way you can. No room for Western etiquette here.

Somehow, Beijing packs fifty percent more passengers into any bus than ever rode any New York City subway car at 5:00 P.M. During slack hours, normal passenger inertia usually accommodates all of the passengers waiting at a stop. At any other time that rider load dictates, standard operating procedure is for one of the ticket sellers—usually two per bus—to jump out as soon as a stop is reached, allow a generous "bite" of passengers to approach the door, and then close ranks to their rear. By all standards, the bus is *already* filled, but that is immaterial. What is reassuring is that since the bus will not leave without the attendant (who also doubles as door closer), all of the people in front of her (sometimes him) will somehow squeeze in.

Ticket attendants occasionally nudge, but rarely push. Instead, they resort to verbal prods such as *"Kuai shang! Kuai shang!* Up fast! Up fast!"

At peak hours, at certain stops, the ticket seller dares not exit the bus. Instead, station-based, arm-banded "stop attendants" do the dirty work. Having no other responsibility—no tickets to sell, no doors to open and close, no bus to ride—they PUSH. They seem to enjoy their work.

Frankly, confronting this "animal crackers" scene every time I needed to get on a bus often got the better of me. On one occasion in the early afternoon, when there was really no need to push, but with native instincts prevailing just the same, I grabbed a particularly aggressive fellow intent on walking through me by the back of his long blue coat, pulled him away from the bus door, and asked him square to his face in Chinese: "Where are your manners?" He didn't have a clue what I was talking about.

Once inside the bus, which is likely to have two sections,

it is easy to revel in your attainment and get a bit complacent. A big mistake. Unless you are traveling just one or two stops, the natural "flow" will take you far from any exit, presaging a mighty struggle when it comes time to leave the bus.

Buying a ticket is a good idea. You could get away without it (in fifty to sixty rides no one ever bothered to check whether I had a ticket). But with city fares ranging between 10 and 20 cents, I mean really...

Getting to pay your fare, though, is sometimes a major undertaking. Sometimes it is dispensed with altogether. Ten days before Christmas saw one of the heaviest snowstorms in years: one to two inches. Beijing vehicles, many of whose tires are bald (never mind snow tires), slowed to a creep. It being rush hour, with buses backed up for miles, the number of passengers at each stop swelled to unabsorbable levels. Once inside the bus, quarters became so tight that one child had to be passed out the window to his waiting dad. On that day, you heard none of the usual, "Tickets. Who needs tickets?" Everyone rode for free.

Even on less festive days, the time to plan your exit is at least one stop in advance. There is no need to signal. With so many people getting on, there is always someone getting off. If you don't plan in advance, you will find yourself in the situation I did one day. Late for an appointment, frustrated, hopelessly grafted to two fellow sufferers too far from any door for any civilized course of action, and not at all in the mood for an extra half-mile walk, I turned football player. Cupping my belongings close to my chest (to avoid people shear), I lowered my head, plowed forward, and leaped out the door. Four startled people—including me—found themselves on the sidewalk. I picked myself up triumphantly and bounded across the street.

The approved technique for exiting a bus in China is of course "slithering." You suck in your stomach, stand on your tiptoes like a groundhog surveying a field, and make like a soap bar—probing with any part of your body for a potential opening. You then slide through any crack that develops, all the while yelling purposefully: "*Xia! Xia!* Getting off! Getting off!"

Despite the zoolike atmosphere, there is an underlying civility to Beijing bus life. Without it, no one could survive day after day. Constant heavy physical contact notwithstanding (some say this is why Beijingers are so slim), in five weeks of riding China's buses, I never once saw tempers flare. And, though they often work in unheated, drafty buses in winter and in stifling heat in summer, most ticket attendants remain cheerful and helpful. On that very snowy evening, after an hour-and-a-half of crawling, the bus suddenly emptied with my stop still a mile away. It turned out the bus was running a short route. When I expressed my bewilderment to the staff, the driver immediately closed the doors and drove me an extra half mile, putting me within walking distance of my destination.

And, there are personal touches. One evening, after a particularly trying day, I boarded the No. 1 bus, headed back toward my hotel. The passenger load was light (it was about 9:00 P.M.) and I was able to get a seat. Immediately, a woman caught my attention. The bus was dark and I really couldn't make out much detail except that she was young and probably attractive. What made her stand out particularly was her white down coat (almost all winter coats in China being dark blue, red, or olive drab in those years). I offered her my seat and she hesitated. When I told her it was an American custom, she relented. It wasn't that way in China, she told me. We got to talking. She was a piano player and music teacher. Though she knew no English, she had an apparent feel for the West. She told me that she had some friends who had moved to San Francisco. It was clear that she secretly wished that she could be there too.

I forget how it started. Maybe I stumbled and she grabbed my hand to steady me...or maybe I grabbed hers. But long after it was necessary, they remained clasped. We didn't know each other's names and, in the dark, could see little more than each other's outline. But it didn't seem to matter; we were both content in our thoughts. After a minute or two, rationality imposed, and I gently withdrew my hand. A stop passed. When the seat next to her emptied, I sat down and we continued to talk quietly. I wanted to ask her name, to see her in daylight, but something inside told me not to. When my stop arrived, I squeezed her hand softly, lingered a bit, and said goodbye.

An interlude...on a Beijing bus.

The Transparent
Yellow Race

□□□

URING WORLD WAR II, the Japanese tell, there was a Chinese agent who infiltrated Japan in search of military secrets. He mastered all the intricate Japanese mannerisms and customs—the bows, the inflections, the deferential mannerisms—to the point that he was indistinguishable from any other Japanese. But one day, washing his face, the story continues, he betrayed his identity. Unlike the Japanese, who cleanse their faces by manipulating their hands, the Chinese leave their hands stationary and move their faces from left to right.

That in fact most Chinese wash relatively stationary faces need not detract from an implicit assumption of the tale: the faces of East Asians are basically the same.

Americans who have infrequent contact with East Asians often ask if Asians themselves can differentiate between Chinese, Koreans, and Japanese. Many of these same questioners assume they will receive a clear-cut answer. And there are crude jokes about the differences in eye-slant direction. On purely physical features alone, however, the fact is that it is virtually impossible to differentiate between groups. Chinese on average may be taller; Koreans may be paler; Japanese women may have shorter, stockier legs (shaped like the Japanese dai-kon radish, some say). While none of these generalizations are false, none approach universal truth. When viewing individuals, they have no practical value.

Genetically, there is little to distinguish between Chinese, Koreans, and Japanese. Han Chinese (who comprise ninety-one percent of mainland Chinese) with long family histories in North China are racially more distant from Han Chinese in the South than from people from Korea (which borders on China's three populous Manchurian provinces). Okinawa, a prefecture of Japan, is much closer to Taiwan than it is to Tokyo.

To see how difficult it is to distinguish between East Asians, ride one of New York's most traveled subway lines, the No. 7 (dubbed the "Orient Express"), from Main Street in Queens to Times Square in Manhattan, at rush hour. Hordes of Chinese who live in and around the Flushing area that has supplanted Manhattan as New York's most populous Chinatown are interspersed with Koreans living in Sunnyside, Flushing, and surrounding neighborhoods. Which are Chinese? Which are Korean?

Dr. Laurel Kendall, a socio-cultural anthropologist and Curator of Asian Ethnology at the American Museum of Natural History in New York, feels that whereas valid observations based on body characteristics can be made for particular groups, there are too many exceptions to be useful. She ventures, however, that, based on body language and facial expression, she could be eighty-seven percent accurate in differentiating between Chinese and Koreans on the No. 7 train. If they stood motionless, however, her success rate would plummet, she qualifies.

Exploring genetic differences between East Asian peoples translates into a very diversified search, extending from classic anthropology to biology and genetics to public health. Genetic similarities between peoples turn out to have implications for studies in epidemiology, immunology, and longevity.

As Dr. Li Jin, a population geneticist formerly at the University of Texas-Houston Human Genetics Center, and now a professor at Fudan University in Shanghai, explains, what people commonly call Chinese, in fact represents two groupings—north and south—that are "much more different genetically than people would suspect." North Chinese are much more similar to Koreans and Japanese than to South Chinese. This prompts him to favor the term, "Northern East Asian," when referring racially to North Chinese, Koreans, and Japanese. Many of his observations derive from the Chinese Human Genome Diversity Project (affiliated with the broader Human Genome Diversity Project, begun in 1991), whose first findings, employing state-of-the-art DNA testing techniques, were published in 1998. Chinese north-south genetic pattern differentiation, Jin feels, will maintain itself for twenty to thirty more years, then gradually "homogenize" as Chinese increasingly migrate on the mainland, encouraged by the loosening of government population control begun in 1979.

In differentiating visually between East Asians, Dr. Jin concentrates on the shape of the forehead, the height of the nose, and the size of the eyes. But distinguishing between Koreans, Japanese, and Chinese on the basis of physical features alone, he feels, would be "really difficult."

WHAT PROMPTED THIS UNLIKELY INQUIRY was a Japanese newspaper article sent me by a Japanese friend during the 1998 World Women's Softball Championships, held in Japan. It told of Utsugi Reika, the third baseman on the Japanese women's national softball team, who had become famous in Japan as she led her team to a qualifying berth in the 2000 Sydney Olympics with a record-breaking four home runs. Utsugi Reika is in fact Chinese, and the former captain of the Chinese national softball team. The Chinese have spent half a century plus hating the Japanese for their World War II crimes of aggression. They still viscerally wave the finger of history in Japanese faces at diplomatic encounters. How a Chinese could take on Japanese identity begged explanation in much the same way that Jews who choose to live in Germany invite sharp questioning.

In 1987, at age twenty-four, Utsugi (her family name) went to Japan, which, as the only country where softball players can earn a professional salary, also attracts American and Australian players. She joined the team sponsored by electrical giant Hitachi, and later became a playing coach for Hitachi. She has been a four-time all-star at first base and a two-time all-star at third base, establishing the Japan League season record for the highest batting average (.500) and most home runs (6). For most of these years, she has been known both officially and informally as Nin-san. *Nin* is the Japanese reading for the Chinese character *ren*, her Chinese family name.

What spurred Ren Yanli to become Utsugi Reika was a 1995 invitation to join the Japanese national team and play in the 1996 Atlanta Olympic Games (the first time softball was to be included in the Olympics). Participating in the Olympics required naturalization—a complex process for foreigners in Japan. Even with the support of the heavyweight Hitachi Company, the conversion took a year to complete. Ren Yanli had first to renounce her Beijing residence certificate (equivalent to renouncing her Chinese citizenship) and to obtain the permission of her father, a career soldier in China's People's Liberation Army. Carrying the instinctive anti-Japanese sentiment typical of his generation, the elder Ren didn't understand why a Chinese would want to become Japanese. He relented when his daughter assured him that the decision was for her future. He still has found himself unable to visit Japan despite numerous invitations.

It might have been expected that Utsugi would go through long periods of inner turmoil as she remolded her identity. But becoming Japanese was something she simply grew into, she says. Despite her anti-Japanese communist education, she exemplified the neutral historical attitude toward Japan characteristic of many of her generation. She worked with Japanese, she had no difficulty eating their food, she spoke their language.

In Utsugi Reika's citizenship application essay, she explained her simple motivations for becoming a Japanese national: her comfort in living with the Japanese people and her desire to play in the Olympics. Were it not for the Olympic Games, she says, she would never have become Japanese in such a rush. Because the one-year minimum wait period after obtaining citizenship could not be satisfied before the 1996 Atlanta Games, Utsugi's participation on the Japanese team required the agreement of her former country, China. China, a world softball powerhouse despite a nationwide base of just two hundred competitive players, and a would-be silver-medal winner at Atlanta, predictably refused. Utsugi instead crowned her softball career at the Sydney Olympics in 2000, where she led Japan to a silver-medal with three home runs. After Sydney, she retired to a life-long position as a coach at Hitachi. But the lure of the 2004 Athens Olympics brought her out of retirement at forty-one as she led Japan to an Olympic softball bronze. Her extra-innings, game-winning double against China in the semifinals gave Japan a 1-0 win, depriving China of a medal in Athens. Following the Athens Games, she made her retirement final and joined Renesas Technology Corp., a semiconductor maker whose major stakeholders are Hitachi and Mitsubishi, as coach.

WHAT IS SO INTRIGUING ABOUT the transition from Chinese to Japanese is how easy it is for Chinese to take on outer Japanese identities, and how Japanese immigration law, in order to preserve a homogeneity reaching the ninety-ninth percentile, facilitates—virtually coerces—the assimilation of those who wish to become Japanese citizens.

The last step before Ren Yanli could become Utsugi Reika was for her to take a Japanese name. In fact, name change is a suggestion rather than a requirement. But, as Utsugi explains, and forms from the Ministry of Justice confirm, there is a space on the form marked "Name after Naturalization," and it is expected that it be filled in. Without a Japanese name, immigration authorities are very unlikely to grant Japanese citizenship.

In fact, there is no practical need for Chinese or Koreans (who comprise more than fifty-five percent of the 1.97 million foreigners [2004 data] registered in Japan) to assume Japanese names when applying for citizenship. Chinese, Japanese, and Koreans all use Chinese characters in their names, and all traditionally place family names before first names. There are, it is true, differences in usage. (Japanese family names overwhelmingly contain two Chinese characters, and Japanese first names most commonly contain two or three Chinese characters. Chinese and Korean names, on the other hand, almost uniformly contain just one Chinese character for the last name and one or two characters for the first name.) Nevertheless, a Japanese reading can always be found for a Chinese character. However, although writing or pronouncing Chinese and Korean names poses no exceptional difficulty at work or in school, the characters Chinese and Koreans use for their names would instantly brand them as foreigners. (Profusely popular Chinese and Korean names such as Li, Chen, Zhang, Wang, and Kim stand out as non-Japanese.) And this undermines the homogeneity that Japan regards as its strength.

Further enhancing the integration of Chinese into Japanese society is the fact that, like Japanese, Chinese (and especially those from the mainland) for the most part profess no formal religious belief. (Koreans are thirty percent Protestant and ten percent Catholic.) Thus, with physical appearance not a factor, for almost all Chinese and for those Koreans without religious beliefs, fluency in Japanese and assuming a Japanese name are the only outward requirements for assimilation into Japanese life.

For Chinese in particular, and despite apparent monumental historical barriers, the path to full integration can take as little as one generation. Slowest to integrate are families in which both parents are Chinese or Korean—preserving the influence of native language and customs. Where one partner is Japanese (and especially in cases where the non-Japanese partner arrives young enough to become fully fluent in relatively unaccented Japanese), the overbearing weight of Japanese culture and the socializing effect of Japanese education quickly dissolve foreign identities. The Japanese work to encourage this in their immigration policy.

Professor Hiroshi Komai of Chukyo Women's University, in Japan, notes that Koreans (who tend to resist assimilation) display much greater attachment to their nationality than do Chinese. This is reflected in the fact that of the roughly 632,000 Koreans residing in Japan as of January 2007, some 449,000 who are non-citizens date their entry into Japan back to World War II, when Korea was colonized by Japan. About 3,000 of the 593,000 Chinese non-citizens are "old-comers," as Professor Komai calls them. In recent years, Japan has marginally relaxed its resistance to granting citizenship to foreigners. Nevertheless, Japan remains highly selective, granting citizenship to just 15,251 foreigners (out of 50,871 applicants) in 2005, according to statistics released by the Ministry of Justice. With ninety-three percent of new citizens being either Korean (64 percent) or Chinese (29 percent), and Koreans and Chinese being the most racially assimilable, the homogeneity that Japanese prize remains secure. These figures and percentages have remained relatively stable over the past ten years.

Contrast the Japanese immigration situation with the situation in the United States. In 2004, in Japan, registered aliens constituted just 1.5 percent (1.97 million) of a population of 127.8 million. In the United States, 12.5 percent (37.55 million of a population of 299 million—2006 U.S. Census Bureau data) was foreign born. With a much smaller pool of foreigners percentage-wise than the United States, the proportion of naturalized to native-born Japanese is much smaller.

While the United States, a homogenized nation, gives prominence to the national origin of its residents and citizens, in Japan, once a foreigner has attained citizenship, he is categorized only as unhyphenated "Japanese." The Japanese release no figures on the national origin of its citizens. Though the figures are old, interestingly, while 66 percent of mainland Chinese and 59 percent of Koreans who immigrated to the U.S. in 1977 had attained U.S. citizenship by 1995, only 17 percent of 1977 Japanese immigrants to the U.S. had been naturalized. Japanese are as reluctant to take on another country's nationality as they are to grant Japanese nationality to foreigners.

AS HER JAPANESE FAMILY NAME (Utsugi), Ren Yanli chose that of her Japanese coach, Ms. Utsugi Taeko, who had befriended her and brought her to Japan. As her first name, Ren Yanli selected *Reika*, *Rei*, the Japanese reading of the second character in her Chinese first name, *li*; *ka*, meaning "China." Together they read as "Beautiful China," melding her past and present. In the office, and on the softball field, she is known as Utsugi Reika; informally, as before, Japanese address her as Nin-san. Chinese call her Ren Yanli.

Ironically, Utsugi finds herself having reversed the immigration path of her Chinese softball coach, Li Minkuan. Coach Li's father was born in Taiwan in 1905. By that time, Japan had colonized Taiwan. The elder Li, though Chinese, used the Japanese name Oda and came to speak a very fluent Japanese. In 1921, at age sixteen, the elder Li moved to Japan, later marrying a Japanese woman from the Tominaga family in the town of Toyota, near Nagoya. Li Minkuan, born in 1937, his two younger brothers, and his two younger sisters were all given unofficial Chinese names. But they were considered Japanese citizens, their mother tongue was Japanese, and their birth certificates and school records all carried the surname of their mother, Tominaga. All four of Coach Li's siblings, most of whom now live in the Osaka region, married Japanese, and their offspring are fully assimilated.

Li Minkuan, the oldest Tominaga child, chose a Chinese path. Inspired ideologically by the 1949 Chinese Communist takeover of the mainland, in 1953, at age fifteen, he traveled alone to China where he slowly went about the process of linguistically and culturally becoming Chinese. Never fully shedding his accent, he later graduated from the Beijing University of Steel and Iron, and eventually became a renowned softball coach in China, shepherding the Chinese national softball team from 1979 to 1996 and winning a silver medal in the 1996 Atlanta Olympic Games. Though fully integrated into Chinese life and a delegate to China's People's Political Consultative Conference since 1993, both of Coach Li's wives (his first wife died when she tragically fell out of a window), each Chinese, have roots in Japan, and his family life remains heavily influenced by his Japanese past.

Li Minkuan is Chinese; his four brothers and sisters (born in the same home, of the same mother and father) are Japanese.

It was Li Minkuan who first taught Utsugi Reika Japanese when she proposed going to Japan in 1985, thereby easing her transition; and it was, in part, Li Minkuan whose opposition, on competitive grounds, postponed her Olympic debut from 1996 to 2000.

As long as Utsugi Reika remains unmarried, she will have little long-range impact on the Japanese national character. Should she marry a Japanese and bear children, however, she will further strengthen the monolith that is the Japanese people.

FENG XIAODONG AND LIU WEIZHI first arrived in Japan from Guangzhou, China in the early 1990s. Feng earned a master's degree in Japanese literature, and Liu went to work for a Japanese premium company producing merchandise (such as commemorative ceramic plates) in China for large corporate Japanese customers.

When we met, Feng Xiaodong had just returned from China, where she had left her two children with her parents. They were to remain there for three years. Though it is far from uncommon for grandparents to raise children in China, the greatest imperative for her and her husband was that their children learn Chinese. The older child had entered Japanese nursery school, where Japanese had become his mother tongue. His parents spoke to each other and to him in Chinese, but, as is universally common where the language of the home differs from the language of the society in which the child lives, he answered in Japanese. A similar pattern awaited the younger child. Feng and Liu hoped to intercept fate.

Feng Xiaodong and her husband had recently been granted Japanese citizenship as a family.

"I am still Chinese," she interjected at the earliest conversation opportunity, reflecting the inner turmoil that had accompanied her decision. For her husband, the consideration was that applying for foreign visas as a Chinese national every time he needed to travel abroad was eroding his business productivity. For Feng Xiaodong, who was about to begin a new job as an editor of the in-house organ of a Japanese company, it was the realization that without Japanese citizenship and a Japanese name, it is very difficult for a foreigner to obtain a job with a Japanese company.

They took the family name Oe, meaning "big river." (Unlike mainland Chinese, a Japanese husband and wife carry the same surname.) Feng Xiaodong took the first name Akiko, combining the Japanese reading of the first character of her Chinese name, meaning "dawn," with the character *ko*, commonly suffixed to feminine Japanese names. Mr. Liu took the Japanese first name Ryuji, meaning "descendant of the Dragon" (a reference to his Chinese birth). Hereafter, professionally, Feng Xiaodong and Liu Weizhi would be known as Oe Akiko and Oe Ryuji.

Feng and Liu's Chinese roots will remain stable. Their ongoing challenge will be to pass along their Chinese heritage to their children when they return to Japan from China. Once the children reenter Japanese schools, it will require enormous stamina to resist becoming Japanese.

Zou Renying, in her mid-forties, from Shanghai, is a manager for the Daitoku Kimono Company, with offices throughout Japan. Her firm fits wedding kimono, which often run thousands of dollars, then ships them to China to be finished at huge labor savings. Zou is fluent in Japanese. Indeed, only after speaking with her in Japanese for a long while did she reveal that she was Chinese. As an executive for a Japanese company, it would be relatively simple for her to achieve the Japanese citizenship that so many Chinese living in Japan yearn for. But a special investor's visa granted her by Japan facilitates her trips between China and Japan. She chooses to leave her children in Shanghai and to retain her Chinese name and identity.

AT EVERY OPPORTUNITY, in China, Japan, and the United States, I sought to differentiate between Japanese, Chinese, and Koreans—scrutinizing their gaits, their mannerisms, their dress, their hairdos.

Japan Airlines flights to and from the U.S. provided a particularly good comparison vantage point. Because so many JAL passengers are from mainland China, several of the flight attendants on these routes are Chinese. Yet dressed identically, it is impossible to tell—even over twelve hours—which flight attendants are Chinese, which Japanese, without looking at name tags. Inevitably, guesses yield surprises.

To verify this budding generality, I decided to randomly photograph large numbers of Chinese, Koreans, and Japanese, eventually selecting sixty-four photographs divided relatively evenly among the three groups. The Chinese were photographed in Manhattan's Chinatown; the Koreans on Manhattan's 32nd Street (the center for Korean supermarkets, bookstores, beauty salons, and restaurants); the Japanese in Japan and around Central Park in Manhattan, where they come in large numbers to see the

Strawberry Fields memorial to John Lennon, created with the support of Lennon's Japanese widow, Yoko Ono. Each subject was asked his nationality before being photographed. The reluctance of many immigrants to be photographed aside (sometimes because of cloudy immigration status), this effort demonstrated the impact that such variables as location, profession, and even time of day can have on sampling. New York's Chinatown is, by and large, populated by working class-Chinese, reflected especially in their dress. Koreans in central Manhattan tend to be dressed more formally. Rural Japanese dress differently than their urban counterparts. Comparing a fruit and vegetable peddler or a farmer with a cosmetician demands a sharper eye than most of us can provide. Similarly, random street photographs taken in mid-afternoon, when most professionals are in their offices, can provide a different population sample than at rush hour, when better-dressed business people are heading home.

As much as practical, the photos were cropped to mask architecture, street signs, store fronts, newspaper type, interior decor (such as ceremonial scrolls), as well as any other elements that would immediately point to a specific East Asian group. A background sign in a store could be an immediate give-away, because Chinese, Japanese, and Koreans all utilize distinctive, easily differentiated, writing scripts.

Of six people asked to identify the sixty-four photographs by nationality, only one was able to correctly select more than half, with 31 the average score. Even for those who scored best, there were incongruities. A physician from Beijing who correctly identified 15 of 20 compatriots, also misidentified 10 non-Chinese as Chinese. The director of the C.V. Starr East Asian Library at Columbia University, a specialist on Japan, correctly identified 18 of 23 subjects as Japanese, but mislabeled 13 non-Japanese as Japanese. Specialists in a particular ethnic group often did worse or no better within their group than outside. A Korean specialist at the Asia Society identified only 6 of 21 Koreans, while recognizing 16 of 23 Japanese. The

Korea-raised librarian of the Korean section at Columbia's East Asian Library identified 10 of 21 Koreans (but 9 of 20 Chinese and 11 of 23 Japanese). A Ph.D. teaching Chinese language and literature at Williams College, who had lived in China for four years, could identify only 9 of 20 Chinese.

Visual differences and cultural clues nevertheless exist. But they are based on facial expression, hairstyle, dress, posture, mannerism. Sometimes clues are as subtle as the portable ashtray a Japanese in his late twenties took out as he smoked a cigarette in Central Park.

Generalizations tempered by many exceptions:

Gait: There is a noticeable difference in the way East Asian and American women walk. Japanese women, in particular, walk with short strides and very little hip swing—often looking like they are slanting sideways as they move forward, much like an airplane angling into the wind to avoid being blown off course. The origin of their shuffle is the traditional kimono, worn with thong socks, which severely limits hip movement and forces toe direction inward. Today, very few Japanese wear kimono except on ceremonial occasions. But the gait inspired by them remains, especially in older women.

Chinese women, too, traditionally wear the hip-restricting *qi pao*, but the slits on the sides allow a bit more body movement than the kimono. When the Communists took over in 1949, traditional dress immediately became counterrevolutionary. Unlike the kimono in Japan, worn across class lines, the *qi pao* was largely limited to upper-class Chinese. Thus the gait it inspired was not equally prevalent among all Chinese. Footbinding, which also restricts gait, disappeared in the early 1900s in China, far earlier than the wane of the kimono as everyday wear in Japan.

Of all of the distinguishing characteristics, gait, regardless of age, remains the most reliable identifying characteristic of women from Japan. I was walking just outside of Central Park one day when I sighted two Japanese women, each well under five feet tall, waddling down the street, toes pointed inward, hips jerking. Camera unavailable, all I could do, as I picked up my pace and passed them, was to pivot and query: "*Nihon-jin desu ka?* Are you Japanese?" Taken aback, the woman to the left raised her head with a quizzical look. "*Hai*, Yes," she confirmed.

A second time, I met an almost identical situation on the other side of the street. This time, the pair was much younger, late twenties it appeared. With taller, slimmer bodies, their jerky hip swing was far less pronounced. But these, too, were Japanese…grateful Japanese…as I pointed out the Dakota apartment building where John Lennon was killed and directed them to the nearest *honya*…bookstore.

Mannerism: Chinese smile and giggle profusely when they are defensive or embarrassed. Japanese nod more than Chinese or Koreans, according to Toshio Okazaki, professor of linguistics at Tsukuba University, who is responsible for teaching Japanese to foreigners and sees no difference in physical features between East Asians.

Eyes: If an Oriental man has had an eye operation to double the fold in his eyelids and give his eyes a more Western look, he is overwhelmingly likely to be Japanese.

Teeth: Adults over age fifty showing gold fillings in their mouth are most likely to be Japanese. The younger generation, however, prefers the white, Western look in teeth.

Cosmetics: Younger women in Japan (confirmed by the Shiseido cosmetic company) tend to use heavier foundation (with white or beige coloring) on their faces than their East Asian sisters, giving them a distinctive pancake or mannequin look. White skin, in the Orient, has traditionally been considered a mark of beauty.

Apparel: If a man wears tinted prescription eyeglasses indoors, he is most likely Chinese. If he keeps the brand label of his suit on his sleeve, he is apt to be Chinese. If he or she leaves the brand tag on his or her sunglasses (even if it impedes vision), the wearer is likely Chinese. China is very much in the nouveau riche phase.

In winter, Chinese men often wear long-sleeved, V-necked sweaters under their suit jackets, reflecting China's underheated winter homes and offices.

As newcomers to affluence, Chinese have fewer articles of clothing in their wardrobe, less access to dry cleaning, and are more apt to wear out-of-date fashions and baggy pants.

Japanese schoolchildren have spiffier backpacks than other East Asian children.

Hair style: Young Chinese men from Hong Kong often shave the back of their head high into the scalp. Hong Kong women, in recent years, have adopted the frizzy look. But mainland Chinese in Guangzhou, to the south, often mimic Hong Kong styles, and occasionally Hong Kong hair styles reach as far north as Beijing.

Japanese women over sixty are highly likely to cut their hair short and comb it back, with modified waving.

Large numbers of Japanese men part their hair in the middle and comb exaggerated pompadours on either side. This is particularly noticeable with the silver-haired set. The Japanese, very concerned about the position of the part, call a style in which the hair is parted at the seventy-percent mark, left to right, *shichi-san*, meaning "7-3." Also characteristically Japanese is the straight-back plastered look (*ooru-bakku*, all-back), popular with politicians. Korean politicians tend to sweep their hair more to the side.

(Leaving nothing to chance in a country where the base cost for a man's haircut is in the $30-range, barber shops in Japan usually have style books, offering dozens of options, so the customer can show the barber the precise cut he wants from rear, side, and front angles.)

Untended sideburns is a mainland Chinese trait among the working class, as are irregularly shaven faces.

ON TOKYO'S TOZAI SUBWAY LINE, one early evening, I overheard two gentlemen chatting in very clear Mandarin. I sought the origin of the two voices and went through my checklist. Short-ish, each wore fashionable, rimless, hexagonal spectacles. I checked their sideburns for neglect, characteristic of main-landers, and found instead sharp razor lines. Their accent disqualified them as Taiwanese, who utter sloppy "sh" and "j" sounds. Hong Kong Chinese speak Cantonese. Their crisply laundered white shirts belied a mainland identity, but that was all that remained.

"Are you from the mainland or from Taiwan?" I intruded.

"The mainland."

"From Beijing?"

"From Manchuria," came back the response.

"From Shenyang?" I led.

"Yes, they said. Are you from the mainland too?"

"From the U.S. mainland," I replied.

After six or seven years in Japan, these two Chinese men, businessmen in their mid-thirties, could pass for any Japanese.

China's Quicksand

□ □ □

...Corruption is a virus... If we lower our guard and allow it to overwhelm us, it has the capacity to bury our Party, to bury our government's mandate, to bury our socialist moderniza-tion endeavor...

... [We must] resolve several key problems. FOR EXAMPLE, the railway system must concentrate on wiping out the use of trains and tickets for private gain...

—President Jiang Zemin
August 21, 1993

THE SECRET TO FLEXIBLE train travel in China, I learned in Henan Province, en route from Luoyang to Kaifeng five months before the campaign to eradi-cate corruption began in August 1993, is purchasing an unnumbered ticket in the hard-seat section and upgrading as necessary. This worked out smoothly on the three-hour trip to Kaifeng, where I was headed to search out descendants of an assimilated nineteenth-century community of Chinese Jews. Positioning myself at trackside with the aid of intelligence input from a platform attendant, I was able to jostle myself to a vacant seat opposite a woman already traveling for thirty-seven hours from Ningxia Autonomous Region on her way to her ancestral home in Anhui Province. The smoke-filled car, littered with wa-termelon seeds, did nothing positive for a lingering cold. But hard-seat travel on China's trains provides easy conversation

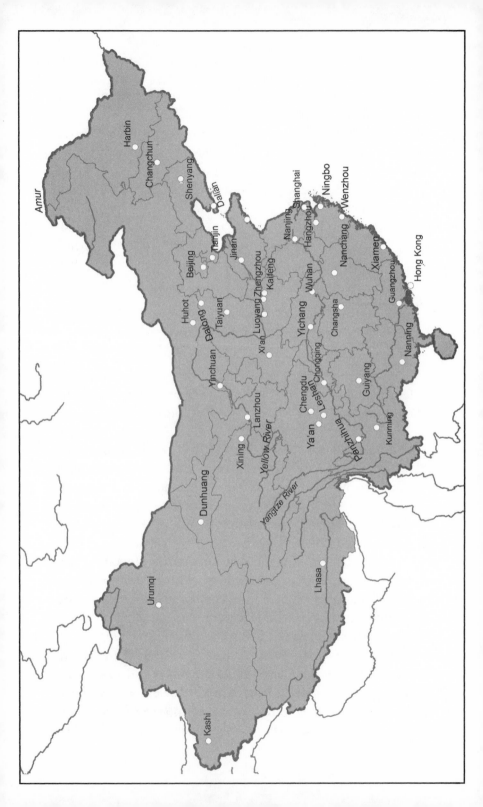

with virtually every segment of the population. Three hours of endurance was a fair price.

The weathered, forty-two-year-old baby-boomer from Ningxia seated on the facing bench put China's heralded prosperity into a certain context. Though she, too, had a color television set and enjoyed the best material standard of her lifetime, "for ninety-nine percent of China," she contended, life remained an exercise in scrimping. Whereas Chinese traveling on business or vacation to other parts of the country now routinely spend $5.00 or $6.00 per night for overnight accommodations, her limit was $1.00. "If we don't find a place for 5 yuan," she said, "we sleep outside."

The 7:45 outbound from Kaifeng two days later—due to arrive in Xi'an at 18:03—provided none of the benefits of the trip in. The most nimble, newly boarding passengers claimed just-vacated seats by slinging valises through the windows. But I spent the first hour standing in the vestibule, unable to make it even into the hard-seat cars fore and aft, whose aisles were packed with expressionless, unwashed faces, perched atop slumping bodies in rumpled clothing. Crowding notwithstanding, a thirtyish woman, toting a toothbrush, managed to slither her way to and from the washroom. And train personnel, pushing carts filled with styrofoam-packaged meals of rice, meat, and vegetables, somehow threaded their way from car to car. There were always buyers.

During the eight-minute stop at Zhengzhou junction, I left the car in search of the train captain, who handled upgrading. Eyeing a foreign face, he quoted 120 yuan ($18) for a soft sleeper to Xi'an. Thirty yuan was the going rate.

Declining, I hurried back to the hard section, where I edged my way down the aisle, past the seating area, until I chanced upon a dripping, trash-filled washbasin, whose counter someone had covered with cardboard and used as a seat. This provided a short-term foot rest solution. A leather salesman from Wenzhou in the same predicament occupied the remaining space in the alcove and began to make conversation. My price for companionship was that he extinguish his cigarette.

Passing by an hour later, the train captain dampened any hopes that a hard seat would free up. The farther west we traveled, he offered, the more crowded the train would become. For 20 yuan, he proposed, I could upgrade to the dining car. This was a privilege of sorts because allowing riders into the dining area unrestricted would fast turn it into another cattle car.

What struck me immediately about the dining car was that the pockets of almost everyone who worked there were stuffed with cash. It came from food and beverage sales to the passengers, from ticket sales to passengers who had switched trains and boarded without tickets, from upgrading. In theory, except for food purchases, all money paid to train attendants was backed up by a sequenced receipt and thus strictly auditable. The problem was that no one monitored the receipts. It is common knowledge in China that many of the receipts issued are *jia piao*—phony. Service personnel demand a fee and produce a receipt. But that doesn't guarantee that it is the proper fee or that it will reach the account of the company nominally issuing it.

Had I paid the 120 yuan originally asked to move directly to a soft sleeper, it would have been duly receipted... and pocketed. Train captain, whose base salary can be augmented several-fold by skimming from the receipts, is the most lucrative position on the train. For the railroad line that means that any revenue produced outside the ticket office is totally unpredictable.

From Shi Lili, thirty-seven, who rode the rails for five years as train captain in Guizhou and Sichuan Provinces before taking a station platform assignment, and whose father spent his entire working career with the railroad, I sought the upper range of the take. Using the five-day, round-trip run from Chengdu (in Sichuan) to Shanghai as her example, she said that the most corrupt of train captains might add several thousand yuan per run to monthly base salaries and performance bonuses totaling 2,800 to 3,000 yuan ($400 to $430). A train crew might make two such runs per month.

Shi Lili's sister, who travels frequently from Chengdu to Chongqing (the Chungking of World War II fame) on business, explained one of the most common ploys passengers use in complicity with rail workers, ultimately depriving the rail lines of huge revenues. For a few yuan, passengers purchase platform tickets, whose intended purpose is to allow friends and relatives to see off and meet passengers. (The absence of platform porters to help with bundles aside, sending off and greeting travelers is a serious—and time-consuming—Chinese ritual.) The platform ticket buys access to the train without a hard-to-come-by reservation, and 50 yuan slipped to a train attendant takes care of the six-hour ride from Chengdu to Chongqing.

A simpler form of corruption is practiced on China's intercity buses. China moves by its railroads. But for most of China, the final miles (or hundreds of miles) home are by drafty, exhaust-belching bus, plying pocked roads that turn to rutted earth or mud without notice.

Most long-distance Chinese buses leave their station of origin full (many, in fact, will not leave until they are full), and most of the receipts from tickets purchased at the station presumably remain there. But every bus makes numerous stops at county hamlets and towns along the way. On the four-hour trip from Chengdu to Leshan (site of the world's tallest Buddha—233 feet), dozens of passengers boarded en route. Some used the bus as the cheapest available transport line, hauling plowshares, rubber tires, aluminum tubing, shovel heads, and wooden moldings into the bus aisle. These way-station passengers paid the quoted fare (not a few objected and left the bus) and were issued a numbered receipt if they requested it. But only the passenger receipt recorded the fare amount; the company stub remained blank. The ticket seller alone knew the precise take from the route—some of which no doubt went to the driver.

I THOUGHT I HAD FOUND A PRECIOUS source to reconcile government anticorruption policy with Chinese realities when I was paired in a sleeping compartment with Mr. Huang Jian, deep into his forties, on the twenty-three-hour train trip from Kunming to Chongqing. Huang had graduated from the Social Sciences Department at Chongqing University, and had risen to head the Propaganda Department of the Communist Party cell of the Fourth Bridge Building Department in Chongqing. Their major client was the railroad. Huang (sufficing, as Chinese often do, with a small hand satchel for his ten-day stay) had just completed a week-long conference in Kunming. As a veteran propaganda chief charged with disseminating the Party line at his plant, Huang had surely read Party Secretary Jiang Zemin's keynote address kicking off the anticorruption campaign.

In this path-marking speech, delivered before the Party's Commission for Discipline Inspection,* Jiang had emphasized three avenues of attack that later in the campaign became formally known as the "three items": (1) top ranking Party and government officials were to take the lead in setting norms of conduct; (2) a group of major corruption cases were to be prosecuted in the legal, administrative, and economic areas; and (3) those "unhealthy winds" at the local level that most vexed the people were to be uncovered and dealt with, with significant progress expected within a year's time.

Among specific areas targeted were the rail system, the banking and financial systems, the department of rural affairs (whose exploitation of peasants through endless and arbitrary tax levies has inspired periodic rural revolt), the customs ser-

---

* The Central Commission for Discipline Inspection of the Chinese Communist Party sets and upholds professional and ethical standards for Party members. It oversees the campaign against corruption.

vice, the public security system, and the justice system. Jiang seemed to be indicting much of China.

Particularly, I wanted Huang's views on how China had become so corrupt. Random observations I solicited had followed no set pattern. A Party sympathizer in his mid-sixties contended that corruption only emerged in China with the Cultural Revolution (1966-1976), when people were forced to fend for themselves. But others noted that this was probably because before the Cultural Revolution everyone was so uniformly poor that there were few material goods available with which to corrupt others. Few disagreed that the concept of "going through the back door" in search of privilege long predated the Cultural Revolution.

An anti-Party hotel manager in Beijing noted that corruption in China likely traced back to the emperors. And that proved to fall not far from Party General Secretary Jiang Zemin's official analysis, passed down to cadres at all levels for study.

Jiang (who at that time was concurrently serving as president of the People's Republic and chairman of the Central Military Commission)* opened his semiclassical, communist exposition by explaining corruption as an end product of the exploitation of the working class. Though there were certainly enlightened emperors and officials who put the country's prosperity at the forefront, Jiang said, "Inevitably, the collapse of each dynasty was inseparable from government corruption."

Shy on specifics, Jiang noted "that there are various complex reasons why corrupt practices still exist in our country under socialism." Significantly, he acknowledged that what China had taken great pains to achieve since opening its borders to the outside world—absorbing coveted Western technology and business techniques, while filtering out the decadent money

---

* At the Sixteenth Communist Party Congress in November 2002, Jiang was replaced as Party general secretary by Hu Jintao, and at the National People's Congress annual legislative session in March 2003, he yielded the presidency to Hu. Jiang relinquished chairmanship of the Party Central Military Commission in September 2004.

worship and greed characteristic of Western values—had run into difficulties. He saw the solution in vigilance and Communist thought education. The same Party leadership that allowed China to eradicate opium and heroine use within three years of the establishment of the People's Republic in 1949, Jiang implied, would wipe out corruption. "The task," however, "will be long-term and arduous."

> ...OF COURSE, we have to clearheadedly acknowledge that there is still a large gap between achievements in the struggle against corruption and the expectations of the public...
>
> —PRIME MINISTER LI PENG
> March 7, 1994

AS THE TRAIN WOUND THROUGH the harsh hills of Yunnan Province into Guizhou Province, sleeper mate Huang turned into a disappointment. He wouldn't show me the letter he carried, allowing him to ride the rails for free. "We don't show foreigners things like that," he said. He was more interested in knowing if every man in the U.S. had two lovers like President Ke-lin-dun; whether American "female comrades" were interested in intermarrying with Chinese "male comrades"; and whether, when traveling around the United States, I too had a *xiao jie* (young miss) to accompany me. I pointed out that since China began its policy of "Reform and Opening to the Outside World" in 1979, the "young miss" phenomenon had rooted there as well, and the Chinese divorce rate had skyrocketed.

By the time Huang had chewed through the third of four sticks of sugarcane he had purchased at Xuanwei Station, he had loosened up enough to admit that his propaganda unit at the Fourth Bridge Building Department, a remnant of Mao's China, was pretty much an anachronism these days. He agreed that the Party had probably chosen to push the anticorruption campaign at this point because Party leaders saw corruption as impeding China's economic growth. But he wasn't able to put Chinese corruption into any perspective, historical or otherwise. About businesses spun off from government administrative offices that had accelerated corruption and were under review, he claimed to know nothing. He was, in fact, little more than an educated parrot, with lingering authority, who slept with his tie on. That his Kunming conference, under the auspices of the Sichuan branch of the Communist Party of China, had been held (counter to Jiang Zemin's clear edict not to squander public funds on travel) in Yunnan Province (instead of in Sichuan, where it belonged), because Kunming ("The City of Spring") had a pleasant vacation climate, indicated that Huang was part of the problem.

Why is the policy unenforceable, I had asked the top official at a Tianjin boat factory traveling to Kunming to liquidate a bankrupt affiliate?

The Chinese have a saying, he replied: "The central government has central policies; local governments have counter-policies."

In the last quarter of 1993, the government announced the prosecution of a series of high profile corruption cases involving embezzlement and bribery. These included the conviction of Li Xiaoshi, vice minister of the State Science and Technology Commission, for taking $5,900 in bribes and embezzling $2,200 in the course of helping the Great Wall Machinery and Electronic Company defraud one hundred thousand investors of more than $110,000,000. Li was sentenced to twenty years in prison. Three senior officials in Henan and Guangdong Provinces (a former mayor, a former head of public security, and a former buildings and real estate administrator) were executed for bribery and smuggling involving sums over $500,000. In the quest for "Party values and honest government," the number of bureaucrats convicted of economic crimes in excess of 10,000 yuan was said to have doubled.

In the years since, the government has periodically publicized a never-ending chain of high-profile cases involving graft and corruption. In 2000, Cheng Kejie, a vice chairman of the National People's Congress, was stripped of his Party membership and sentenced to death for taking $4.7 million in bribes over a period of six years. In one instance, he used his position as governor of the Guangxi Zhuang Autonomous Region to sell prime government land at an undervalued price to shopping center developers; in others, he manipulated loans to his personal advantage. At his side was a consort by the name of Li Ping, adding adultery to the tawdry mix. In that same year, in the southeastern port city of Xiamen, in what came to be dubbed China's "Number One Smuggling Case," China cracked open a scheme involving the smuggling of cars and trucks, crude oil, vegetable oil, and firearms, running into the billions of dollars, in which the police, banks, and customs were complicitors. In all, eleven conspirators were sentenced to death. The ringleader, Lai Changxing, fled to Canada and became China's "most wanted man."

In January 2007, an arrest order was put out for former Kunming vice mayor Hu Xing, who had a bribe-taking wrap sheet stretching back to 1993 that ran past $5 million. With the police on his heels, Hu set out on a three-month odyssey that took him overland from Kunming to Guangdong. After picking up one million yuan delivered to him by a crony, he continued by plane to Shanghai. From there, using a passport from Nauru (a Pacific island country eight square miles in size), he traveled to Singapore, then Hong Kong. Refused entry in London, he returned to Singapore, where he was arrested and deported to China to face charges.*

---

* A 2004 report by the Chinese Ministry of Commerce said some four thousand Chinese officials suspected of crimes involving $50 billion had fled overseas since China launched economic reforms in 1978. According to the Supreme People's Procuratorate, the legal supervision body in China, from 2003 to July 2007, 136,570 cases of bribery and graft were opened against government officials.

The Party Commission for Discipline Inspection has logged thousands of such cases involving Party members at all levels.*

THE HIGHEST PROFILE ANTICORRUPTION case of all involved the 1998 conviction of former Politburo member and former Beijing mayor and Party head Chen Xitong on charges of dereliction of duty and corruption that netted him $10 to $20 million in cash as well as numerous apartment buildings and private homes. In deference to his rank and connections, he was sentenced to sixteen years in prison and permitted to return home to a lenient house arrest after serving just a third of his sentence. Of almost equal stature, in 2006, Shanghai Party boss Chen Liangyu was stripped of his Shanghai post, suspended from the Politburo, and expelled from the Party for manipulating public pension funds on a grand scale to enrich himself and his family.

... No matter who is involved, no matter how lofty the position, let each person receive the punishment he deserves. If he deserves a heavy sentence, don't go easy on him. Otherwise, we will never stamp out corruption...

—PRESIDENT JIANG ZEMIN
January 14, 2000

The highly publicized anticorruption campaign notwithstanding, the uniform view on the street across China remains that corruption has never been more rampant. A series of show cases has been paraded before the public. The government is good at making headlines. The government controls the headlines. With so many blatant cases to prosecute, a determined

---

* In September 2007, China established a National Corruption Preventative Agency, with branches throughout the country, that would coordinate anticorruption efforts throughout China, and target civilian corruption as well as corrupt government and Party officials.

central government might even make serious headway in combating grand-scale malfeasance. But the grassroots corruption affecting everyday life that "vexed the public" and leached people's energies—from purchasing a train ticket, to installing a telephone, to healing a wound—remained untouched and untouchable. This was the real "democracy" Chinese craved. Any anticorruption gains realized by the government would only be temporary, they felt.

WHAT IS DISARMING ABOUT CORRUPT service personnel in China is that many of those with hands in your pockets are basically kindhearted individuals.

The No. 110 Yangtze River Liner, destined for Yichang, which I boarded in Chongqing, is known as the "peasant ship." A large percentage of its four hundred passengers are peasants from remote villages of Sichuan and Hubei Provinces headed for China's large cities to look for work. Officer Yuan, one of two ship policemen, who asked me into his cabin to present my passport soon after boarding, called it the worst ship in the fleet. My fourth-class quarters were in a narrow dormitory with five, double-decked, plywood bunks on either side of a narrow aisle—twenty beds per cabin—which stretched across the ship's deck. While some tried to sleep, others whiled away the hours in the dingy quarters by playing cards or engaging in drinking games.

Yuan and the ship's Party supervisor took me under their wings, fixing me a bowl of noodles and tea, and cluing me into the subtleties of river life that are changing radically as China moves along with the Yangtze River dam project that will flood the valley and displace one million people. After several hours of talk, interrupted by occasional port calls, I had returned to Dormitory No. 2 a bit past eleven, resigned to a fitful night, when Yuan entered the room and nudged me out of the first stages of sleep.

"Sleep in our room," he said.

I gathered my belongings and made my way across the deck, carefully stepping over the dozens of dozing peasants blanketing the hallway floor, some huddled together in twos and threes for warmth and physical support, and entered the police quarters, which had four bunk beds.

Officer Yuan wasted no time in suggesting that this service required a "fee."

"Do you have U.S. dollars?"

I needed them, I told him.

He mentioned 100 Chinese yuan, about $12.00. In no mood for bargaining the price of a night's sleep, I said quietly that it would be best if I returned to the dormitory and moved toward the door.

"No, no," he stopped me. "How much can you pay?"

"Twenty yuan," I said.

"Give the money to him," Yuan said, gesturing to his partner.

There wasn't a trace of tension between us the next morning. Public Security Officer Yuan escorted me to the front of the ship, answered my river questions, and positioned me at the best vantage point with minimum wind sweep to observe the fast-approaching Qutang Gorge, the first of three Yangtze River gorges, which people travel from all over the world to see.

Yuan's was a hard life, and he had recently put in for land duty. For twelve years he had been riding the river boats up and down the Yangtze for seven days at a clip with only one day off after each cycle. Squeezing a few hundred extra yuan out of a month's journeys when opportunity presented itself compensated him a bit for his meager salary and wretched work conditions, and made life a little sweeter for his family. It was as much a part of his work as arresting the petty looters who preyed on sleeping passengers from time to time. Neither necessity had leathered his personality.

TWO DAYS LATER—tired, grubby, and hungry—I reached the river port at Yichang, after passing through the last of the three gorges.

Contrary to what I had been assured on the boat, I found that train tickets on the overnight to Wuhan via the "Three Gorges Express" were *bu hao mai*—not easy to buy. After standing on the ticket queue for an hour at Yichang Station, the window agent told me that all of the tickets had been sold. Up and down the queue, profiteers were scalping tickets, known as "black tickets" in Chinese. But in dim evening light, I would never have been able to differentiate between an authentic ticket and a phony ticket. In theory, I should have been able to buy a standing room ticket on the train and then upgrade. But that would require another hour on a different line with serious risk of missing my train. And if I missed my train, I would miss my plane to Shanghai. Even the 200 yuan I threw at the ticket seller in desperation would not produce a ticket.

When I was finally allowed onto the platform to speak to the station duty officer, I found a smiling face very secure in her ability to help me. But when she escorted me to the waiting lounge, she added a caveat. "Would I be willing," she asked "to up the price?" Miss Fang suggested 200 yuan.

"My pockets aren't so deep," I responded, and suggested 150 yuan, which she accepted. She returned five minutes later with a middle-berth, hard-sleeper ticket and 76 yuan change.

"Because your pockets aren't so deep," she said, "I got you a ticket at the domestic price [instead of one adding the fifty percent surcharge usually charged foreigners*], and you don't have to pay our 20 yuan service charge."

From a heavy equipment salesman who worked in Yichang and lived in Wuhan, and rode the overnight train frequently, I learned in the waiting room that in fact there are *never* any sleeper berths available on this train route at the ticket window. All of the sleeper tickets out of Yichang are purchased at service charges with the assistance of Miss Fang and the other station duty officers.

---

* Differential ticket pricing for Chinese and foreigners has since been abolished.

Often, when seeking assistance in purchasing a transportation ticket in China (large organizations and hotels all have such "specialists"), you are told by the purchasing agent that, aside from simply going to the ticket office to purchase a ticket, "We have another way." Miss Fang, I finally understood, was that "other way."

(Five months earlier, at an anticorruption work session held by the State Council [the government Cabinet], the official in charge of the Railway Bureau announced that the practice of indiscriminately soliciting extra fees and jacking up prices had been "fundamentally brought to a halt.")

IT WAS ONLY A YEAR AFTER THE FACT that I was able to insert context into an incident regarding a train ticket purchased in Luoyang. The missing link was that, in addition to the grand larceny the central government was targeting, and the petty corruption that was leaching the country, local governments in China were themselves squeezing their citizens.

I arranged with the front desk at the Peony Hotel in Luoyang to purchase my ticket to Kaifeng. I had already been to the train station without success the previous evening, and paying a 10-yuan service charge to the hotel would eliminate the need to return to the station after eight that evening when standing room tickets for the following day's trains would be put on sale.

The Kaifeng ticket was estimated at 20 yuan and I gave the reception clerk a 50-yuan deposit to cover the ticket, the service charge, and "extras." (In China, deposits normally exceed the cost of transactions.) When I returned that evening to pick up my ticket, the "ticket man" produced a ticket pasted on a receipt from the railroad noting the cost of the ticket as 19 yuan; three 2-yuan coupons—total, 6 yuan—for an "air conditioning fee"; and 9 yuan worth of receipt coupons for no discernible purpose. Then he sped off. Exclusive of the legitimate 10-yuan hotel ticket service charge, I had paid a 15-yuan service charge for my 19-yuan ticket.

At a cost exceeding any conceivable loss I might recoup, I faxed the Peony Hotel upon returning to New York, accusing them of issuing phony tickets. They faxed me back. After their own investigation, they issued this clarification: In addition to the 6-yuan air-conditioning fee, there was a 9-yuan city construction fee mandated by the city of Luoyang for each train ticket sold in Luoyang. "Because from Luoyang to Kaifeng was in a short-distance, so maybe the additional fees was higher than the original fee," summarized the Peony in English. Exploitation was being practiced at so many levels, it was often difficult to identify the culprit. This was what the leaders in Beijing meant by "wildly levying fees."

All over China, random fees were proliferating, turning services that the government in Beijing thought ought to be free into paying services. Road tolls are a ready example. Whereas China has increasing numbers of toll roads to airports and along its fast-growing national highway system, many tolls are arbitrarily imposed by local counties, who place barriers on low-grade roads and send a straw-hatted man out to collect 10 yuan. With intercity trade flourishing, this provides a windfall. A driver in Chongqing reported that he spent 300 yuan in tolls on a motor trip from Guangzhou to Chongqing. Is this corruption? "The government already paid for these roads," he snapped.

"The central government has central policies; local governments have counterpolicies."

MY BAPTISM TO GRASSROOTS Chinese corruption had come in the wake of a vigorous but short-lived Chinese campaign to counter "peaceful evolution," which had reached its climax way back in August 1991, following a failed Soviet coup attempt, whose aim was to reverse the reforms of Soviet president Mikhail Gorbachev. Peaceful evolution as a concept has its origins in the cold war and the policies of John Foster Dulles in the 1950s. But it really only began to assume prime relevance in China as the Chinese tried to refute the international onslaught in reaction to suppression of the student-worker rebellion at Tian'anmen in the spring of 1989.

By "peaceful evolution," the government meant the use of nonbelligerent tools by the Western world to undermine the country's ability to carry out what the Chinese term "China's special brand of socialism," thereby eroding the confidence of the Chinese people in their own system. These tools included linking improvement of human rights with granting most favored nation status, withholding technical and economic assistance, and the inimical use of Voice of America.

Significantly, it was the vaguely defined but repeatedly cited corruption issue that spurred Beijing workers to ally with protesting students in the spring of 1989. And it was this alliance that lead to the bloody suppression on June 4th, which in turn incubated the peaceful evolution campaign. "Bribery is Everywhere," "Down with Graft" were some of the protest signs toted by workers at a time when all roads in Beijing led to Tian'anmen.

By November 1991, when I returned to Lanzhou, capital of Gansu Province, with Bao (a Communist Party member and more communist than most), after a visit to her peasant village five hours from Lanzhou, the campaign against peaceful evolution had been abruptly dropped, not to resurface. But the corruption that helped trigger it remained of continuing interest. On the train back to Lanzhou, a free-flowing debate with Bao and her cousin, a college physics teacher, had bogged down over the issue of whether, without open discussion and public accountability, corruption could ever be wiped out in China.

The theme crystallized the next night over how I would get to the airport for my morning flight to Chengdu. We were sipping tea and picking at watermelon seeds before dinner in the fifth floor walk-up of Bao's friend, Hua, when Hua announced with a smile: "Your corrupt car has been arranged." Hua's daughter had just made a telephone call.

I returned a quizzical look.

"To the airport," Hua added.

When I had arrived in Lanzhou from Beijing, Bao and her husband had met me in a recent-model, four-wheel drive, van. The woman in the front seat, sitting next to the driver, was Hua. The question of the van settled on my mind instantly because it was forty-five miles from Lanzhou Airport to the city. Hiring such a car would run about $50. I told Bao explicitly when we got to her apartment that I wanted to pay for the car. "*Bu yong*," she replied, "it wasn't necessary."

But I wasn't yet at peace. A car from the airport would have eaten up one-and-a-half month's worth of family income.

"No," Bao assured me, Hua had arranged it. Someone at her government office job had access to a car.

Almost no one in China at the time, with the exception of movie stars and pop singers, had private cars, nor could many afford to rent one for a day. So, when someone said that he "had a car," it was assumed to be a company car diverted to personal use. *A corrupt car.* It wasn't hard to get used to such things.

One of the chief ways to fight peaceful evolution, Party leader Jiang Zemin had emphasized, was to eliminate corruption. Public service television commercials in Beijing flashed license plate numbers of offending cars with the announcement: "If you see this car, turn it in. It is being used for personal purposes." But it was a hopeless fight. Access to a car was a crucial part of a person's *guanxi wang*, his "network of privilege." Knowing people who could do favors for you—corrupt or uncorrupt—was what made life tolerable.

Even before I arrived in China, Bao had dipped into her own "network" to arrange my air ticket from Beijing to Lanzhou. I hadn't been able to clear the ticket in New York, and by the time I got to China none might be available through normal outlets. Zhang, the husband of Bao's classmate, worked at a travel agency in Beijing. Travel agency connections are particularly valuable in China because, to stay in business, they must have a ready supply of air and train tickets. One reason why tickets are sometimes scarce is that employees who work for the railroad or for air carriers remove a percentage of unsold tickets from public sale. It is common to go up to a ticket counter and be told that all the tickets have been sold, only to later board, after obtaining a ticket from another source, and find empty seats.

It can be argued that "network of privilege"—corruption itself—is one of the reasons why there is no clamor for radical political change; why the Tian'anmen revolt, galvanized against corruption, has been all but forgotten in prospering China, while memories linger in the United States like a persistent cough. "Going through the back door" is such a refined Chinese art that instituting a democratic system based on equity would undermine the entire fabric of Chinese life. Everyone in China complains about corruption. But many feed off it as well. If times were hard, there might be a different cry. But for almost everyone in China, these are the best of times.

> There are still many too many loopholes....Some people are exploiting loopholes in the law to engage in corrupt practices, accept bribes, and pillage the State's coffers...
>
> —PRIME MINISTER LI PENG
> December 22, 1996

Far from recoiling, many Chinese rationalize unprecedented, pervasive, personal corruption—skimming, chiseling, cheating to augment salary—as an effective means of overcoming inadequate government salaries and maintaining buying power. During the past five years, there have been aggressive salary increases, and monthly working salaries now commonly range between $200 and $1,000. (With increased salaries has come

China's first tax on personal monthly income above 800 yuan [$107], raised to 1,600 yuan in 2005.) But many, including policemen, daycare workers, factory workers, and non-professional hospital staff, have been left behind.

In the space of little more than a decade, China has moved from a country with a basically flat salary curve, with few earning more than $200 a month, to a country with a vast salary differential. As of 2005, there were more than 320,000 millionaires in China according to a Merrill Lynch estimate. At the same time, the take-home pay for a research physicist with graduate degrees and training abroad can be as low as $250 per month. The recurrent observation, whenever the subject of galloping corruption arises, is that if the "nouveau have-nots" had a more equal share of the pie, there would be less need for corruption.

THE TRADITIONAL CHINESE PREOCCUPATION has always been food; now it is money. Everyone is angling to become an entrepreneur.

"How can I get rich?" a bicycle rider in his mid-twenties employed as a salesman purveying Chinese and Western medicine stopped and asked me outside of Tongji Hospital in the city of Wuhan. "That," he said, "is the major topic of conversation in China today." He was planning on entering graduate school for career advancement and wondered if he could get rich by reading books. Maybe this *lao wai*—foreigner—had some insight to offer.

"If you have a nose for business," I told him, "you'll find a way to make money. If you have to ask me, anything I tell you probably won't help very much."

"To go to sea," *xia hai*, is the Chinese euphemism for going into business, a play on the migration toward China's coastal cities which, through preferential economic policies, have prospered significantly more than China's heartland. The ideal way to go to sea, a college professor allowed, is "to bring along your safety net"—all of your connections—thereby minimizing risk. The limiting factor is that the majority of the population can only whiff money and dream dreams. Whatever the classic egalitarian communist ideal, "letting part of the population get rich first" is now a reality in China, the government acknowledges.

But not everyone's trip to sea is voluntary. An estimated one-third of large state-owned businesses in China, some of which employ as many as one hundred thousand people, are money losers and are downsizing to increase profitability. Because most of their workers were hired with "iron rice bowl" (life-long) benefits, these workers cannot be let go. Instead, they are laid off at sixty percent of wages and are free to seek supplementary employment. Most often they turn to street-side peddling: cheap tote bags, combs, socks, underwear, footwear, CDs, anything that can be easily transported. In Wuhan, one of China's largest industrial cities, the entire city, it seemed, had turned into a never-ending flea market with peddlers blanketing every street, overpass, and vacant space where potential customers pass.

The lurking danger is that if the wealth gap is not soon narrowed, what the Chinese call "red eye disease"—jealousy—will incubate to epidemic proportions, threatening both civil order and prosperity.

FIFTEEN YEARS AGO, there were two basic classes in China among the urban population: a working class on government salary, and a small emerging class of entrepreneurs, entertainers, and managers beginning to break away from the pack. The major lament then came from the underpaid professional class: "The person who sells eggs makes more than the person who develops the atomic bomb. The person who wields the barber's blade makes more than the person who wields the scalpel."

Today, there are five identifiable classes: (1) a fixed-salary class (i.e., bus drivers), (2) a fixed-salary class with honestly augmentable income (i.e., teachers), (3) a fixed-salary class with corruptibly augmentable income (i.e., physicians), (4) a burgeoning middle class (i.e., small private businessmen, accountants, lawyers), and (5) a class of super rich (i.e., businessmen, entertainers, investors).

Physicians, especially doctors who do operations or procedures, as well as those who assist them, are a prime example of salaried workers whose under-the table pay exceeds what they find in their official monthly pay envelope.

Zhang Xiuyun, forty-four, underwent a laparoscopic procedure to remove a uterine fibroid at Beijing Obstetrics and Gynecology Hospital. The all-inclusive cost for the procedure, including three days in the hospital, came to about 9,000 yuan ($1,200), two-thirds of which was covered by the insurance provided by her employer (a private Singapore school that prepared Chinese to work abroad), and a third of which she had to pay on her own.

Then, there were the additional charges, forbidden by regulation, but accepted as "normal": 1,000 yuan to the head of the GYN Department, the aunt of her classmate, who arranged the hospital stay and chose the surgeon for her; 1,000 yuan to her classmate for connecting Zhang with her aunt; and 1,000 to the surgeon. An additional 500 yuan went to the night-shift nurse. To a $1,200 surgery bill, $500 had to be added under the table, hiking Zhang's out-of-pocket from $400 to $900.

Had Zhang Xiuyun been unwilling to put up these "extras," she would have found herself waiting on a surgery queue for weeks, if not months. Had she not tipped the night shift nurse, the call button in her room would have gone unanswered or been answered less frequently.

This institutionally-approved under-the-table practice not only increases the monthly salary of a senior surgeon from $800 to between $2,500 and $3,000,* it also helps put access to medical care out of the reach of many if not most ordinary Chinese. There is simply no provision in Chinese hospitals, almost all of which are government run, for patients who do not have the means to pay their bill. Before hospitalization, a patient is required to make a deposit; if that deposit is not or cannot be made, the patient is not admitted. Once admitted, the surgeon will come to the patient's room before surgery and tell him how much of the bill will not be covered by his insurance. Any non-reimbursable charges *must* be paid in cash before surgery. If the money is not paid, the surgery will not be performed.**

Although the practice of ingratiation is largely limited to the surgical staff, a non-surgical physician or nurse can line his

---

* For a few aggressive surgeons at China's better hospitals, true riches await moonlighters. A senior thoracic surgeon I know at a top Shanghai hospital dedicated virtually every weekend to surgical procedures in neighboring cities. To conserve his energy, he hired a car and a driver so that he could sleep en route. Performing lymph-node biopsies and lung lobectomies, he was able to pocket between $2,500 and $3,000 per weekend, $125,000 to $150,000 per year. He did this for three years, after which he was able to buy three luxury apartments, two as investments.

** In addition to extra ingratiation outlays that must be paid to hospital workers, the billing and insurance practices of Chinese hospitals contribute heavily to putting advanced care out of reach of ordinary Chinese. Take as an example a spinal surgery performed at a Beijing hospital to decompress herniated disks at four levels and fuse five lumbar vertebrae, billed at 122,500 yuan ($16,300). Under the table payments to two surgeons (1,800 yuan), anesthesiologist (1,000 yuan), and floor nurse (500 yuan) added $440 to the cost of this surgery. In addition, of the billed sum, the patient, a woman in her mid-seventies, needed to pay 59,980 yuan ($8,000) in costs not covered by her insurance. Among the items for which the patient was fully responsible, with no insurance reimbursement whatsoever, were: artificial bone, fluoroscopy to assist in surgery, and a gel to stop bleeding—all basic surgery necessities. Total cost to patient: $1,693. Among the items that were fifty percent reimbursable: imported surgical rods and hardware to stabilize the spine (patient's share: $5,000) and membrane to shield spinal nerves (patient's share: $1,213). Chinese versions of these imported items were available, but they weren't durable. Presented with this burden, most Chinese choose a less-expensive procedure or, more often, none at all. In today's money-driven China, every enterprise is out to squeeze as much money for itself as it can. The sole bargain in Chinese hospital care is the daily ward room charge: as low as $15 per day in a double room.

pockets by arranging an early appointment with a specialist, or a hospital bed, which is usually in short supply.

THE SALARY GAP THAT FUELS CORRUPTION would close substantially if business taxes were collected as prescribed. But as the often-seen sign IT IS EVERY CITIZEN'S RESPONSIBILITY TO PAY TAXES hints, this is not the case. I happened to be riding in a cab in North Beijing when the driver switched to a radio program discussing the gross receipts tax on taxi fares—then twelve percent. "No one pays it," he said unequivocally. Tax evasion is not corruption, but corrupt tax collectors are.

As early as January 1994, China instituted a string of nationwide value-added, consumer, industrial, commercial, real estate, and natural resource taxes. Yet, to this point, and despite some improvement, most of China still has no aggressive enforcement mechanism for the tax, business, and consumer protection laws being written to counter fraud and corruption.

OFTEN IGNORED WHEN DISCUSSING the widening wage gap in China's cities is the income differential between the 562 million Chinese (43 percent of the population) who live in urban areas and the 745 million Chinese (57 percent) who live in rural China.* Without media representation, with little political influence, the interests of China's farmers are easy to sidestep. In 1993, China's peasants, per capita, earned only 36 percent of what city dwellers earned. In 2005, China's peasants had

---

* The proportion of Chinese living in rural villages is elusive. Before China's modernization drive began in 1979, 82 percent of China lived in rural areas. From 1995 to 2005, the percentage dropped from 71 percent to 57 percent. Some of this change reflects the one hundred to two hundred million "floating population"—villagers who have moved to Chinese cities looking for higher wages. To complicate matters, an indeterminable number of peasants who now work in cities return to their villages for a portion of the year. In many cases, village households continue to function while the man of the house is away, with wives doing the farm work. A second factor is that rural China is itself urbanizing, with many county towns installing factories on all scales. Source: National Bureau of Statistics of China (2006).

only 31 percent of the income of urban Chinese. Though most of China's peasants have the additional benefit of being able to raise their own food, they constitute, as the government is beginning to recognize, China's hidden time bomb for civil unrest—lacking the resources to make the basic investments in education, equipment, and infrastructure, which would enable them to close the urban-rural income gap.

I chanced upon a group of fifteen one Sunday afternoon in Tongxian, at Beijing's eastern edge. These were men and women in their twenties who, having traveled two nights by train from distant Hubei Province, were literally walking into China's capital to join the three-and-a-half million transients already there. Some wore sneakers or shoes, others simple cloth slip-ons with thin rubber soles. They carried burlap bags with sleeping quilts, flimsy travel bags with a change or two of clothing, and trade implements. Two men balanced their burdens, tied with ropes to the ends of splintered tree branches, across their shoulders. A couple carried two canvas bags, one perched atop the other, shifting hands periodically to relieve the strain. Every few hundred yards, the group would pause to recoup energies.

One job the women in the group were not seeking, I was told right off the bat, was the traditional female peasant position of nanny, paying just a few hundred yuan per month plus food and lodging.

Having reached Beijing and bedded down among other transients from Hubei in makeshift "Hubei Village," some of those in the group would find long-term work in factories or on construction sites at salaries of 500 yuan per month and up. Others would find themselves curbside at established labor markets in the city where, competing with dozens of migrants from the far reaches of China, they would place paper placards on the ground advertising their skills—carpentry, tile masonry, painting, cement work. A small minority would turn to lawbreaking. (Those without Beijing residence cards commit a disproportionate percentage of Beijing's crimes.) Not a few would find the going too rough and return home. For the most part, a construction engineer in the boom Pudong District of Shanghai who hires such laborers told me, rather than displace skilled city labor, these rural laborers would free more highly trained city workers for more sophisticated tasks.

THE PRESSURE TO EARN MONEY IS SO PERVASIVE in China today that whether corruption or fraud enters the picture frequently depends upon whether a particular job presents opportunities for corruption, and whether equally lucrative but honest alternative opportunities are available.

The 5,000 to 6,000-yuan ($650 to $800) monthly salary for university full professors, for example, requires ten to twelve hours of teaching per week. But, particularly in the case of foreign language courses, which are in heavy demand, 2,500 to 5,000 yuan ($350 to $700) can be added to monthly pay by teaching six additional hours of evening classes weekly. Consultant work, especially among those who teach engineering, design, and law subjects that have practical business applications, might yield additional thousands of yuan per month. With most rents on either side of $150 per month (and as low as $15 if a recent graduate chooses to live in a dormitory), with a spouse's supplementary salary, life in China can be very comfortable at $1,000 to $1,500 per month.

Across China, workers are finding ways to augment salaries. Directors and cameramen at government film studios supplement their incomes by hundreds or thousands of yuan per month by producing commercials for Chinese businesses. Government-employed plumbers and electricians do work on the side. In the staid, state-run Chinese sports system, after-school coaches add to their salaries by recruiting aggressively and sharing in the activity fee paid by parents.

With business energy bursting spectacularly in China's cities, it took a visit to a couple in downtown Shanghai, currently China's most dynamic city, to impress upon me that getting rich is largely an activity of the young. Liu was fifty-nine and a worker in a Chinese traditional medicine factory. His wife was fifty-four and for thirty years had taught elementary school. Zi Zhong Street, where they lived, chock-full of vendors hawking everything from fruit to live fish, was considered one of the least safe streets in Shanghai; late at night, homeless transients with makeshift body coverings could be seen sleeping among the vacated stalls. Their two-room, unheated, cold-water flat, without toilet facilities, predated the revolution. The term "comfort" is irrelevant here. With cooking done in the courtyard, and a loft added to the front room, a hopelessly cramped living area has been made at best utilitarian. Certainly there was no room for a bookshelf. Since riding Shanghai's buses is so debilitating, Mr. Liu's wife often walked the forty-five minutes to work. There wasn't enough energy left at the end of a day for a second job. Popular impressions notwithstanding, "Most people in China," she took pains to stress, "have only one source of income."

In a year, both husband and wife will retire. Their building is scheduled to be razed to make way for urban renewal, and eventually they will be given a new apartment, adding comfort to their lives. But they will forever be cash poor.

Even among those in their thirties, many are left behind. Of three editors from a magazine affiliated with the 73.5 million-member Communist Youth League, who asked my opinion on turning the dozens of Youth League bases throughout China into summer camps for foreigners, only Li had an enterprising sideline. He was busy writing books about animals for children. He had an inscribed copy and a business card in my hand in an instant, together with a pitch about the universal appeal of his books. The other two had no business impulse and unhelpfully pure instincts. As they admitted when the discussion turned to corruption, even if they were interested in turning money under the table, they had nothing to sell that anyone would want.

The first-grade teacher at an elementary school in the north-east section of Chengdu, capital of Sichuan Province, lacks neither opportunity nor inclination. He is busy marketing his students' futures. From the moment they enter school, Chinese children are under enormous pressure to perform. Even for a seven-year-old, a score of 70 or 80 is considered a red flag. As elsewhere in China, first graders in Chengdu do homework until eight in the evening. I witnessed a young mother berating her little girl, Qing Qing, for only showing her mother her good grades while withholding the weak ones. Qing Qing—arms rigid, eyes focused on a distant wall—wilted under her mother's tongue. Then, on Saturday night, after six days of classes, it was into her room to practice penmanship.

Qing Qing's teacher had let parents know that for their children to do well, they have to pay. Otherwise, there would be retribution: students would be ridiculed before classmates, made to copy sentences dozens of times in their notebooks, or ignored. With fifty students in a class, it wasn't difficult to ignore a child. According to the education system in Chengdu, this first-grade teacher will stay with his class through grade five. Falling out of his favor would affect the child's entire life.

Qing Qing's mother, who runs a successful shoe store, was paying $50 per month to satisfy this teacher's appetite, a healthy supplement to the teacher's monthly salary. Far from being content with his goldmine, he had just telephoned the afternoon I visited, asking unashamedly for a loan of 10,000 yuan ($1,250). When he couldn't reach Qing Qing's mother, he called her ex-husband with the same request.

The parents of almost every pupil in Qing Qing's class—most with modest incomes in a far-from-affluent neighborhood—pay this teacher at least 50 yuan per month. Why don't they band together and expose the teacher? Why don't they change school districts? "It is the same everywhere in Chengdu," Qing Qing's mother said. "Ninety percent of the parents are timid, including me."

The educational climate in Chengdu and elsewhere in China pressures parents to open their pockets to safeguard the futures of their children. From kindergarten onward, teachers are given gifts of squid, house'paint, gold jewelry, and paintings in the spirit of ingratiation. Television commercials picture students giving teachers bottles of Sunshine Spirit Oral Tonic—a traditional potion made from snake, chicken, and other extracts—on Teacher's Day, reinforcing the sense of obligation.

> ...But the broad masses are STILL not happy...Unscrupulous road tolls, unjustifiable traffic fines, arbitrary school fees, milking farmers...exploiting connections, going through the "back door."
>
> —CENTRAL PARTY COMMISSION
> FOR DISCIPLINE INSPECTION
> January 23, 1995

CHENGDU, ONE OF THE FIRST CITIES in China to embrace economic reform, is a vanguard when it comes to educational graft. In Beijing, teacher ingratiation is limited to small gifts. But there are kindred parallels between Beijing and Chengdu regarding school "fees." Because schools vary widely in quality, certain "key" schools are in particular demand. As in Chengdu, the transfer fee in Beijing, for children whose parents want them to study outside of their district, runs high. At Beijing's No. 159 Junior and Senior High School, a tariff posted in the main corridor lists the transfer fee as "not to exceed $4,000." Corruption potential lies in how the transfer money is distributed and in temptations placed before "have-not" parents without the honest means to provide their child with the same opportunity "have" families can provide.

Temptations to milk every opportunity for extra cash in order to provide equal opportunities for their children will grow as private elementary schools, introduced in Chengdu for the first time in 1992, and springing up in cities nationwide, begin to siphon off the best teachers. And they will widen further as access to higher education, until recently among the purest areas of Chinese life, increasingly becomes based on one's ability to pay.

THE HUNGER FOR MONEY in China sometimes encourages illicit practices that would never merit even an unscrupulous person's attention in a more developed economy. I became alerted to the problem of fake products, which are far from new in China, at a least opportune moment. I had just returned from an unforgettable trip to the Three Gorges on the Yangtze River and had taken in several rolls of film to develop. When I returned to collect the prints, I discovered something that would never have occurred to me: three of five rolls of Fuji film, purchased in different parts of China, turned out to be phony, which was readily apparent from the print quality.

The ploy is labor intensive, but rewarding: The discarded cassettes in which the exposed film is housed are bought from local processing labs together with the plastic containers. Non-Fuji film, purchased in bulk from Chinese film manufacturers, is then rewound into the used Fuji cassettes. The only visible dissimilarity between authentic and inauthentic, undeveloped film is the color of the inch or two of film that protrudes from the cassette before use. An innocent could never detect the difference. Sometimes, counterfeiters purchase authentic Fuji cardboard boxes from photo labs; sometimes they print their own boxes; sometimes the film is sold unboxed.

For retailers of fake goods, most of whom operate private stands in tourist areas, the incentive is enticing. Instead of paying a middleman 15.50 yuan for a roll of authentic, 36-exposure Fuji film, which they would retail for a suggested 20 yuan, they pay 12 yuan for a roll of fake Fuji and market it at full retail.

Fraud or corruption? With 480,000 rolls of fake Fuji film confiscated in the Beijing area in one police swoop, this is big business. To secure the quantity of cassettes from processing labs needed to make the scheme viable requires large-scale complicity, as does the cooperation of Chinese film manufacturers, middlemen, and retailers. Are government workers and agencies on the take? "In China, anything is possible," sighed Peter Wong, Fuji Sales Division Manager for China Trade, fingering a stack of complaints.

China is at work on the problem, and Consumer's Day, March 15, is observed nationally. But the instant feeling one is left with after shooting three rolls of counterfeit film is that every purchase in China is suspect.*

THE PROBLEM WITH ADULTERATED Chinese food and medicine hit the international headlines in the spring of 2007, when it was discovered that melamine, a toxic chemical at certain levels, had been added to wheat gluten sold to U.S. pet-food manufacturers in order to artificially boost the protein level of the pet food. Sixteen dogs and cats died, and thousands were sickened, leading to one of the biggest pet-food recalls in American history. On the heels of the pet-food scandal came warnings and recalls in the United States, Panama, and Nicaragua about toothpaste made in China containing a toxic chemical called diethylene glycol, used in antifreeze, and a cheap substitute for glycerin. Faced with questions about the safety of its food and drug exports, the Chinese scrambled to heighten food and drug inspection and enforcement, closing 180 food plants.

None of these revelations were news to China's top leadership.

In the spring of 2004, a particularly gruesome example of bogus products shook China. In Anhui Province, 13 babies

---

* Sometimes, no effort at all is made to cover up counterfeit goods. Standing prominently beside a display of Rolex watches priced at $100 in a shop in the Jinglun, one of Beijing's better hotels, was the following sign: THESE WATCHES ARE FAKE.

died and 171 were hospitalized. All had developed "big head disease," the end result of ingesting nutrient-deficient baby formula, which contained just two percent protein in place of the standard twelve percent. Instead of being nourished by the formula, the babies were starving to death. Dozens of brands of substandard baby formula were subsequently discovered, with many arrests. But it had taken a year since reports about the formula had first surfaced for the government to take action.

In 2006, in a special session, China's State Council took up the issue of fake pharmaceuticals. It targeted the Qiqihar Second Pharmaceutical Company, found to have manufactured bogus antibiotics that caused the deaths of eleven people.*

These were extreme examples. In many more less prominent cases, manufacturers with sharp pencils simply chiseled a few percent here and a few percent there, to significant cumulative economic advantage. Cheap steel, subgrade cement, watered-down medicine—the victims might never know that they had been duped.

In July 2007, Zheng Xiaoyu, who ran China's Food and Drug Administration from 1998 to 2005, was executed by the Beijing No. 1 People's Intermediate Court. Included among bribery and corruption charges calculated at about $850,000 was a determination that Zheng had taken bribes to approve drug production licenses for companies marketing untested medicine. The swiftness with which the sentence was carried out, as well as its severity, can be seen as an effort to prove to the outside world that China is serious about food and drug safety.

THE CATALOGUE OF CORRUPTION CONTINUES: to the judicial system, to loan officers in banks, to coaches who accept athletes' bribes for places on provincial sports teams.

---

* In a twist, in 2006, the editorial writers at the *People's Daily*, the Party organ, called Procter & Gamble to task for including two toxic heavy metals in the formula of its SK-II skin cream, marketed in China. It accused P&G of treating China as a second-class market by selling inferior formulations to unknowing Chinese.

Chinese often cite judges as being amenable to softened sentences in return for cash, and the fact that General Secretary Jiang Zemin earmarked the justice system for reform early in his anticorruption campaign suggests a widespread phenomenon. But direct contact with active participants proved hard to come by.* I had, however, been clued into graft in the Chinese penal system through the prison letter written by her brother, Peter Chen, that Sharon Strothman had sent to me in 1991. Peter (Chen Wuchuan) was serving the fifth year of a seven-year sentence for beating someone up in conjunction with a robbery staged to finance repayment of a gambling debt. The Sichuan facility in which he was incarcerated, like many others, was known as "The Coal Mine," because the "reform through labor" practiced there centered around mining. Conditions were harsh.

The details in Peter Chen's letter were specific. Contributions made by the family to prison authorities had kept him out of the mines, enabling him to recover his health. Yearly visits by the family verified this. An additional $800 would reduce his sentence by one year.

CRITICS WHO DISMISS CHINA'S LIBERALIZATION out of hand—because it doesn't extend to free elections or a free press—ignore China's telephone revolution. Not many years ago, almost no one in China, with the exception of high officials, had a telephone. The only place a person could be reached by phone was during work hours. By the early 1990s, many of the Chinese I keep in touch with had acquired home phones (at $950 in Beijing), eliminating the need for colleagues to climb flights of stairs or neighbors to pedal blocks to deliver messages.

This form of freedom, however, didn't come without supplementary costs. A friend in Chengdu waited four months before being made to understand that an additional 1,500 yuan ($270)

---

* In December 2000, the Chinese minister of justice, Gao Changli, was removed from office. Though never officially confirmed, corruption is the rumored reason.

under the table was due an installer from the telecommunications office for the physical hookup. Another friend, a doctor, told how her life's dream of getting into a residency program in plastic surgery was rebuffed in 1988, because her family was unable to meet the demands of the contact at the Plastic Surgery Hospital: that the friend's family arrange a home phone for the contact.

This type of corruption, like other computerized domains (e.g., airline reservations and passport issuance), has been marginalized by advancing technology. By the late 1990s, China had become one of the hottest markets for cell phones, and today there is hardly a progressive adult in China who does not have one. Tens of millions of Chinese, in fact, have leaped directly from out-of-touch to wireless. There are countless villages in China where mobile is the only telephone service available. Since there is no connection involved, the corruption opportunity evaporates.

THAT CHINESE COACHES WOULD BE PAID OFF for places on a sports team seemed implausible when it was first raised over lunch in Beijing by one of China's star national athletes. The Sichuan provincial soccer team was offered as a blatant example. The life of a Chinese athlete is one of endless regimentation and Spartan living. For a run-of-the-mill athlete, there is no glory and little recognition. From the team's perspective, adding a substandard athlete would place a drag on the team's performance. Nevertheless, this widely confirmed phenomenon is nationwide and pervasive—most commonly at the provincial level, where marginal players buy their way onto teams at sums of up to 20,000 yuan.

Pocket-dipping coaches and players each have dual motivations. For the coach: personal greed or an opportunity to obtain sponsorship support for his team by a parent whose child likes sports but isn't quite up to the provincial level. In budget-squeezed provinces, such support can sometimes keep the team going and preserve the coach's job. For parents of children who aren't good students, membership on a provincial team assures them entry onto the government payroll. For, the moment an athlete joins the provincial team, he is guaranteed a job after his playing days are over.

During a week's stay with seven hundred athletes at China's largest sports camp in Kunming, I met up with a coach from Sichuan, a long-time acquaintance. He was willing to expand upon what he termed the Chinese sports world's "open secret" and help me reconcile lingering communist practices with China's new, money-oriented direction.

"Even though a family might be well-off," he said, "what parents still want most is for their child to have a secure job." And buying their way onto a provincial team continues to provide such security. The numbers, of necessity, remain small (at most, one or two players per team) because, aside from affecting a team's playing level, pay-to-play athletes are harder to discipline. China's iron rice bowl is rusting (many jobs that previously guaranteed lifetime tenure are now backed only by limited-term contracts); but for former athletes it still holds rice.

This Sichuan coach led me to a gate I could not enter. He had heard that two of the athletes currently training in Kunming had purchased their way onto their provincial team. I knew the team's coach, and I knew one of the team's star players. I had spent several days at their provincial base. This trail led too close to home to be pursued vigorously.

An additional incentive for buying one's way onto a provincial team is residence status (*hukou*, in Chinese). Since the Communist takeover in 1949, China has distinguished between two classes of citizens: *peasants* (who have access to the land and are thus deemed capable of providing for themselves without government assistance) and *city dwellers*. Many of the athletes who buy their way onto provincial teams, only to drop out after two or three years, are peasants who automatically become official residents of the provincial capital, with its quality of life benefits.

CHINA'S SYSTEM OF SUMMARY JUSTICE for misdemeanors, without appeal, creates irresistible skimming temptations. I first happened upon this when a busload of glaring passengers spilled out onto a Beijing sidewalk near the Friendship Store, surrounding a fare beater as two conductors extracted 10 yuan from the scoundrel.

A repeat on-the-spot episode took place in the vast plaza in front of Beijing Railway Station—a raucous, not-quite-seedy expanse with hundreds of people, hunched over bundled parcels, awaiting outgoing trains or pondering where to spend their first night in the big city. An announcement had just blared over the loudspeaker. DEAR PASSENGERS: BEIJING STATION IS AN IMPORTANT GATEWAY WHERE VISITORS GATHER THEIR FIRST IMPRESSION OF OUR CITY. IT IS IMPORTANT TO MAINTAIN HEALTH STANDARDS. Even before the words had evaporated into the air, two fiftyish women, each sporting a badge reading PUBLIC HEALTH, briskly swooped down on a trousered woman in her early thirties. A moment later, she could be seen handing over five one-yuan notes.

"Fine?" I asked.

"Spitting," they smirked, and huffed off with the money.

Most often cited at the top of the list of corrupt Chinese public servants are the traffic policemen who collect their fines on the spot. Not many years ago, the bulk of moving vehicles in China were buses and bicycles. The bikes maintained their outer lanes; the buses and other motorized vehicles their inner lanes. With prosperity have come motorbikes and motorcycles; a several-fold increase in taxis; a rapid increase in truck numbers; minibuses to provide a less crowded, more expensive alternative to public buses; China's first generation of privately owned passenger cars; and, in a grand reversion to pre-Communist times, the large-scale reintroduction of privately owned, human-powered pedicabs. Traffic congestion has become so acute in China's biggest cities that Guangzhou and Shanghai, two of the country's most pulsating metropolises, have enacted restrictions on use of the hallowed bicycle in their city centers. With inadequate traffic-light systems, with pedestrians and bicycle riders long in the habit of weaving between moving vehicles, with traffic at times restricted by day of the week to even or odd license-plate numbers on main thoroughfares, traffic violations aren't hard to find or trump up.

Traffic policemen, however, have both superiors and fine quotas to consider, so all they pocket is not theirs to keep. But, without auditing, it is always an easy matter to pocket from a few to 100 yuan without receipt in place of an official fine. Or—a common practice—to quote a much higher fine than the offense merits and keep the overcharge. Traffic policemen particularly prey on cab drivers because they are anxious to avoid tickets. Cab drivers polled in Beijing and Chongqing say that, anticorruption campaign or not, traffic cops have become more corrupt than ever.

> At present, instances of corruption are **still** fairly prominent, creating a situation where corruption can easily proliferate. The struggle against corruption is **still** severe and the responsibility to fight against corruption **still** onerous."*
>
> —PARTY SECRETARY HU JINTAO
> February 19, 2003

FOR CERTAIN SERVICES IN CHINA, bribery remains discretionary. Considerations are urgency, resources, patience, and stamina.

Regal attempts have been made to ease the lives of ordinary

---

* This came to be known as "the three *stills*," newly chosen Party General Secretary Hu Jintao's maiden entry into the fray against corruption.

Chinese in recent years, and in some areas, genuine progress has been made. Obtaining a passport from the Public Security Bureau, for example, used to involve multiple applications and approvals (from the employer, the police, and the local government), a wearying process that could take up to two months. Many Chinese found it easier to slip a few bills under the table and save steps. In recent years, though, in Shanghai, Beijing, and a few other large cities, obtaining a passport has become a one-stop process, and the intention is to extend the simplified process nationwide.

Progress notwithstanding, in many areas, China remains a nation of official seals and mandarins (the original bureaucrats), who have refined the art of redundancy. Example: a pathologist who had graduated from Shanghai Medical University and qualified as a physician in the United States needed a copy of her medical school records. The request floated around for months until she located a person in the proper office who, for $100, was able to walk her request through. One of the sticking points was a school rule that only the dean of the medical school could affix the seal that would authenticate the records. The dean of a medical school is a busy man. And so he designates specific hours, one day per week, for affixing his seal. Should he happen to be busy that day, out of town, or on vacation, the documents wait until the following week.

A similar situation involved the request from a former attending radiologist at a Beijing hospital to authenticate that she had done her residency at the hospital. The petitioner's supervisor took the form to the personnel department to affix the hospital seal. The personnel department refused the request because the former attending physician no longer worked at the hospital. The supervisor—the chairman of her department—couldn't very well pay off the personnel department. The solution: the supervisor filled out the form under her own seal; the personnel department then attested, using the hospital seal, that the supervisor was in fact the supervisor.

IT WAS YAN LILI, in a Christmas note, who, a year earlier, had first spurred my interest in China's accelerating corruption, hinting that there had been significant changes since my previous trip. But when I rang her up soon after arriving in Beijing and asked her to elaborate, she mentioned only a lot of new bridges. She also recommended a visit to Beijing's two newest upscale, joint-venture* department stores, featuring $200 electric shavers, $30 neckties, air conditioners, and Snickers bars.

After three weeks of travel around the country, I was back in Beijing at the Central Newsreel and Documentary Film Studio, one of the main government film studios, where Yan Lili worked. Yan asked, as she always did, if I had found what I was looking for, and I pulled out the list of corruptions I had compiled, forgetting for the moment that I was sitting in a government propaganda mill. Yan didn't flinch. She added her bit.

Yan, thirty-three, is good with words. Once prompted, she can talk for a long time. Trained in the arts—song, dance, narration—her aspiration is to write and direct.

Temporarily, she had been sidetracked into a bureaucrat position at the studio in charge of documenting government activities—always in a positive light. Propaganda.

"The first big change," Yan said, "is that we are here on the inside talking." On a previous visit, she had given me a revealing talk on the political study sessions held inside the studio. But that was a private lecture delivered in her apartment, and she had taken the precaution of closing a second door so that nothing "counterrevolutionary" would seep through the walls. This time, two colleagues were sitting across the desk, one a senior director. On the oversized wall map, I noted, China—the "Middle Kingdom"—was positioned in the center. That these were all card-carrying Communist Party members was assumed.

The senior director, in her mid-thirties, had returned invigorated the day before from an eighteen-day stint filming the

---

* Jointly owned by Chinese and foreigners. China used to insist that the Chinese side hold a controlling interest, but this is no longer the case.

yearly National People's Congress. She reported a major departure from previous Congresses on the propaganda front. In the past, only the central Chinese news agencies and major newspapers were authorized to attend. This time, local reporters from throughout China had been accredited. Their dispatches back home stressed local issues and gave identity to local legislators—even if they weren't popularly elected. Such identity provided "addresses" toward which dissatisfaction with corruption and other matters could be directed. "Seek the truth" was now hard-core Party doctrine, even if the truth couldn't always be fully reported.

During the Congress, the film director observed a second outgrowth of a more pluralistic Chinese press: the brisk sale of political documents to foreign journalists by Chinese journalists.

Yan was on leave at the time from her public relations work to attend a four-and-a-half- month course at the Central Communist Party School. Hers was a class of fifty, comprised of younger echelon bureaucrats and editors. This was the Party's latest strategy to maintain its hold on China: to gather together the mouthpieces of public information and give them a sense that the Party was responding to the country's practical wants.

Attendance at Party School was mandatory. Yet despite her dislike for regimentation and her anti-communist sentiments (her Party membership notwithstanding), Yan seemed to find interest in the practical class discussions and the philosophical wordplay they begat. Under Mao and all the traditional hardliners who walked in his wake, Yan pointed out in one of her revealing semantic digressions, the emphasis was on resolving contradictions within society that obstructed China from following a predestined socialist path. And she voiced the Chinese word for "contradiction," *mao-dun*. *Mao*, which means "spear," could, with no change in intonation, also refer to Mao Zedong. But under problem-oriented Deng Xiaoping's "socialist market economy," she continued, the emphasis had turned to *MAO-dun*, again voicing the word *mao-dun*, but changing the intonation. *MAO* in this usage meant "cat."

"It doesn't matter whether a cat is black or white," Deng had said, referring to the capitalism versus communism debate. "If it catches mice, it is a good cat."

"Even the best cats have fleas," annotated Yan, nudging closer to the corruption issue.

China was now a thoroughly practical country, and everyone was looking for his own advantage. There was unequal distribution of wealth. Rampant corruption on the personal level was an outgrowth. The pragmatic way to eradicate corruption in official Chinese eyes was to run an anticorruption campaign. The pragmatic way to deal with corruption in ordinary Chinese eyes was to prosper personally. Taxi drivers were working fourteen-hour, seven-day, tax-free weeks to build a nest egg and move on to saner opportunities. School teachers were learning to run bakeries on school time and later exploiting the experience by opening up their own private shops. Traffic cops were skimming traffic fines and some were using the money to buy pianos for their daughters. In a very short period, China had donned a coat of many colors.

Yan herself, as she admitted, was somewhat of a contradiction. Although she didn't think she would ever be much good at making money, her years in propaganda had turned her into a devout realist. She had become a specialist at trading favors. She spoke often of how many "friends" she had all over China who could provide a hotel room, transportation, or inside information. I had already cashed in on a few of those favors myself. In a year or a few years, Yan reasoned, China would be forced by the pace of progress to charter additional national television networks. She was busily positioning herself so that, when the opportunity was ripe, she could move aggressively from propaganda to art.

Index

A

Acupuncture, 212–213
Afghanistan, 192, 193
Agriculture. See Farmers and farming
Ai clan of Kaifeng, 200
Ai Jun, 198
Air travel, 314–315. See also Tourism
Albert, Tom, 260
Angwang Qupi, 120
Anhui Province, 297, 327–328
Ao Fan, 24
APEC (Asia-Pacific Economic Cooperation), 189
Aphrodisiacs, 243–244
Apparel. See Clothing and fashion
Architecture, 102, 113, 133–134, 137–138, 147–148. See also Art
Armstrong International Corporate Identity Co., 163–169
Army, 36, 37, 284
Art, 115, 165. See also Architecture
A San Restaurant, 246
Asians, as a race, 281–296
Asia-Pacific Economic Cooperation (APEC), 189
Assimilation. See also Intermarriage
of Bai, Yi, and Muslim minorities, 126
of Chinese into Japanese, 285
intermarriage and, 128
of Jews of Kaifeng, 198, 200–208
through language, 142–143

as result of education, 104–105, 106–107
of Tibetans, 112
Atchi-la-tsa, 130
Athens Olympics, 226, 227, 285
Athletics. See Sports and leisure
Atlanta Olympics, 2, 219–224, 227, 284–285
Australia
    prime minister, 61
    softball team
        Atlanta Olympics, 220, 221, 222, 223–224
        Beijing Olympics, 231–232
        pre-Beijing Olympics tournament, 230
        Sydney Olympics, 227, 283, 285
Automobiles. See Cars

B

Babies. See Children; Family planning
Baby formula, 328
Backpacks, 295
Bai minority, 126
Baixingying Village, 44, 46–47
Baiyang, 87
Banking system, 302
Bao (Communist Party member), 313–315
Barefoot Temple Village (Chijiaosi), 41–47
Baseball, 229 (note)
Bastian, Michael, 228–230

Bathing. *See* Hygiene and bathing
  habits
Beijing
  administration and structure, 40
    (note), 276 (note)
  Beijing City Communist Party
    School, 58–60
  "floating population", 320 (note),
    321–322
  Guan Yuan Agricultural Market,
    233–234
  Israeli embassy, 204
  Olympics, 37, 163–169, 225–232,
    276
  "Peking" transformed into,
    239–240, 241
  population, 276
  teacher ingratiation, 325–326
  tourism, 269–270
  traffic policemen, 333
  transportation services, 269–274,
    276, 332–333
Beijing Evening News, 269, 273
Beijing Literary Theme Park, 271
Beijing Long Distance Bus
  Company, 270–274
Beijing Medical University Hospital,
  253, 259–260
Belgrade, 191
Beth Israel Medical Center, 211
Betting salons, 179. *See also*
  Gambling
Betty (Huang Zhanghong), 23, 31
  (note)
Bicycles, 275–276, 332, 333
Big Black Mountain (Da Hei Shan),
  125, 129
Birds, 234
Boats, 308–309. *See also*
  Transportation
Bodhisattva, 114
Boxx, Gillian, 224
Brainwashing. *See* Propaganda
Bribery. *See* Corruption
Brookstone, Dr., 253
Brothels, 246
Brown, Joanne, 220
Buddhism, 91, 97, 114–115, 120
Bureaucracy, 334

Burials. *See* Death and burial
  practices
Buses, 269–274, 275–280, 301–302,
  332. *See also* Transportation
Bush, George W., 189
Business. *See* Economy and trade
Business (B-1) visas, 8–10
Bybee, David, 31

C
Cabs. *See* Taxis
Cadre rotation, 49
Camera film, 326–327
Canton(ese), 244, 296. *See also*
  Guangzhou
Capitalism, 39, 53. *See also* Land
  reform
Carmichael, Umpire, 224
Cars, 313–314, 332–333. *See also*
  Transportation
Catholics, 286
Caves, 83–85, 87, 89–90
CCTV (China Central Television),
  75, 193
Cell phones, 330
Central Commission for Discipline
  Inspection, 302
Central Committee Communist
  Party School, 57–58,
  60–62, 68–69, 336. *See
  also* Communism and the
  Communist Party
Central Newsreel and Documentary
  Film Studio, 335–337
Central Park, NY, 291–292
Chao Tzu-yang, 240
Chen family (parents of Sharon
  Strothman), 1, 16, 249–251.
  See also Chen Wuchuan
  (Peter); Strothman smuggling
  operation
Chengdu, Sichuan
  Green Sheep Palace Dog Market,
    236
  Strothman smuggling operation,
    4–5, 6–7, 10–11, 18–24
  teacher salaries, 324–326
  Yang Suping meeting, 94–95
Cheng Kejie, 306

Chen Guoji, 60–62
Chen Jun. *See* Strothman smuggling operation
Chen Liangyu, 307
Chen Lixin, 52–53
Chen Menchu (Teacher Chen), 125, 129–146, 150–153, 155–158, 160
Chen Weiming, 16, 19, 21
Chen Wuchuan (Peter), 5–6, 7–8, 16, 28, 30 (note), 329
Chen Xitong, 307
Chiang Ch'ing, 240
Chijiaosi. *See* Barefoot Temple Village
Children. *See also* Education; Family planning
adulterated baby formula, 328
backpacks of Japanese children, 295
dogs as pets for, 233, 236
nannies for, 321
preventive care for, 84–85, 152
China Central Television (CCTV), 75, 193
Chinatown, NY, 193, 282, 291–293
Chinese Human Genome Diversity Project, 283
Chinese knot, 165
Chinese language. *See* Language
Chinese medicine, 186, 216–217, 243–246. *See also* Health and medicine
Chinese National Softball Team
Athens Olympics, 285
Atlanta Olympics, 219–224, 227, 284–285, 289
Doha Asian Games, 230
Kunming training facilities, 214, 215–217
Li Minkuan (Coach), 2, 17–18, 221, 222–224, 228, 288–289
recruitment for, 227, 229–230
salaries and bonuses of players, 226, 231
Sharon Chen as player, 1–3
Sydney Olympics, 227, 283, 285
tension between team leaders and coaching staff, 228–229

training for Beijing Olympics, 225–232
Utsugi Reika as former captain of, 283–285
Chinese Olympic baseball camp, 229 (note)
Chinese Sports Commission, 75. *See also* Sports and leisure
General Sports Administration, 213, 227
Chong cao, 104
Chongqing, 40 (note), 253 (note), 333
Christiane (Strothman case informant), 4–5, 6, 7, 8, 9–10, 13–14, 16
Cities. *See* Urbanization and urban areas
Class (economic), 315–326. *See also* Standards of living
Clinton, President, 304
Clothing and fashion
cosmetics, 294
gait affected by, 293
hairstyles, 295–296
Long Ding, 156
Lu E, 149, 150–152, 155, 156–157
physical differences between East Asians, 294–296
Tibetan, 96, 120–121
traditional dress as counterrevolutionary, 293
urban trends, 151
winter coats, 279
"The Coal Mine", 329
Coal mines, 171–179
corruption within process, 178
deaths and danger associated with, 171, 176, 177
process, 176–178
Coastal cities, 316–317
Cohen, Dr., 217
Cold War, 312–313
Communications, 192, 329–330. *See also* Media and entertainment
Communism and the Communist Party, 33–71. *See also specific members and leaders by name*

adaptation to modern society, 35
career patterns within, 49, 67–69
Central Commission for
    Discipline Inspection, 302
China defined as "socialist" by, 48
"collective self", 76
corruption within, 56, 305–308,
    311–312
discipline imposed by, 46
dynastic cycle reinstated by, 36–37
government controlled by, 36, 37
lack of transparency within,
    48–50, 56–57
land reform policies, 39–47,
    50–55
of Litang, 109–111
in Lu E, 153
membership as expedient to job
    advancement, 153
membership figures, 38 (note)
minorities within, 66
Panchen Lama hand-picked by, 91
party building, 37, 64
People's Daily, 56–57, 328 (note)
personal information of Chinese
    officials, 48–50
Propaganda Department, 190–
    191. See also Propaganda
schools, 57–62, 67–68, 68–69
"seek the truth", 221, 231, 336
senior leadership, 36
Seventeenth Party Congress, 57
    (note)
Shijiazhuang Village as model
    village of, 52
Sixteenth Chinese Communist
    Party Congress, 33, 34–36,
    47–50, 91–93, 303 (note)
"thought unification" by, 37–38, 69
"Three Represents", 38–40, 46, 63
"Three Stills", 333
traditional dress determined to be
    counterrevolutionary by, 293
United Front Work Department,
    55–56
Youth League, 34, 323
Zhuolu County, 39–47
Computers. See Internet
Consumer's Day, 327

Cooperatives, 51–55. See also Land
    reform
Corn, 41–44
Corruption, 297–337. See also
    Crime; Scams
campaign against corruption. See
    Jiang Zemin
coaching salaries, 322, 330–332
economic classes and, 317–326
fake products, 326–328
within government and
    Communist Party, 56,
    305–308, 311–312
government anticorruption
    policies, 297, 302–309, 314,
    328, 329, 333
within justice system, 329
within medical practices, 318–320
within mining process, 178
overview of, 303, 337
peaceful evolution, 312
rationalization of, 314–316
refined art of redundancy, 334
summary justice for
    misdemeanors, 332–333
tax collections, 320
teacher ingratiation, 324–326
Tian'anmen revolt vs., 315
within transportation systems,
    297–302, 308–312, 315, 325
Cosmetics, 294
Counterfeit products, 326–328
Countryside. See Villages
Cremation, 139
Crime, 321, 332–333. See also
    Corruption; Justice system;
    Scams
Cross, Larry, 24
Cui Shuping, 200–201
Cultural Revolution, 259, 303
Culture. See Architecture; Art;
    Food and dietary practices;
    Language; Media and
    entertainment
Customs service, 302

D
Da Hei Shan, 125, 129
Dai, Dr., 216–217

Dai minority, 126
Daitoku Kimono Company, 291
Dalai Lama, 91, 113, 114
Dancing Beijing, 163–169
Dao, 163–164
Datong, 174
Death and burial practices, 96–97, 139, 159
Deforestation. *See* Forestland
Dell, Michael, 61
Deng Mei, 20–21, 25–27
Deng Xiaoping
  communist "reign" of, 37
  on socialism, 47–48, 53, 336–337
  "thought unification" by, 38
  transcription of name into English, 240
Dengzhu Zeren, 114–115
Dentistry
  adulterated toothpaste made in China, 327
  fillings, 294
  jaw reconstruction (Mei Mei case), 251–267
Derong, 100
Dharamsala, India, 113–114
Dialects. *See* Language
Di (American Jew in Kaifeng), 207
Dietary practices. *See* Food and dietary practices
Diethylene glycol, 327
Discipline. *See* "Thought unification"
Discovery Pub, 23–24
Discrimination, 144
Divorce rates, 304
Djoma, 116–118
Dog meat, 233
Dogs as pets, 233–237
Doha Asian Games, 230
Doji, 118
Dragons, 166–167
Drug use, 304
Du Fu, 21
Dui ge, 153–155
Dulles, John Foster, 312
Dupes, 181–188
Dynastic principle, 36–37

E
East Shuangtang, 54–55
Economics Institute in Boulder, 24
Economy and trade. *See also* Salaries; Standards of living
  within Beijing, 270
  business (B-1) visas, 8–10
  capitalism, 39, 53
  corruption within financial systems, 302
  downsizing, 317
  economic classes, 315–326
  GDP, 63
  market days, 136–137, 187–188
  market economy, 37
  privately-owned businesses, 33–34, 250–251
  socialism
    corruption and, 303–304, 313
    Deng Xiaoping on, 53, 336–337
    Jiang Zemin on, 37
    Ma Fu on, 33–34
    nature of China's socialism, 48
  taxes, 320
  World Trade Organization (WTO) membership, 37, 189
  xia hai ("to go to sea"), 316–317
Education. *See also* Children
  assimilation of minorities as result of, 104–105, 106–107
  backpacks of Japanese children, 295
  bilingual, 141
  Communist Party schools, 57–62, 67–69
  cultural, 146
  English studies, 113
  Hui Min Elementary School (Tibet), 96
  Lu E, 138–145
  Ma Fu's proposal for Guyuan, 88, 90
  National Minorities University, 98
  Pinyin transcription, 141
  private elementary schools, 326
  teacher salaries, 318, 322, 324–326
Elderly, 45–46
Electricians, 322

Electricity. *See also* Technology
within caves, 84, 85
Jiawa Township, 117
Long Ding, 156, 157
Lu E lacking, 138, 141
provided by administrative
villages, 152–153
stingy use of light bulbs, 53
Embezzlement. *See* Corruption
England, 61
English language, 113, 239–241
Entertainment. *See* Media and
entertainment
Entrepreneurs, 317–318
Eyes and eyesight, 152, 294–295,
296

F
F-1 (student) visas, 8–9
Faces. *See* Hygiene and bathing
habits; Physical differences
between East Asians
Fake products, 326–328
Family planning, 82, 116–117, 140,
283
Fang, Miss, 310–311
Farmers and farming. *See also*
specific villages by name;
Villages
cooperatives, 51–55
harvest festivals, 155
herding, 101–102, 111
irrigation systems, 77, 87
land reform, 33–34, 39–47,
50–55, 122–123
placement of fields on mountains,
155
rice terraces, 148–149
Fashion. *See* Clothing and fashion
Feng Xiaodong, 289–291
Fernandez, Lisa, 220, 221
Film (camera), 326–327
Films. *See* Media and entertainment
Finance. *See* Economy and trade
Finland, 205
Fish as food, 97
Fish as pets, 234
Food and dietary practices
adulterated, 327–328

dog meat, 233
Hani minority, 133, 134–135, 157
Jews of Kaifeng, 197, 200, 208
snake meat, 243–246
Tibetan, 96–97
Footbinding, 293
Forestland, 99, 105, 130–131, 156
Fortunetellers, 246–247. *See also*
Scams
Fraud. *See* Corruption; Scams
Freund, Michael, 207
Fruit crops, 43–44
Fuji film, 326–327
Fukienese, 244

G
Gambling, 179, 186
Gansu Province, 107, 313–315
Ganzi Prefecture, 91–124. *See also*
Tibet and Tibetans
described, 91–93
ethnic breakdown, 97
forestland, 99
herding vs. agriculture, 101–102
Kangding County, 94–96, 97,
99–100, 114–115
Litang County, 198–123
map, 92 (map)
population, 97
tourism, 99
traditional herb gathering, 104
Yaijiang County, 98, 99–101,
104–105, 108
Gao Changli, 329 (note)
Gao Chao, 208
Gao clan, 200
GDP, 63. *See also* Economy and
trade
Gecuo, 115
Gejiu, 128
General Electric, 61
General Sports Administration of
China, 213, 227
Genetic differences between East
Asians, 282
Gesang Yangjing. *See* Yang Suping
Gorbachev, Mikhail, 312
Grapes, 43–44
Great Britain, 61

Great Hall of the People, 35
Great Wall scam, 269–274
Greece. *See* Athens Olympics
Green Sheep Palace Dog Market, 236
Grein, Cindi, 8, 16
Guangdong Province, 305
Guangzhou (Canton), 121, 333. *See also* Cantonese
Guankou Village, 86–87
Guan Yuan Agricultural Market, 233–234
Guo, Mr. (dog seller), 234–235
Guo Chunning, 164–169
Guo (husband of Zhao Chunmei), 53
Guo ("One Day, Five Site" tourist), 269
Guo Tongxi, 20–21
Guralnick, Walter, 257, 258–259, 266–267
Guyuan, Ningxia, 71–90. *See also* Ningxia Hui Autonomous Region
    described, 65–67, 73, 77–78, 86–87, 89–90
    health and medical care within, 81–83, 84–85, 87
    Ma Fu's free education proposal, 88, 90
    map, 72 (map)
    minorities within, 66
    Second People's Hospital, 78–79

H

Haigeng Sports Training Center, 214, 215
Hai, Dr. (Jiaocha Clinic), 82
Haim, Yehoyada, 204
Hainan Island spy-plane incident, 191, 193
Hairstyles, 295
Hai Xiuke, 86–87
Hakkas, 244
Hani minority, 125–162. *See also* Language; Lu E
Han Zhiren, 87
Hao Yue, 19–21, 22
Health and medicine
    acupuncture, 212–213

adulterated, 327–328
American model, 258
Chinese medicine scams, 186
dental fillings, 294
economic class of physicians, 318–320
eyesight, 152
herbal medicines, 104, 186, 216–217, 243–246
hospital system, 257–266, 318–319
jaw reconstruction (Mei Mei case), 251–267
life spans, 84–85, 152
of pets, 236–237
pre-op procedures, 262–263
preventive care, 84–85, 152
within rural villages, 81–83, 84–85, 87
sexually transmitted diseases, 246
snake meat, benefits of, 243–246, 325
Hebei Province, 39–47, 42 (map), 172 (map)
He (driver), 80, 83
He Liping, 219
Henan Province, 197 (map), 305. *See also* Kaifeng
Heni Township, 116–118
Hepatitis B, 84–85
Herbal medicines, 186, 216–217, 243–246. *See also* Health and medicine
Herding, 101–102, 111, 116–118, 122–123
Heroine, 304
Hitachi Company, 284, 285
Homes. *See* Architecture
Hongge, 227
Honghe (Red River) Prefecture, 127 (map)
Hong Kong, 40 (note), 244, 296
Hospitals. *See* Health and medicine
Hua (friend of Bao), 313–314
Huang Gaoqu, 213–214, 215, 217
Huang Jian, 302–305
Huang pao, 155
Huang Zhanghong (Betty), 23, 31 (note)
Hua Weili, 38

Huaxi Jie. *See* Snake Alley
Hua Zui coal mine, 176–178
"Hubei Village", 321–322
Huffaker, Carl, 4
Hui Min Elementary School, 96
Hui Muslim population, 40 (note),
    66, 82, 126, 186–187. *See also*
    Muslims
Hu Jintao
    biographical information, 48, 303
        (note)
    "Building a Harmonious Society
        through a Scientific
        Outlook", 57 (note)
    China's integration into the world
        economy led by, 37
    Communist Youth League
        position, 34
    on corruption, 333
    as Party secretary in Tibet, 91
    "Three Represents", 38
    "Three Stills", 333
Human Genome Diversity Project,
    283
Hurst, Bruce, 229 (note)
Hu Xing, 306
Hu Yao-pang (Hu Yaobang), 240
Hygiene and bathing habits
    Chinese customs of face washing,
        281
    East Shuangtang, 54
    Japanese customs, 281
    Lu E, 138–140, 150–152
    Tibet, 107–108, 112, 113
    Zhuolu County, 43

I
Immigration to Japan, 283–286,
    289–291, 296
Immigration to the United States.
    See also Strothman smuggling
        operation
    Immigration and Naturalization
        Service (INS) investigation of
        Strothman smuggling ring
    flaws in investigation, 8, 10–15
    Hao Yue caught by, 22
    identities of illegals revealed to,
        16–18

indictment of Strothmans, 30
    McSpadden's statement, 7, 23
    Zhang Longxue reaction to, 28
    marriage as means to, 249–251
    statistics, 287
    visas used by illegal immigrants,
        8–10
Immunizations, 84–85, 152
Imperial era, 36–37
Income. *See* Salaries; Standards of
    living
India, 113
Industrialization, 50–52. *See also*
    Urbanization and urban areas
Intermarriage. *See also* Assimilation
    assimilation as result, 128
    between Chinese and Americans,
        304
    between Chinese, Koreans, and
        Japanese, 287
    by Jews of Kaifeng, 200–201
Internet
    chat rooms, 192
    as connection to the world, 64
    Internet cafes, 239
Iran, 192
Iraq, 192
Irrigation systems, 77, 86–87. *See
    also* Water resources
Islam. *See* Muslims
Israel
    ambassadors to China, 202, 203,
        204
    Jewish revival in Kaifeng and,
        205–207
    presence in China, 199
    weapons and military expertise,
        192

J
Japan Airlines (JAL), 214, 291
Japan and Japanese people
    bathing customs, 281
    clothing and jewelry, 293
    foreigners living within, 283–286,
        287, 296
    Hani legend about, 158
    homogeneity, 286–288
    immigrants to China, 289

immigrants to U.S., 288
mannerisms, 294
names, 286, 290
national softball team, 219, 226,
  232, 283–285
Okinawa, 282
physical differences between
  East Asians, 281–283, 286,
  291–296
religion, 286
Taiwan colonized by, 288
wars, 55, 221, 281, 283–284
writing system, 165
Jaw reconstruction (Mei Mei case),
  251–267
Jews of Kaifeng, 195–208. *See also*
  Minorities
assimilation of, 198, 200–208
dietary practices, 197, 200, 208
intermarriage, 200–201
Kaifeng Museum, 195–196, 199,
  204
official status of, 201–202,
  203–204
recent history of, 197, 199–208
revival movement, 206–208
train travel to Kaifeng, 297–300,
  311–312
visits by foreign tourists, 204–207
Jiang Qing, 240
Jiang Xiuyun, 228–229, 230
Jiang Zemin
anticorruption campaign, 297,
  302–304, 305, 307, 314, 329
APEC meeting with Bush, 189
communist "reign" of, 37
land reform proposals, 45
Marx's basic theory adapted by,
  47–48
Party Congress Report, 62–63
at Sixteenth Communist Party
  Congress, 303
"thought unification" by, 38
"Three Represents", 38, 46, 63
Jianlibao Company, 183–185
Jianziwan, Mount, 109
Jiaocha Township, 80–88
Jiawa Township, 110–111, 116
Jiefang cao (liberation grass), 131

Jin City, 187–188
Jin clan of Kaifeng, 200
The Jin Dai Restaurant, 245
Jin Denglian, 83–85
Jin (East Shuangtang), 54–55
Jingang Temple, 114–115
Jing Guang, 24
Jinghai County, 51 (map)
Jing Jing, 233, 235
Jinglun, 327 (note)
Jin Guangyuan, 205
Jinning County, 181–188, 182
  (map)
Journalism. *See* Media and
  entertainment
Justice system, 303, 329. *See also*
  Crime

K
Kaifeng. *See* Jews of Kaifeng
Kane, Karen, 256
Kang, 43, 84
Kangding County, 94–96, 97,
  99–100, 114–115. *See also*
  Ganzi Prefecture
"Kanding Love Song", 95
Kaniang, 110–115
Ke-lin-dun (Clinton), President,
  304
Kendall, Laurel, 282
Kimonos, 293
Komai, Hiroshi, 287
Korea and Korean people
attachment to nationality, 287
colonization of, 287
foreigners living within Japan,
  286, 287
immigrants to U.S., 288
mannerisms, 294
names, 286
physical differences between
  East Asians, 281–283, 286,
  291–296
religion, 286
writing system, 165
Kosovo, 191
Kucine, Allan, 256
Kunming City
betting scams, 186

bus scam, 181–185
Haigeng Sports Training Center,
    214, 215–217
map, 182 (map)
vacation climate, 305
Kunyang bus, 181–185
Kuomintang (Nationalist Party), 55

L
Lai Changxing, 306
Land reform, 33–34, 39–47, 50–55,
    122–123. See also Farmers and
    farming
Language
  assimilation through, 142–143
  bilingual education, 141
  Cantonese dialect, 296
  cultural oppression, 144, 145
  Cultural Revolution, 259, 303
  English language, 113, 239–241
  Han language, 126
  Hani language, 126, 138, 141,
      142, 156, 158
  Hong Kong dialect, 296
  Mandarin dialect, 93, 96, 106–
      107, 122, 125, 140–142, 145,
      185, 296
  Pinyin transcription, 141, 240
  Sichuan dialect, 11, 17, 26, 106,
      122
  Taiwanese dialect, 296
  within Tibet, 106–107, 112
  writing system, 165–166
  Yunnan dialect, 185
Lanzhou, 313–315
Laobaixing, 37. See also Villages
Lefebvre, Jim, 229 (note)
Lei Donghui, 231
Lei Xingkuei, 89–90
Lennon, John, 292
Lhasa, 120
"Liberation grass" (jiefang cao), 131
Libya, 192
Li clan of Kaifeng, 200
Li (coal truck driver), 172, 173
Li (editor), 323
Life spans, 84–85, 152
Light. See Electricity
Li Jia, 6–7, 10, 22–23, 31 (note)

Li Jin, 283
Li Kexiu, 195
Li Meifang (Mei Mei), 249–267
Li Mimi, 21–22
Li Minkuan (Coach)
  Atlanta Olympics, 221, 222–224
  immigration path, 288–289
  on Michael Bastian, 228
  Sharon Strothman and, 2, 17–18
Lin, Florence, 246
Li Peng, 304, 315
Li Ping, 306
Li Pingquan, 6
Li Shiyou, 20–21
Litang County, 108–123
  altitude, 100
  Communist Party, 109–111
  Heni Township, 116–118
  land reform, 122–123
  Wu Yali, 119–122
Li Tiejun, 35–36
Little Fang, 41–44, 53
Liu, Christie, 219–220, 221, 222
Liu Bing, 172, 173, 179
Liu (medicine factory worker), 323
Liu Weizhi, 289–291
Liu Xingyuan, 128
Liu Yaju, 219
Liu Yaming, 17–18
Liu Yan, 100
Liu (Zhuolu County Party
    Secretary), 44–45, 46–47
Li Wen, 24. See also Zhang Longxue
Li Xiaoshi, 305
Li Yunmei, 157
LM (Strothman illegal), 9, 20–21, 22
Local government, 34–35
Long Ding, 152, 155–157
Long Weiyou, 132–140
Lüchun County, 125–162, 127
    (map)
Lu E and Hani people, 125–162
  architecture of homes, 133–134,
      137–138, 146–148
  bathing rituals, 138–139, 150–151
  brick making, 147–148
  Chinese names used by, 142
  clothing and jewelry, 149, 155,
      156–157

Community Party members, 153
described, 126
diet, 133, 134–135, 157
entertainment and festivals,
153–155
hauling done by women, 149–150
isolation of, 143
language, 126, 141, 142
legend of Japanese people, 158
market days, 136–137
marriage traditions, 133, 154
mountain journey to and from,
129–132, 155–162
names and naming practices, 133
rice paddies, 135, 140, 144, 147,
148, 153, 155, 161
schools, 138–145
separate identity maintained by,
156–157
standards of living, 144–145, 156
stoicism, 151–152
village sizes limited by, 157–158
water sources, 148–149, 150
Zhao line, 133
Luodengba, 116
Luorong Pengcuo, 110–111
Luorong Yapi, 111
Luo Yang (Chen's ex-wife), 7
Luoyang (city), 196, 311–312
Luo Zhongmin, 59–60
Lu Wei, 231

M
Macao, 40 (note)
Ma Fu
education proposal, 88, 90
as mayor of Guyuan City, 65–67,
71–80, 87–90
Ningxia visit with, 62–80
political career of, 67–69
at Sixteenth Chinese Communist
Party Congress, 33–34
Wu Haiying (wife), 65, 69–70,
71, 89
Yinchuan City Communist Party
School speech, 62–63
Mahjong, 179
Ma (Jin Denglian's neighbor), 85
Ma Laran, 128–129

Ma (mayor of Jiaocha), 85–86
Manchuria, 54
Mandarin dialect. See Language
Mao-dun (spear), 336–337
Mao Zedong
base in caves of Yen'an, 83
communist "reign" of, 37
mao-dun (spear), 336–337
Marx's basic theory adapted by,
47–48
revolution initiated in villages, 40
"seek the truth", 221, 231, 336
"thought unification", 38
transcription of name into
English, 241
Market days, 136–137, 187–188
Market economy, 37
Marriage. See also Intermarriage
divorce rates, 304
Hani traditions, 133, 149, 154,
156, 157
as means to legally emigrate to
U.S., 249–251
surnames kept by women, 133
Tibetan wedding customs, 120
Martin, W. A. P., 198
Marx, 47–48
Ma Sanbao (Zheng He), 186–187
Matsch, Richard P., 6 (note), 31–32
Mayo Clinic, 211–212
Ma Zhenggao, 84–85
McDonald, Shan, 227
McSpadden, Phil, 7, 23, 31 (note)
Meals. See Food and dietary
practices
Media and entertainment
China Central Television, 75, 193
Communist Party control of, 36
entertainment class, 317–318, 322
government film studios, 335–337
Internet chat rooms, 192
music and singing in rural
villages, 95, 96, 112, 153–155
People's Daily, 56–57, 328 (note)
political documents sold to
foreign journalists, 336
propaganda via, 191, 193
satellite dishes, 105
SinoVision, 193

Medical care. *See* Health and medicine
Melamine, 327
Melton, Eddie, 8, 10–14, 16–17, 23
Mental discipline. *See* "Thought unification"
Miao minority, 126
Middle class, 318. *See also* Economic classes
"Middle Kingdom", 335
Migrant workers, 54, 269–270, 320 (note), 321–322
Military. *See* Army
Milosevic, Slobodan, 191
Min Chunxiu, 22–23
Ming Dynasty, 187, 271
Minibuses, 332. *See also* Buses
Mining. *See* Coal mines
Minorities. *See also specific minorities by group*
  assimilation
    of Bai, Yi, and Muslim minorities, 126
    intermarriage and, 128
    of Jews of Kaifeng, 198, 200–208
    through language, 142–143
    as result of education, 104–105, 106–107
    of Tibetans, 112
  child limitations for, 82, 116–117, 140, 283
  cultural oppression of, 144, 145, 146
  kept in check by Chinese presence, 97
  Museum of National Minorities, 185–186
  National Minorities University, 98
  political careers of, 66
  population figures, 126
Motorbikes and motorcycles, 332
"Mountain High Blush" (song), 96
MTV, 112
Museum of National Minorities, 185–186
Music. *See* Media and entertainment
Muslims. *See also* Minorities
  American treatment of, 64

Arab world favored by China, 192
assimilation, 126–128
Great Eastern Mosque, 198
Hui Muslim population, 40 (note), 66, 82, 126, 186–187
Myopia, 152, 161

N

Names and naming practices
  Chinese characters within Chinese, Japanese, and Korean names, 286
  Hani, 142
  Japanese, 290
  surnames kept by women after marriage, 133
Nanjing University, 107 (note)
Nannies, 321
National American University, 20, 30
National Corruption Preventative Agency, 307 (note)
National highway system, 175, 312, 325
Nationalist Party (Kuomintang), 55
National Minorities University, 98
National People's Congress, 89, 303, 306, 336
National Sports Research Institute, 213–214
NATO, 191
The Netherlands, 219
New York City, 193, 282, 291–293
The New York Times Magazine, 75
9/11 Terror attacks, 64, 189–193
Nine Dragon Amusement Park, 271–272
Ningxia Academy of Social Sciences, 89
Ningxia Hui Autonomous Region, 62–70. *See also* Guyuan, Ningxia
  administration of, 40 (note)
  GDP, 63
  Hui Muslim population, 40 (note)
  map, 72 (map)
  Ningxia Communist Party School, 67–68
Nin-san (Utsugi Reika), 283–286, 288, 289

Nomads, 116–118, 122–123. *See also* Herding
North China Music Bar, 173–174
Northglenn, Colorado, 7–8, 12–13, 16
No. 9 People's Hospital, 259, 260
No. 110 Yangtze River Liner, 308–309
Nuclear weapons, 192
Nu minority, 126

O

Oe Akiko and Oe Ryuji, 290
Okazaki, Toshio, 294
Okinawa, 282
Oklahoma City University, 2–4, 7, 10, 23, **31 (note)**
Olympics. *See also* Chinese National Softball Team; Sports and leisure
　Athens, 226, 227, 285
　Atlanta, 2, 219–224, 227, 284–285
　Beijing, 37, 163–169, 225–232, 276
　Olympic baseball camp, **229 (note)**
　Sydney, 227, 283, 285
　Tokyo, 165
"One Day, Five Site" tour, 269–274
Ong, Mr., 244
Ono, Yoko, 292
Opium, 304
Oral surgery (Mei Mei case), 251–267
"Orient Express", 282
Outhouses. *See* Hygiene and bathing habits
Ou-Yang Dan, 21

P

Pacific Gateways English Academy, 9
Pakistan, 192
Panchen Lama, 91, 114
Pan (softball catcher), 226
Panzhihua Olympic softball training camp, 225–232
Park, Keum M., 9

Passports, 19, 20, 22, 28, 306, 308, 316, 330, 334
Patten, Chris, 61
Peaceful evolution, 312–316
Pears, 44
Peasants. *See* Villages
Pedicabs, 333
Peking (Beijing), 239–240, 241
Penal system. *See* Crime
Peng Guoquan, 20–21, 25–27
Pengyang County, **72 (map)**, 79–88
Peony Hotel, 311–312
People's Daily, 56–57, **328 (note)**
Pets and pet food, 233, 234, 236–237, 327
Pharmaceuticals. *See* Health and medicine
Phony products, 326–328
Physical differences between East Asians, 281–287, 291–296
Physicians. *See* Health and medicine
Pinghe, 128
Pinyin transcription, 141, 240
Plumbers, 322
Poker, 179
Police
　Communism and the Communist Party control of, 36, 37
　corrupt, 178, 306, 308–309, 332–333, 334
　Deputy Police Chief Zhang, 11, 19, 23, 26–29
　salaries, 316
　as township service, 80 **(note)**
Politics. *See* Communism and the Communist Party
Population control policies. *See* Family planning
Population relocation, 90
Privately-owned businesses, 33–34, 250–251. *See also* Economy and trade
Procter & Gamble, **328 (note)**
Professional class, 317–320
Professors, salaries of, 322
Propaganda
　achievement by declaration, 62–63

anticorruption campaign,
  307–308
Communist Party schools as tool,
  57–62
media role, 191, 193, 335–337
model citizens as delegates to
    Communist Party Congress,
    35–36
Propaganda Department, 190–191
on September 11 terror attacks,
    189–193
"thought unification", 37–38, 69
Prosperity. See Wealth
Protestants, 286
Provinces, described, 40–41
Public Security Bureau. See also
    Police
  corruption within, 334
  Strothman smuggling operation
      investigation, 11, 20, 25, 26
Public transportation. See
    Transportation
Puerto Rico, 220
Puppies, 233–237
Pu Yulian, 104–108

Q
Qi, 163–164
Qianmen Station, 269, 270, 273
Qin (Beijing City Communist Party
    School), 59
Qinghai, 107
Qing Ming Jie, 159
Qing Qing, 324
Qin Shi Huangdi, Emperor, 37
Qi pao, 293
Qiqihar Second Pharmaceutical
    Company, 328
Qiu Weiliu, 259

R
Race, yellow, 281–296
Racial differences, 281–283
Railway system, corruption within,
    297–301, 302, 309–312,
    315, 332–333. See also
    Transportation
Rainfall, 86, 89–90. See also Water
    resources

Ranching. See Herding
Raymond, Ralph, 222
Red light districts, 246
Red River Prefecture, 126–129
Religion. See Minorities; specific
    religions by name
Relocation of populations, 90
Ren, Dr., 214–215
Renesas Technology Corp., 285
Ren Yanli, 284, 288, 289
Retirement, 45–46
Rice paddies, 135, 140, 144, 147,
    148, 153, 155, 161
Rice terraces. See Rice paddies
Richardson, Dot, 221, 224
Ringling Bros. circus act, 275
River life, 308–309
Road tolls, 175, 312, 325
Rolex watches, 327 (note)
Rong Rong, 235, 237
Roser, Steven, 257, 259
Rural villages. See Villages

S
Sakyamuni, 114
Salaries. See also Standards of living
  of coaches, 226, 322, 330–332
  economic classes, 315–326
  increases in, 299, 315–316
  teacher salaries, 318, 322, 324–326
  urban-rural income gap, 320–322
San Francisco Airport, 10–11
Sanying, 78
Scams. See also Corruption;
    Fortunetellers
  Great Wall scam, 269–274
  Jinning County, 181–188
Schools. See Education
Schweyer, Rob, 226
Sechiuma, 116–118
Second People's Hospital of
    Guyuan, 78–79
Second Sino-Japanese War, 55, 221,
    281, 283–284
Senior citizens, 45–46
September 11 terror attacks, 64,
    189–193
Seventeenth Communist Party
    Congress, 57 (note)

Sexually transmitted diseases, 246
Shaanxi, 83
Shangbao, Feng, **231 (note)**
Shanghai
  administration of, **40 (note)**
  bicycle restrictions, 333
  Israeli consulate, 204
  No. 9 People's Hospital, 259, 260
  standards of living, 63, 322–323
Shanghai Medical University, 334
Shangri-La, 100
Shavei Israel, 205, 207
Shen Jun, 11–12, 24. *See also* Zhang
    Longxue
Shen Yong, 29
Shi clan of Kaifeng, 200
Shih Lin market, 246
Shijiazhuang Village, 50–52, 55
Shi Lei, 205–206
Shi Lili, 300–301
Shi Mingxia, 208
Shinya, Hiromi, 211
Ships, 187, 308–309. *See also*
    Transportation
Shi Xinguang, 202–203, 206
Shi Zhongyu, 201–202, 203, 206
Shui minority, 126
Sichuan Province. *See also*
    Chengdu, Sichuan
  Chongqing, **253 (note)**
  "The Coal Mine", 329
  delegation to Sixteenth Chinese
    Communist Party Congress,
    91–93
  language and culture, 106–107,
    122
  map, **92 (map)**
  Panzhihua Olympic softball
    training camp, 225–232
  population, 93, 252
  provincial soccer team, 330–331
  Yang Suping (Gesang Yangjing),
    91, 101, 103, 108
Sichuan University, 24
SinoVision, 193
Sixteenth Chinese Communist
    Party Congress, 33, 34–36,
    47–50, **303 (note)**
Smuggling Chinese into the U.S.

See Strothman smuggling
    operation
Snake Alley, 243–247
Snake oil, 325
Snakes, 243–247
Snow, 278, 279
Soccer, 330–331
Socialism
  corruption and, 303–304, 313
  Deng Xiaoping on, 53, 336–337
  Jiang Zemin on, 37
  Ma Fu on, 33–34
  nature of China's socialism, 48
Softball (Chinese team). *See*
    Chinese National Softball Team
Softball (U.S. team), 220–224, 226,
    227, 230, 232
Song and dance. *See* Media and
    entertainment
Song Chuan, 7, 9, 16, **30 (note)**
Song Dynasty, 198
Southwestern University of Finance
    and Economics, 24
Soviet Union, 312
Spear (*mao-dun*), 336–337
Spinal surgery, **319 (note)**
Sports and leisure. *See also*
    Olympics; *specific sports by*
    name
  betting salons, 179
  Chinese Sports Commission, 75
  General Sports Administration of
    China, 213, 227
  Haigeng Sports Training Center,
    214, 215–217
  National Sports Research Institute,
    213–214
  residential status of players,
    331–332
  salaries and bonuses of players,
    226, 231
  salaries of coaches, 226, 322,
    330–332
  state-run sports system, 1–2
  Tibet, 97
Spurdle, Sarah, 246
Standards of living. *See also*
    Salaries; *specific cities and*
    villages by name

economic classes, 315–326
transportation expenses and, 299
State police, 37
Steiner, Dr., 258
Stony Brook, 256
Strawberry Fields memorial, 292
Strothman smuggling operation,
  1–32. *See also* Chen family
  (parents of Sharon Strothman)
  Christiane (Strothman case
    informant), 4–5, 6, 7, 8,
    9–10, 13–14, 16
  Connie Strothman, 6 (note), 32
    (note)
  criminal history of Sharon's
    brother, 5, 7–8, 16, 28, 329
  Frederick B. Strothman, 3, 9, 16,
    21, 25, 32 (note)
  investigation within China, 17–30
  Jim (James) Strothman
    charges, sentencing, and
      punishment, 6 (note), 30–32
    marriage to Sharon, 4
    role in smuggling operation,
      4–6, 7, 10, 15–16, 17, 18,
      20, 21
  money laundering and sheltered
    assets, 15, 16
  Sharon Strothman
    attempts to gag customers, 30
      (note)
    call to author, 29–30
    charges, sentencing and
      punishment vs., 30–32
    college scholarship, 2–3, 249
    Discovery Pub dispute, 23–24
    family home in Ya'an, 1
    marriage, 3–4
  Student (F-1) visas, 8–9
Subway system, 276. *See also*
  Transportation
Sufot, Abe, 202, 203
Sun, Dr., 210–211
Sunglasses, 294–295
Sun Li, 231
Sunshine Spirit Oral Tonic, 325
Surgeons. *See* Health and
  medicine
Sydney Olympics, 227, 283, 285

T
Taipei, 243–247
Taiwan
  administration of, 40 (note)
  colonization, 288
  dialects, 296
  media coverage of, 193
  snake meat, 244
  softball team, 219, 220, 230
Tao Hua, 221
Taxes, 320
Taxis, 275, 320, 332, 333
Teachers. *See* Education
Technology. *See also* Electricity;
    Media and entertainment
  Internet as connection to the
    world, 64
  Internet cafes, 239
  Internet chat rooms, 192
  satellite dishes, 105
  telephone revolution, 329–330
Teeth. *See* Dentistry
Telephones, 329–330
Televisions. *See also* Media and
    entertainment
  China Central Television (CCTV),
    75, 193
  Long Ding, 156
  satellite dishes, 105
  SinoVision, 193
  VCD (video CD), 112
Teng Hsiao-p'ing. *See* Deng
    Xiaoping
Terrorism, 64, 189–193
Thatched Hut of Du Fu, 21
"Thought unification", 37–38, 69
"Three Gorges Express", 310–311
"Three Represents", 38–40, 46, 63
"Three Stills", 333
Tian'anmen bus stop, 276
Tian'anmen revolt, 313, 315
Tianjin Municipality, 47–55, 60
  administration of, 40 (note)
  delegation to Sixteenth Chinese
    Communist Party Congress,
    47–50
  East Shuangtang, 54–55
  map, 51 (map)
  Shijiazhuang Village, 50–52

transcription of name into English, 241
West Shuangtang, 52–54, 55
Tian ma, 216–217
Tibet and Tibetans, 91–124. *See also* Ganzi Prefecture; Kanding County; Litang County; Yaijiang County
  altitude and topography, 99–100
  architecture and artistry, 102–103, 104, 105, 110, 115, 147–148
  Buddhism, 91, 97, 114–115, 120
  Chinese perception of, 102
  clothing and jewelry, 120–121
  described, 93
  diaspora communities in China, 107
  Ganzi Tibetan Autonomous Prefecture, **92 (map)**
  Kangding County, 94–96, 97, 99–100, 114–115
  language and culture, 96–97, 103, 106–107, 122
  Litang County, 108–123
  names, 103
  nomads, 116–118, 122–123
  population within Ganzi Tibetan Autonomous Prefecture, 97
  Sixteenth Chinese Communist Party Congress delegation, 91–93
  wedding customs, 120
  Yaijiang County, 98, 99–101, 104–105, 108
  yak-butter tea, 103
  Yang Suping (Gesang Yangjing), 91, 101, 103, 108, 122–124
Tientsin. *See* Tianjin
Timber. *See* Forestland
Time zones, **107 (note)**
"To go to sea" (*xia hai*), 316–317
Tokayer, Rabbi Marvin, 205
Tokyo, 165. *See also* Japan
Toll roads, 175, 312, 325
"Tommy John" elbow surgery, 231
Tongxian, 321
Toothpaste, 327
Tourism. *See also* Transportation
  to Beijing, 269–274

differential ticket pricing for Chinese and foreigners, **310 (note)**
  fake film sold to tourists, 326–327
  Ganzi Tibetan Autonomous Prefecture, 99
  Great Wall scam, 269–274
  Jewish tourists to Kaifeng, 204–207
  Jinning County scams, 181–188
  snake trade, 243–244
  travel agencies, corruption within, 314–315
Townships, **80 (note)**
Traffic. *See* Transportation
Trains. *See* Railway system
Transparency within politics, 48–50, 56–57
Transportation. *See also* Tourism
  bicycles, 275–276
  buses, 269–274, 275–280, 301–302, 332
  "corrupt cars", 313–314
  corruption within systems, 297–302, 308–312, 315, 325
  fixed-salary class of drivers, 317–318
  motorbikes and motorcycles, 332
  national highway system, 175, 312, 325
  pedicabs, 333
  railway system, 297–301, 302, 309–312, 315, 332–333
  ships, 187, 308–309
  subway system, 276
  taxis, 275, 320
  traffic violations, 332–333
  travel agencies, corruption within, 314–315
  trolleys, 276
Trees. *See* Forestland
Trolleys, 276. *See also* Transportation
Trucks, 332
Tubal ligations, 82. *See also* Family planning
TV Guide, 75

U

Uighurs, 126
United Front Work Department,
    55–56
United States. *See also* English
    language
  Atlanta Olympics, 2, 219–224,
      227, 284–285
  Chinatown, NY, 193, 282,
      291–293
  foreign-born population, 287–288
  Hainan Island spy-plane incident,
      191, 193
  Immigration and Naturalization
      Service (INS), 7, 8, 10–15,
      16–18, 22, 23, 28, 30, 64
  immigration to, 8–10, 249–251,
      287. *See also* Strothman
      smuggling operation
  intermarriage with Chinese, 304
  Kosovo bombing, 191
  national softball team, 220–224,
      226, 227, 230, 232
  pet food sold to, 327
  September 11 terror attacks, 64,
      189–193
  SinoVision, 193
  toothpaste sold to, 327
  treatment of Muslims, 64
Urbanization and urban areas. *See
    also specific cities by name*
  child limitations within, 82
  clothing and jewelry trends, 151
  coastal cities, 316–317
  cremation practices, 139
  dogs prohibited as pets within,
      233
  economic classes within,
      317–318
  "floating population", 320 (note),
      321–322
  industrialization, 50–52
  land reform and, 45, 50
  residential status of sports players,
      331–332
  urban-rural income gap, 320–322
U.S. Department of Homeland
    Security, 8
U.S. Department of Justice.

See Immigration and
    Naturalization Service (INS)
Utsugi Reika (Nin-san), 283–286,
    288, 289
Utsugi Taeko, 288

V

Vaccinations, 84–85, 152
VCD (video CD), 112
Vietnam, 165
Villages. *See also* Farmers and
    farming; *specific villages by name*
  cell phone usage, 330
  characteristics of, 40–41
  clothes washing rituals, 150–152
  clothing and jewelry, 149, 151,
      155, 156–157
  dogs permitted as pets within, 233
  electricity provided, 152–153
  exploitation of peasants, 144, 302
  family planning, 116–117, 140
  health and medical care within,
      81–83, 84–85, 87
  Mao's revolution initiated in, 40
  migrant workers from, 54, 269–
      270, **320 (note)**, 321–322
  music and singing within, 95, 96,
      112, 153–155
  population relocation, 90
  population size limited in Hani
      villages, 157–158
  residential status of sports players,
      331–332
  townships, **80 (note)**
  urbanization of, **320 (note)**
  urban-rural income gap, 320–322
Visas used by illegal immigrants, 8–10

W

Wagner, Marsha, 246
Wa Na, 157–160
Wang, Danny, 23–24
Wang Dazhang, 258–259
Wang Dongshou, 104–108
Wang (Kunyang bus passenger),
    185, 186, 187
Wang Lihong, 222, 223–224, 226,
    228, 230
Wang Mingchen, 18

Wangmo, 113–114
Wang Pei, 120
Wang Xing, 260–261, 262–266
Wang Yisha, 199–201
Wan Li, Emperor, 271
War of Resistance, 55, 221, 281,
    283–284
Washrooms. *See* Hygiene and
    bathing habits
Watches, **327 (note)**
Water resources
  Baiyang, 87
  Guyuan, 77, 86, 89–90
  Lu E, 131, 148–149, 150
  river life, 308–309
  Yangtze River, 90, 308
  Yellow River, 77, 90, 198
  Zhe E River, 125, 129
Wealth. *See* Salaries; Standards of
    living
Wedding customs, 120. *See also*
    Marriage
West Shuangtang, 52–54, 55
White, Bishop William, **196 (note)**,
    199
Wiggs, Dr., 212
Wing Lam, 10
Women. *See also* Clothing and
    fashion; Family planning;
    Marriage
  gait, 293–294
  retirement age, **45 (note)**
  surnames kept after marriage, 133
Wong, Peter, 327
Worker salaries. *See* Salaries
World Trade Center terror attacks,
    64, 189–193
World Trade Organization (WTO),
    37, 189
World War II, 281, 283–284, 287
World Women's Softball
    Championships, 283
Writing system, 165–166
Wu Haiying (wife of Ma Fu), 65,
    69–70, 71, 89
Wuhan, 310, 316, 317
Wu Jiang, 253–254, 256–257, 258,
    259, 260–261, 265
Wu Yali, 119–122

X

Xia Baolong, 47–50, 73
Xia hai ("to go to sea"), 316–317
Xiamen, 306
Xi'an, 200
Xiazhongzi, 101
Xinjiang Uighur Autonomous
    Region, 126
Xizhimen Bridge, 234
Xu, Mr. "Puppy Sales", 234
Xuanhua, 172–174, 179
Xu Ling, 256–257
Xu Xin, **203 (note)**

Y

Ya'an, 1, 20, 250–251
Yage, 208
Yaijiang County, 98, 99–101,
    104–105, 108
Yan Fang, 222, 223, 224
Yang Deqing, 41
Yang (East Shuangtang), 54–55
Yang Suping (Gesang Yangjing), 91,
    101, 103, 108, 122–124
Yangtze River, 90, 308, 309, 326
Yang Zhihui, 81
Yan Lili, 335–337
Yan Xiaoyu, **30 (note)**
Ya Zhou Restaurant, 245
Yellow race, 281–296
Yellow River, 77, 90, 198
Yen'an, 83, 221
Yichang, 309–311
Yin, Mr., 246–247
Yinchuan, 66
Yinchuan City Communist Party
    School, 62–63
Yong Le, 187
Yu, Karen, 246
Yu, Vice President (Yu Yunyao), 61
Yuan, Officer, 308–309
Yuan (Hui Min Elementary School
    principal), 96
Yu County, **172 (map)**, 174–178
Yunnan Province, 107, 126–128,
    127 (map), 181, **182 (map)**,
    186
Yu Yanhong, 226, 229
Yu Yunyao, 60

Z

ZB (Strothman illegal), 9, 13–14, 17, 22, 24, 30 (note), 31
Zeidman, Andrew, 252–253, 257
Zhagalazha Village, 118–119, 120
Zhagen Aduo, 110–115
Zhai Lijun, 270
Zhang Chunfang, 220–221, 222, 224
Zhang Guoqiang, 171–175, 178–179
Zhang (husband of Bao's classmate), 314–315
Zhangjiakou City, 41, 42 (map), 172 (map), 172–174, 179
Zhang (Laif Fu Restaurant owner), 173
Zhang Longxue, 11, 19, 23, 26–29
Zhang Rui, 27, 30 (note)
Zhang (Second People's Hospital), 79–80, 88
Zhang Wu, 163–169
Zhang Xiuyun, 318
Zhang Zhenkang, 260–264, 265–266, 267
Zhang (Zhuolu County Party Secretary), 44–45, 46
Zhang (Zhuolu County train passenger), 40
Zhao Chunmei, 53

Zhao clan of Kaifeng, 200
Zhao Niangma
family and lifestyle, 132–140, 148, 155
Hani names and naming practices, 142
isolation of, 143
taxes paid by, 144
Zhao Pingyu, 200
Zhao Xiangru, 203–204
Zhao Yunzhong, 199
Zhao Zhoufa, 145–147
Zhao Ziyang, 240
Zhaxi Ciren (monk), 114–115
Zhaxi Ciren (Yajiang contact), 108
Zhaxi (Tibetan host), 102–104
Zhe E River, 125, 129
Zheng He (Ma Sanbao), 186–187
Zheng (West Shuangtang Village), 53, 54
Zheng Xiaoyu, 328
Zhou Zhi, 101
Zhu, Dr. (Second People's Hospital), 78–79
Zhu Huiqiang, 16. See also Chen family (mother of Sharon Strothman)
Zhuolu County, 39–47, 42 (map)
Zhu Weiqun, 55–57
Zou Renying, 291